"Greg LeRoy brings this arcane debate out of the shadows of economic theory by telling the stories of real businesses from across the United States. He draws on years of experience to suggest how subsidies can work better for American workers and for our communities."
>—Congressman **Earl Blumenauer**, founder and co-chair, U.S. House of Representatives Livable Communities Task Force

"*The Great American Jobs Scam* is one-stop shopping for every citizen who wants to understand why and how corporate welfare doesn't work. And when Greg LeRoy describes how Wal-Mart got over $1 billion in taxpayer deals at only 244 of its facilities as 'the tip of the iceberg,' he's inviting all of us to discover the rest of the iceberg—and melt it."
>—**Joe Trippi**, author of *The Revolution Will Not Be Televised: Democracy, the Internet, and the Overthrow of Everything*

"Greg LeRoy not only tells us what's wrong with job subsidies—he shows us what we can do about it, so we can get our priorities straight and our democracy back."
>—**Si Kahn**, coauthor of *The Fox in the Henhouse: How Privatization Threatens Democracy*, and Executive Director, Grassroots Leadership

"LeRoy does a wonderful job of pulling back the curtain and revealing the truth behind the broken promises of great riches that are sold to communities and taxpayers across America. Perhaps most valuable are his clear suggestions and solutions—absolutely critical tools for the policymaker or citizen activist."
>—**Chellie Pingree**, President and CEO, Common Cause, and former Majority Leader, Maine State Senate

"LeRoy has written an important book on an issue that is of vital concern to working Americans."
>—**John Sweeney**, President, AFL-CIO

"Americans know the economy is not working, but most don't know why. This book outlines the problems, proposes concrete solutions, and offers strategies for moving forward toward policies that create and support family-wage jobs. A must-read for all of us."
>—**Kim Bobo**, Executive Director, Interfaith Worker Justice, and author of *Organizing for Social Change*

"This book fills a pressing national need for a comprehensive analysis and criticism of the economic 'incentives,' or should we say 'subsidy,' issue afflicting the United States. Taxpayers—particularly small and middle-sized businesses—should be outraged."
>   —**Robert F. Orr**, Executive Director, North Carolina Institute for Constitutional Law, and retired Justice, North Carolina Supreme Court

"Finally, a book that will propel policymakers to end the hemorrhaging of public treasuries from bidding wars. LeRoy exposes the disjuncture between the rhetoric of job creation and the reality of huge subsidies for paltry numbers of jobs, often fleeting and usually underpaid. He doesn't just leave us shaking our heads—he offers us a full course menu of smart and doable remedies."
>   —Professor **Ann Markusen**, University of Minnesota and author of *Second Tier Cities*

"*The Great American Jobs Scam* offers a lively chronicle of the exploits of corporate mercenaries who have mastered the art of bait-and-switch in the name of job creation and economic development. LeRoy shows us how our communities can battle back to achieve the good life for families and more livable communities."
>   —**Don Chen**, Executive Director, Smart Growth America

"By showing how the tax-dodging system works, [this] book will empower taxpayers to hold their elected officials (and the corporate special interests) accountable. It should be required reading for governors, mayors and legislators around the country who want to invest their citizens' money wisely and effectively."
>   —**Robert S. McIntyre**, Citizens for Tax Justice

"Anyone concerned about sustainable economic development, decent schools, urban sprawl, or their children's future should read this book."
>   —**Mike Matejka**, Alderman, City of Bloomington, Illinois

"SEIU enthusiastically supports Greg LeRoy's new book . . . No one has helped the labor movement more than Greg LeRoy to learn how to investigate these subsidies and leverage them for working families."
>   —**Andrew L. Stern**, Service Employees International Union

"I like Greg's stuff immensely; he cuts through the jargon with incredible skill, presents the issues, brings them alive."
>   —Professor **William W. Goldsmith**, Chairman, Department of City and Regional Planning, Cornell University

THE GREAT AMERICAN JOBS SCAM

Greg LeRoy

The Great American

JobsScam

★ Corporate Tax Dodging and the Myth of Job Creation ★

BK

BERRETT-KOEHLER PUBLISHERS, INC.
San Francisco
a BK Currents book

Berrett-Koehler Publishers, Inc.
235 Montgomery Street, Suite 650
San Francisco, CA 94104-2916
Tel: (415) 288-0260; Fax: (415) 362-2512
www.bkconnection.com

Ordering Information

Quantity sales. Special discounts are available on quantity purchases by corporations, associations, and others. For details, contact the "Special Sales Department" at the Berrett-Koehler address above.

Individual sales. Berrett-Koehler publications are available through most bookstores. They can also be ordered directly from Berrett-Koehler: Tel: (800) 929-2929; Fax: (802) 864-7626; www.bkconnection.com

Orders for college textbook/course adoption use. Please contact Berrett-Koehler: Tel: (800) 929-2929; Fax: (802) 864-7626.

Orders by U.S. trade bookstores and wholesalers. Please contact Publishers Group West, 1700 Fourth Street, Berkeley, CA 94710. Tel: (510) 528-1444; Fax (510) 528-3444.

Berrett-Koehler and the BK logo are registered trademarks of Berrett-Koehler Publishers, Inc.

Printed in the United States of America

Berrett-Koehler books are printed on long-lasting acid-free paper. When it is available, we choose paper that has been manufactured by environmentally responsible processes. These may include using trees grown in sustainable forests, incor porating recycled paper, minimizing chlorine in bleaching, or recycling the energy produced at the paper mill.

Library of Congress Cataloging-in-Publication Data

LeRoy, Greg.
   The great American jobs scam : corporate tax dodging and the myth of job creation / by Greg LeRoy.
      p. cm.
   Includes index.
   ISBN-10: 1-57675-315-8; ISBN-13: 978-1-57675-315-6
      1. Corporations—Corrupt practices—United States.   2. Corporations—Taxation—United States.   3. Tax evasion—United States.   4. Tax incentives—United States.
5. Job Creation—United States.   I. Title.

HV6769.L47 2005
336.2'07'0973—dc22   20050401107

First Edition

10 09 08 07 06 05   10 9 8 7 6 5 4 3 2 1

Project Manager: BookMatters, Berkeley; Copyeditor: Kristi Hein, Pictures & Words; Proofreader: Janet Reed Blake; Indexer: Hope Steele; Interior Designer: Jennifer Kelly-Dewitt, BookMatters *for Shoon and Ellie*

The trouble with people is not that they don't know
but that they know so much that ain't so.

—*Josh Billings*

Contents

Foreword

William Greider

Some scandals in American political life are difficult to see because they are not hidden. The "scam" that this tough-minded book describes in rather shocking detail is visible to all—if they will take the trouble to examine the public record—but the subject is largely excluded from political discussion. The essence of the crime, as Greg LeRoy explains, can be described as either extortion or bribery, depending on where you sit. A branch of government—state and local, often federal too—bribes a corporation with real money to locate its facility in their jurisdiction, sometimes paying hundreds of thousands for a single job. Or the company may extort the money from the same government as the price of not moving its factory elsewhere. Often the exchange is so transparently fraudulent, it is difficult to say who is the culprit and who is the victim.

The formal name given this scam is "economic development"—fostering new enterprise, creating more jobs—and who could be against that? Taxpayers and workers. They are the true "mark." Vast sums of public financing are squandered across the nation in transactions that are often no more than a friendly handshake and a press release. Scarce tax revenue is diverted to private interests with no real guarantee that anything at all will be created for the common good. Citizens discover their school systems or hospitals are starved for funding as a result. Workers find that the "new" jobs do not actually appear or that the jobs are, in fact, quite lousy—creating workers without a living wage and thus dependent on tax-financed healthcare or other public relief systems. Or the company decides soon enough to move the factory again to yet another location willing to pay another, still larger bribe. As LeRoy explains, the competition for employment among cities, counties, and states is so intense, the companies typically arrange an auction among them—who will pay the largest bribe?—that is often phony itself, since the company executives have already decided where they intend to locate the plant. They merely jiggle the appetites of mayors and governors so these officials will bid up the price that taxpayers must pay.

This scandal is seldom discussed in politics because most politicians participate in it, both Republicans and Democrats, conservatives as well as liberals. With some regularity, communities discover what's happening and local protests are mobilized. Sometimes they win redress, manage to block the payoffs, or even retrieve their money from companies that have swindled them. On the whole, however, the American governing system is ensnared by this lose-lose process. The public loses the tax resources to do something real. It loses again when the "deal" turns out to be fraudulent development. This book, I hope, will broaden the ranks of Americans who are actively engaged in stopping the crimes and restoring authentic meaning to the processes of economic development.

Here is a simple proposition to consider as you absorb the facts of the scam: public money should be devoted to public purposes, ideally to long-term improvements that can be expected to benefit everyone, including future generations. After all, that is a central element of why we have government. We need its capacity to undertake large, widely shared projects—achievements that individuals are unable to do alone. This is why government builds highways and sewer systems and schools or creates the infrastructure that will foster genuine economic development. Private enterprise gains enormously from this public investment, in both profits and personal fortunes. Government, in fact, creates business opportunities that private enterprise will pursue and expand.

But the subsidy system in American governance has now become so distorted—actually deranged—that it largely amounts to a corrupt pork barrel of private favors at public expense. Challenging this larger scandal—forcing both political parties to get honest about the true damage to the public interest—is obviously most difficult politics. It is going to require a sustained, smart, and patient movement that unites people across party lines and diverse interests.

If this book makes you angry, as I expect it will, that is a good thing. Anger is the first step toward action. Get angry and join the diverse army of citizens forming up to reclaim the public good.

William Greider is author of The Soul of Capitalism: Opening Paths to a Moral Economy (Simon & Schuster) and national affairs correspondent for The Nation magazine.

Money for Nothing

Lurking within the records of most cities and states in America there lies a scandal. A tax scandal. A jobs scandal. A corporate and political scandal.

Look up the names of corporations that have received taxpayer subsidies in the name of jobs. Almost every big company has gotten them. In fact, the average state now has more than thirty economic development subsidies, many of which are locally granted by cities and counties. These subsidies include property tax abatements, corporate income tax credits, sales and excise tax exemptions, tax increment financing, low-interest loans and loan guarantees, free land and land write-downs, training grants, infrastructure aid—and just plain cash grants.

Chances are you will find companies—many companies—that have failed to create or retain as many jobs as they said they would. Companies that are paying poverty wages or failing to provide healthcare to their employees. Companies that are abandoning our cities and sprawling onto farmland and natural spaces. Even companies that are outsourcing jobs offshore.

Dig a little deeper and you'll undoubtedly find companies that have not created *any* new jobs—even some that have actually *laid*

1

people off since they got the subsidies. Other companies that have gotten paid just to move existing jobs from one place to another, where they are proclaimed to be "new jobs."

How can companies get away with this? Because the system is rigged. Corporations have it down to a science. They have learned how to chant "jobs, jobs, jobs" to win huge corporate tax breaks—and still do whatever they wanted to all along.

That's the Great American Jobs Scam: an intentionally constructed system that enables corporations to exact huge taxpayer subsidies by promising quality jobs—and then lets them fail to deliver. The other benefit often promised—higher tax revenues—often proves false or exaggerated as well.

This system costs taxpayers an estimated *$50 billion a year* in total spending by states and cities.[1] The bottom of the iceberg—in every sense of the word—is the tax breaks. Those granted by states—income, sales, and excise taxes—are the least visible, least accountable, and most corrosive means by which states fund job creation. Those granted locally—in particular, property tax abatements and diversions—are especially harmful to schools.

This system has a long history and many moving parts. It can be traced at least as far back as the Great Depression, but it really matured by the 1970s. By then, most of the key actors were in place: secretive site location consultants who specialize in playing states and cities against each other; "business climate" experts, with their highly politicized interpretations of tax and jobs data; and an organized corporate network orchestrating attacks on state tax systems.

Today, this $50 billion-a-year pot has attracted an even more elaborate cast of characters: rented consultants proffering rosy projections about job creation and tax revenue; subsidy-tracking consultants to help companies avoid leaving money on the table; and even an embryonic industry that's helping businesses buy and sell economic development tax credits.

Perhaps we could overlook all this chicanery if the rising tide of money were lifting all the boats. But in return for all our taxpayer dollars we are *not* getting higher wages, better benefits, a stronger tax base, or better public services. Instead, for the last quarter century, most workers' wages have stagnated or fallen, healthcare has become less affordable and available, and pensions have shrunk in number and value. States and cities have developed structural budget deficits, forcing cutbacks in everything from school programs to infrastructure maintenance.

The only clear winners are large corporations. In return for building new facilities in many states, companies are actually getting *negative* income taxes. Subsidy packages routinely exceed $100,000 per job. Guess who's getting stuck with the tab. When the big boys pay less, either the rest of us pay more or the quality of our public services declines—and usually it's some of both.

At the core of this scandal are corrupted definitions of "competition" that obscure cause and effect. We must create no-tax zones for factories, say the governors, to be competitive with other states— even though the whole country is bleeding manufacturing jobs and the obvious issue is globalization. We have to create a new TIF district (that's "tax increment financing") and steal shoppers from neighboring suburbs, say the mayors, to compete for tax base—even though malls in older areas are dying.

Those who peddle and those who buy into these corrupted definitions salute the corporate bottom line while thumbing their noses at common sense, social science, and good government. These corruptions are the deliberate creations of a 50-year campaign by corporations to divide and conquer the states—as well as the suburbs. This corporate gospel of competition preaches that governments at all levels must not be allowed to cooperate with each other. Public relations campaigns, consulting studies, lobbying of federal and state legislators, litigation all the way to the Supreme Court—companies will do whatever it takes, but governments must not be allowed to work together against the corporate assault. They must be kept in the dark and allowed into the room only when it's time to talk about subsidies.

To that end, according to the gospel, states must not be allowed to compare notes to determine whether companies are lying about competing subsidy bids or cheating on their income taxes. Instead, states must only be allowed to compete to see which will tax the least corporate income, or which will give the biggest tax gift to a trophy deal.

Cities and suburbs must not be allowed to cooperate either, even though their fates hinge upon the health of their *regional* economies, not upon individual deals. Instead, localities must compete for tax base by pirating jobs and retail sales from each other, even though this means chewing up farmland for wasteful sprawl and throwing away older areas, poor people, and past infrastructure investments.

As public officials internalize these corrupted definitions, governments deliberately fail to cooperate with each other in the taxpayers' interest. Business becomes the alpha constituent. In these "public-private partnerships," government gets to play a single role: the dispenser of dollars. Blindfolded public officials practice job creation guided by wolves posing as Seeing Eye dogs.

At every level, this system demeans and degrades public officials: the economic development official forced to bid for an unknown company against unknown competing sites; the school board members who have no say in the property tax abatements that will corrode their budget; the revenue director whose sober advice is upstaged by the frothy projections of an economist rented by the Chamber of Commerce; the governor who overspends on a "trophy" project because she so fears being known as "the governor who lost us Mercedes-Benz." Those who would dare to ask an impertinent question are quickly singled out for ridicule and isolation: they must be against jobs.

Besides creating corporate windfalls, the Great American Jobs Scam is causing all manner of collateral damage. It was used to blunt calls for trade reform long before NAFTA. It bankrolls the pirating of one state's jobs by another state. It corrodes state budgets. It subsidizes private for-profit prisons—and hundreds of Wal-Mart facilities. The Great American Jobs Scam is used to help bust unions. It subsidizes poverty-wage companies that saddle us with hidden taxpayer costs such as Medicaid and Children's Health Insurance Program bills. It is helping create a massive tax-burden shift away from big companies onto working families and small businesses. It is diverting precious resources away from the two investments that really do grow good jobs—skills and infrastructure. And just don't get me started about stadiums.

The scam has also created mass confusion about true cause and effect—about how little difference tax cuts and subsidies really make when it comes to jobs. The prevailing "business climate" ideology that plagues us today is a hangover from the meanest elements of the Old Economy. Our beliefs about taxes and jobs were shaped by a very politicized series of studies in the 1970s and 1980s that served the lobbying agenda of footloose manufacturers looking for cheap labor in the South on their way to Mexico or China. That agenda had no value for the rest of the economy then, and it is just what we *don't* need to succeed in the New Economy today.

Much of our prevailing ideology about jobs and land is a hangover from a manufacturing site location bias against cities and from a post-war consensus built around "white flight" from cities, concentrated poverty among people of color in older areas, and lots of subsidies for jobs out by the interstate—be they factory, office park, or Wal-Mart jobs. That consensus has left us with a sprawling, dysfunctional built environment that is harming our health and our economic competitiveness.

That the scam could get this far out of hand suggests a profound breakdown in whatever consensus we ever had about corporate responsibility to our society. The way you handle your money *is your value system*. By their rampant tax dodging, large corporations are collectively saying: We don't care if the schools fall apart and the bridges are crumbling and the public health systems are impoverished and college is becoming unaffordable. We are not all in this together. We are not investing in our communities' futures. We are disinvesting.

The Great American Jobs Scam belongs in the dustbin of history. To put it there, we need strict accountability measures that will curtail private disinvestment and restore public reinvestment. By getting our taxpayer dollars out of private deals and into public goods, and by integrating our jobs strategy with land-use planning, we can spend less and get more.

We must eradicate the subsidy scams that have grown up around the corrupted definition of competition and replace them with a healthy new form of competition in which places compete based on their assets—their skilled labor base, their infrastructure, their schools and universities, their entrepreneurial culture, their quality of life—which are made equally available to all employers.

Fortunately, despite the siege of disinformation, there is a rich bipartisan history of reform that has created proven precedents for dismantling the scam. The most important of these is disclosure. When more information is available about the costs and benefits of the scam, many more people will get involved—and that's the scammers' darkest nightmare.

Getting a lot more people involved is the only way to challenge the prevailing ideology. You can see that ideology for yourself by going to any conference of economic development professionals and watching the public officials. You will never hear them crow about how well their working families are doing, about rising median incomes or declining dependency on Medicaid or fewer children suffering from asthma. But you will hear them touting big deals.

And you will see them courting site location consultants and corporate vice presidents.

This is what economic development in the United States has become. Welcome to the Great American Jobs Scam.

Chapter One

The Tax Dodgers Are Coming!
The Tax Dodgers Are Coming!

The Great American Jobs Scam is actually a collection of scams that have evolved over the past half-century and especially over the past three decades. These scams both rely upon—and reinforce—several factors. They rely on taxpayer confusion about the causes and effects of job creation. These scams thrive when the purported benefits—especially jobs benefits—of tax cuts and other subsidies are played up, so companies must exaggerate the positive impact while the business basics of location behavior are played down. They rely on taxpayer costs being kept vague, understated, or hidden. They need program rules to stay loose and unaccountable so that when a company fails to deliver, it suffers no consequences. They flourish when governments fail to monitor the real outcomes on jobs, wages, and other benefits. And most of all, these scams are built upon a corporate-controlled definition of "competition" that prevents government officials from cooperating in taxpayers' best interests.

Scam #1: Job Blackmail or
How to Get Paid to Do What You Planned to Do Anyway

A textbook chapter in the Great American Jobs Scam unfolded in 1995 in Massachusetts. All the characters from Central Casting were there: the high-profile company that threatens to leave unless it gets big tax breaks; the business lobby; the business lobby's "rented economist" whose dire prediction or rosy forecast gets far more attention than the sober findings of a government commission; the former gubernatorial aide-turned-lobbyist; and even a union of workers convinced—for the moment at least—that a big tax break will secure their jobs. And oh yes: *lots* of rhetoric about jobs, jobs, jobs, with loopholes hidden in the fine print.

Lexington-based defense contractor Raytheon Corp.—then the state's biggest private employer—triggered this row of dominoes in February 1995 by threatening to move its defense operations out of Massachusetts unless it got 12 tax cuts and utility deals from the state and concessions from its unionized workers. With the end of the cold war and sharp cuts in Pentagon procurement spending, the company had been downsizing; almost a third of its remaining 60,000 jobs were in the Bay State. To make sure everyone got the message, Raytheon's chief defense executive had lunch in Nashville with the governor of Tennessee, where the company already had three plants.[1]

Of the tax breaks Raytheon originally sought, the most costly was a new law called Single Sales Factor. SSF would change the way a multistate company determines how much of its profits are to be taxed in Massachusetts. For companies like Raytheon that have a lot of property and payroll in the state but sell most of their products outside the state, SSF results in a huge income tax cut (see chapter 4 for more). Raytheon estimated SSF would cut its income tax bill by three-fourths, from $28.1 million a year to $7 million.[2]

But Raytheon's first push for the tax cuts came across as "an awkwardly attempted holdup," as one journalist put it, and the company gained little support at the capitol on Beacon Hill.[3] Other big manufacturers didn't join in, and newspaper editorialists called it blackmail.[4] Neither the Republican governor, William Weld, nor the Democrats who controlled the legislature backed Raytheon. So the company hired a new lobbying team, including Democratic operative John Sasso, who had been chief secretary and presidential campaign aide to former governor Michael Dukakis.

Sasso and the new lobbying team engineered a public relations campaign that turned a corporate tax cut into a jobs program. Suddenly it wasn't the Raytheon tax cut bill; it was the "defense initiative" to help save 117,000 defense jobs in the state—well-paying blue-collar jobs that enabled people without a college education to make a decent living. Suddenly statistics abounded about the positive ripple effects of Raytheon's payroll and the state's high cost of doing business. "The heart and soul of our defense business" is here, a company executive wrote in a masterly op-ed article; but, he lamented, "[we have a] 20 percent cost gap created by being in Massachusetts."[5]

Sasso's connections reportedly helped the company formalize the support of the International Brotherhood of Electrical Workers (IBEW) Local 1505, which represented most of Raytheon's hourly employees in Massachusetts. That, in turn, brought the state AFL-CIO on board. Through the summer of 1995, Sasso and the Raytheon team honed the message; their efforts included a series of private meetings with legislators. The mantra that this was a blue-collar jobs bill resonated especially well with key leaders, such as House Speaker Charles Flaherty, a Democrat. Even those who had opposed it at first came on board. By September, Governor Weld had his line down pat: This is "a jobs package, not a Raytheon package."[6]

The demand for SSF quickly expanded from defense contractors to all manufacturing companies. The state's business lobby, Associated Industries of Massachusetts (AIM), went into high gear. It pointed out that the state had lost a third of its factory jobs in the last decade and was lagging in new capital investment.[7]

Raytheon hired three studies to boost its campaign: two by academics and another by DRI/McGraw-Hill, a prominent economic consulting firm (now Standard & Poor's/DRI). [8]

The DRI/McGraw-Hill study said that "[e]nactment of the defense initiative would save the jobs that are today at risk, and would create a substantial number of new jobs as well." But it used two dire scenarios for its baseline numbers: the impact on the state economy if Raytheon pulled 10,000 of its jobs, and the impact if all of the prime defense contractors in the state pulled 50,000 jobs. Setting the bars so very low and then assuming the tax cuts would save all the jobs at risk, the study found positive job benefits from SSF. However, DRI/McGraw-Hill refused to disclose its economic model, saying it was proprietary. And the vast majority of the projected job benefits consisted of *saved* defense jobs and ripple-effect jobs, not newly created jobs.[9]

The company and its allies repeatedly recycled the DRI/McGraw-Hill study findings, upstaging another study—staffed by economists at the Federal Reserve Bank of Boston—that found Massachusetts' business tax burden to be very average.[10]

Was it plausible to assume the tax breaks would save 100 percent of the jobs? Raytheon never made such a pledge, and AIM (the business lobby) was quite frank about the prospects for defense jobs. "Will the Single Sales Factor for Defense Firms Promote Job Growth?" an AIM fact sheet asked. "It is extremely doubtful. This proposal may help Massachusetts to retain a portion of its share of the defense industry, but there is no reason to believe that the federal government will be increasing its defense procurements in the foreseeable future." In other words, Pentagon demand would determine how many jobs there would be.[11]

Raytheon's political-style campaign peaked in November, when the SSF bill passed both houses of the legislature by large margins. Defense contractors got the whole break as of 1996; other manufacturers got it phased in over five years.

The assumption that the tax breaks would save all of the Raytheon jobs quickly proved wrong. In May 1996—just five months after SSF took effect—the company reportedly offered buyouts to 4,400 of its hourly employees in Massachusetts.[12] By January 1998—two years after SSF took effect and about three years after Raytheon first threatened to leave—the company had reduced its Massachusetts headcount by 4,100 people or 21 percent. Having merged with or acquired three other companies, Raytheon would restructure.[13]

The 1995 law creating SSF in Massachusetts had a provision that was supposed to make sure companies that got the tax break didn't lay off lots of people. But the law had two big loopholes. First, it said a company using SSF had to sustain its Massachusetts *dollar payroll, not its headcount,* at a minimum of 90 percent of 1995 levels through 1999. But the law did not account for wage inflation, and since it was tied to dollars, not workers, Raytheon was free to lay off lower-paid production workers and replace them with a smaller number of higher-paid white-collar workers and still meet the 90-percent payroll rule.

By mid-1999, Raytheon had shed another 1,600 Bay Staters, and union members bore the brunt: IBEW Local 1505 membership had shrunk by more than 40 percent. Now the workers felt betrayed. They had testified in favor of SSF in 1995, agreed to the 1996 buyout offer, and suffered a big layoff as well in 1996; now entire product lines were leaving. The state AFL-CIO president Robert Haynes said Raytheon had reneged on its 1995 deal. Barry Richards, a Raytheon employee for 21 years, said, "Ever since [SSF] passed, they have done nothing but decimate our ranks."[14]

The unions backed legislation to strip the company of the tax break unless it met a job-retention rule tied to headcount instead of payroll. Quoting all of the company's 1995 rhetoric about jobs, they said it was time to fix the loophole. But Raytheon said it was in compliance. "We never, ever offered any guarantees of specific employment numbers," the company's CFO said.[15] Despite all the rhetoric about jobs, "Raytheon never promised not to lay people off," recalled state representative James Marzilli, adding that he tried to get company executives to make such a pledge during hearings, but they would not.[16]

The proposal to fill the jobs loophole was defeated, and when 1999 ended, Massachusetts manufacturers entered SSF heaven: they got to keep taking the big tax cut year after year—but were no longer obligated to maintain even 90 percent of payroll. In other words, the job benefits were temporary; the taxpayer costs became permanent.

Lobbying records later revealed that the 1995 campaign cost Raytheon $573,539, including $107,972 to Sasso and $76,796 to DRI/McGraw-Hill.[17] For this, they got a tax break the company said at the time would save it $21 million a year—an astronomical, irresistible rate of return.[18]

Scam #2: Create a Bogus Competitor

Companies often know where they want to go (or stay), but they create a bogus competitor in order to "whipsaw" locations against each other and get more subsidies from the place they intended to go to all along.

A retired North Carolina construction executive who had used this scam admitted during a lawsuit deposition:

> I hate to give the example, but we decided very early in the game we were going to locate somewhere in the Winston-Salem/Greensboro area and narrowed it down to Kernersville rather rapidly; but spent a lot of time in Siler City and Asheboro and other communities hearing their story, primarily to use as a leverage to get all we could out of Winston-Salem. Now I give you that as a local example. But a more recent one—in Dickson, Tennessee, we had about ten west Tennessee municipalities chasing us with all kinds of offers; although we knew through the whole process it was going to be Dickson. And it was unfair and probably, as bad as it sounds, we used the others to get what we could out of where we were going in the first place. . . . you know, I've been around it a long time; but to me it's the process. Usually, you know early where you are going, and you use your leverage.[19]

The same game may have been used in a high-profile "retention" episode, in which a state granted subsidies even though information leaked suggesting it was all a bluff. Marriott International, Inc., the huge hotel chain, played Virginia against Maryland from late 1997 to mid-1999. It said it might move its headquarters with about 4,000 employees from Bethesda, Maryland (a suburb of Washington, DC) to suburban Virginia.

Some were skeptical that Marriott was really serious about Virginia. Commuting from Maryland into Northern Virginia is tedious because so few bridges span the Potomac River, and four-fifths of the headquarters employees lived in Maryland—including two-thirds of its highest-paid executives.[20] Two Virginia counties offered packages worth about $12 million and $17 million, plus possible sales tax breaks and the potential for a cash grant from the "Governor's Opportunity Fund." (Some states give governors the ability to make cash grants as "deal closers"; I think of these more as "photo opportunity funds.")[21]

Maryland and Montgomery County officials had to counter. Who could afford to become known as the governor or the county executive who lost Marriott? They mounted an offer of multiple subsidies estimated at $49 million to $74 million, depending on the company's future growth. The package included "Sunny Day" funds, training funds, state and local tax credits, and County Economic Development Fund loans.[22] Marriott accepted the bid at a March 1999 press conference. The Maryland General Assembly would officially enact the package in about a month.

But then came a glitch. Jay Hancock, an investigative reporter at the *Baltimore Sun*, went to Richmond and read the Virginia files. A Marriott executive had phoned a senior Virginia official a month before the Maryland press conference—to say the company wasn't moving. The story's headline: MARRIOTT USED VA. AS A RUSE TO RAISE MD. BID.[23] The Virginia official noted: "He expects an agreement to be ma[d]e and they will stay in Maryland. He ask[ed] me to keep this confidential so that Maryland will not start to back off if they feel we are no longer a competitor. To me this confirms that they were merely using us as leverage."[24] Indeed, the files indicate that the Virginia officials had long been skeptical.[25]

The *Baltimore Sun* bombshell caused much gnashing of teeth in Annapolis, where some legislators wondered about the company's ethics and the state's competence. Despite the revelations, they passed the $49 to $74 million package for Marriott. "It's terrible public policy to throw money at businesses to get them to stay in the state or locate here," said state senator Brian Frosh. "It's an invitation for every other Maryland business to say, 'Stick 'em up.'"[26]

Scam #3: Payoffs for Layoffs or How to Collect Taxpayer Subsidies While Downsizing

Whether you look at particular programs, cities, or states, it's not unusual to find companies that have received subsidies and then, instead of creating jobs, actually laid people off.

New York City must hold the record for such episodes, though it is hardly alone. One study of 80 companies that had received "retention" subsidies from the Big Apple found that at least 39 had later announced major layoffs, or they had entered into large-scale mergers or put themselves up for sale—events that usually trigger mass layoffs.[27] A detailed analysis of 10 subsidized companies found they had a total loss of more than 3,000 jobs.[28]

Bank of America received two "job retention" subsidies from New York City, in 1993 and in 2004. The 1993 subsidy was given to induce the bank to move employees into the World Trade Center following the 1993 bombing. In exchange for at least $18 million in benefits, the bank promised to retain at least 1,700 jobs in Tower One for 15 years. Instead, it laid off at least 800 people in 1997 after merging with Security Pacific National Bank. This was such a severe drop in employment that the city canceled the subsidy in 1998, but didn't require Bank of America to refund any past subsidies.[29]

After it was displaced by the attacks of September 11, 2001, Bank of America won a new subsidy in 2004 for the consolidation of several offices into a new headquarters building in midtown Manhattan. The deal is supposed to retain 2,995 jobs and create as many new jobs over 25 years. The state and city offered a total package of $82.6 million. The Bank also got $650 million in triple-tax-exempt "Liberty Bonds," special low-interest loans enacted for New York City following the September 11 attacks. But shortly after the deal closed, Bank of America merged with Fleet Bank (which had also received an NYC job-retention subsidy). The new entity announced it would cut a total of 17,000 jobs nationwide. The overall job impact on New York City was unknown as of late 2004.[30]

Getting payoffs for layoffs has played out differently for IBM in upstate New York. In 2000, the company received a subsidy package of at least $659 million for the construction of a new microchip plant in East Fishkill, apparently the largest subsidy package ever granted in New York State. About $475 million, or three-fourths of the subsidy, came from New York's "Empire Zone" program, meaning that the plant would operate nearly tax free for perhaps 10 years, thanks to wage tax credits, investment tax credits, job creation tax credits, property tax abatements, and sales tax exemptions—even something called a "tax reduction credit."[31]

A typical enterprise zone program is limited to areas that are hurting economically. But East Fishkill was hardly depressed; in 2000, its unemployment rate averaged only about 3 percent. So why had parts of East Fishkill and surrounding Dutchess County been declared an Empire Zone? Because of an obscure change made to the Empire Zone law as a direct result of IBM announcing huge layoffs in the area!

In 1993, IBM had laid off more than 7,000 people in the Hudson Valley, about a third of its workforce there.[32] In response, the New York State legislature soon amended its zone program, adding new eligibility criteria for "sudden and severe disruptions." The new criteria said that even if an area had below-average unemployment, if there were major layoffs or were likely to be major layoffs within three years, the area could become a zone. Governor Mario Cuomo specifically referred to the IBM layoffs in his approval message.[33]

Seven years later, in a perverse reward for its own mass layoffs, IBM cashed in.

Scam #4: Take the Money and Run

Call centers—offices where people make outbound calls trying to sell things or receive inbound calls for customer service—are a major source of employment in the United States. Trade associations claim they account for about three million jobs.[34] They are often touted for their job creation in small cities and rural areas. Requiring inexpensive equipment that takes little time to set up, call centers can create jobs quickly, especially now that fiber-optic telephone lines are more common. But they can also leave town just as fast.

Tampa-based Sykes Enterprises Inc. operates call centers in the United States and abroad. The company has a widespread history of receiving subsidies, typically in small cities or rural areas. Indeed, a company vice president once said: "Every one of our locations is a result of some incentive plan. If a community is inviting Sykes to build a call center, they are expected to deed the land for two call centers to us, and give incentives of at least $2.5 million."[35]

The trouble is, employment in the facilities fluctuates a lot, and the company has closed many of them.

In Greeley, Colorado, Sykes announced a new center in 1994, with subsidies from state and local governments totaling about $915,000—for six acres of land, site improvements, training grants, a no-interest loan, and local tax and fee waivers. Employment later peaked at 580, but in January 2002, Sykes announced it would close—and with that closure, 400 jobs were lost.[36]

In Klamath Falls, Oregon, Sykes announced a planned center in 1995. It received $800,000 in cash, 52 acres of land, $250,000 worth of road construction, and a three-year property tax exemption. It was projected to generate 432 jobs, but peaked higher, at 650. By late 2003, however, employment was down to 80 workers, and those were laid off in early 2004.[37]

Bismarck, North Dakota, approved a package for Sykes in 1995 that included up to $2 million from Bismarck's "Vision Fund," 18 acres of city-owned property, utility breaks and other concessions, plus a five-year property tax exemption. In 1996, the state even gave Sykes a five-year exemption from state corporate income taxes. A second Bismarck center was announced in early 1997, subsidized by $2 million from the city's "Vision Fund." In 1998, public opposition to a third city offer—for free land, improvements and another $2.5 million—caused Sykes to drop plans for a third Bismarck call center. In January 2002, the company closed one of the centers, transferring jobs to the other, and in May 2002 Sykes said 316 more jobs would be lost. By August 2003, layoffs reduced employment at the surviving Bismarck call center to about 150.[38]

The farm town of Milton-Freewater, Oregon, borrowed $2.2 million in 1998 to make a $2.7 million cash grant to Sykes for 400 projected jobs. The city also provided free land, utility services, and tax credits, plus $1 million in state funds for road improvements. Businesses just across the state line in Washington even chipped in $200,000 in private funds. The facility eventually employed almost 500 people, but in May 2004 Sykes closed it and terminated the 264 remaining jobs. (An unexpected contract caused the facility to re-open later in 2004 with a small crew.)[39]

Manhattan, Kansas, and the state of Kansas offered Sykes a subsidy package of about $6.2 million in 1998 for an estimated 432 jobs. From the city came a $2.6 million cash grant, free land, $500,000 for site improvements, and property tax reductions for five years. The state provided $550,000 from an "Economic Opportunity" fund, enterprise zone tax breaks worth nearly $1.8 million, and a project and training grant of $800,000. In June 2004, the remaining 256 workers lost their jobs when Sykes moved the work to Asia and Latin America. The Manhattan plant closed only six months after the enterprise zone tax breaks expired.[40]

In 1996, business leaders in Hays, Kansas, contributed $1 million of their own money to gain a Sykes call center, on top of $2.35 million and 20 acres of free land provided by state and local government. As many as 650 new jobs were anticipated. The city of Hays even agreed to repay the state's $600,000 contribution if the company failed to meet minimum job creation targets. However, neither private sector nor government support could keep the Hays center open, which employed 370 people in August 2003. After Sykes closed the center in 2004, the customer service company that took over its Hays facility had trouble recruiting potential workers made insecure by their experience with Sykes.[41]

In Ada, Oklahoma, Sykes opened a center in 1999 with about 440 jobs after the city gave it $2.5 million in a cash grant plus land. But in January 2004 Sykes announced the Ada center's closure, with the loss of more than 400 jobs.[42]

Scottsbluff, Nebraska, gave Sykes $1 million from its federal Community Development Block Grant and $500,000 in local funds in 1999 to subsidize construction and infrastructure. After peaking at 393 jobs in late 1999, the Scottsbluff center was closed in 2002 with 240 layoffs.[43]

Hazard, Kentucky, helped Sykes in 1999 with a package of about $4 million, mostly state training money, for a potential 432 jobs. The state also spent $6 million on the Coalfields Business Park, where Sykes located. Employment peaked at 650 in 2001, but the facility was closed in late 2003, with the loss of 393 jobs.[44]

Pikeville, Kentucky, provided Sykes with almost $4 million from local funds in 1999, mostly for training, plus infrastructure and site preparation. The company also received a five-year property tax abatement. Sykes closed the facility in April 2004, with the loss of 324 jobs. Pikeville city manager Donovan Blackburn was bewildered: "We put together a lucrative incentive package for Sykes. And then when the package ended, they just ran."[45]

In 2000, Eveleth, Minnesota, provided Sykes with a $3 million cash grant, plus $1 million worth of site preparation improvements and 22 acres of free land. Employment never exceeded 300 at the 432-seat facility, and Sykes announced it would close the facility in

2002, with 200 layoffs. Matt Sjoberg—then an official of a Minnesota regional development agency, Iron Range Resources—said, "Sykes came in. They tried to make a go of this. They put the money in their back pocket, and they ran."

Sykes's 2000 subsidies from the city of Palatka and Putnam County, Florida, included $3 million from the County, a five-year property tax exemption, and 22 acres of free land. About 200 workers lost their jobs when Sykes closed the facility in the fall of 2004. Local attorney Timothy Keyser wasn't surprised: "That seems to be how that corporation makes its money. They dangle jobs to jurisdictions that pay them tax money."[46]

The Sykes call center in Marianna, Florida, was expected to employ over 560 people within three years of its 2000 opening. Jackson County and Marianna provided $2.1 million in subsidies, and the state another $2 million for land and infrastructure. In July 2004, Sykes announced the center would close, with 266 remaining workers laid off. In a rare show of generosity, Sykes donated $1 million worth of land and some equipment to Marianna in late 2004.[47]

Do we detect a pattern here?

Many of the U.S. closures coincided with Sykes's growth offshore. In late 2004, the company said it had 10,000 workstations in low-cost countries such as Costa Rica and the Philippines (up 82 percent in the last year) compared with 2,700 workstations in the United States (down 45 percent)—and only half the domestic stations were staffed.[48]

Scam #5: Exploit the War Among the States or How the Auto-Plant Sweepstakes Got Used to Blunt Trade Reform

James "Big Jim" Thompson, then-governor of Illinois, stands about six-foot-six. So it must have startled Mitsubishi Motors president Toyoo Tate when Thompson got down on his hands and knees to spread out a big map of Illinois. The lanky governor spoke of his vision for an "auto corridor" along Route 51 from Bloomington-

Normal to Rockford—if only Mitsubishi would agree to choose Illinois for its Diamond-Star auto assembly plant, a joint venture with Chrysler.

"I thought at first that President Tate might think I was violating the normal rules of reserve governing Japanese business relationships by crawling around his floor. Yet I wanted him to see that we really cared about their plant, our highway and our state," Thompson explained. The resulting 1985 subsidy deal weighed in at $249 million—the biggest in Illinois history and then the biggest package ever given to an auto assembly plant in the United States.[49] The factory was part of the first big wave of foreign direct investment in U.S. "transplants," or auto-assembly factories, by Japanese automakers.

But Thompson's Diamond-Star deal caused some other midwestern officials to roll their eyes; I remember one Michigan official clucking condescendingly. There were other forces at play that explained why so many transplants were suddenly cropping up—forces that were obvious to people in the Motor City who knew auto politics. The strong yen made Japanese labor just as expensive as U.S. labor. But the really big threat was protectionism: public resentment at rising auto imports prompted the U.S. House of Representatives to pass legislation in 1983 that would have required certain levels of domestic content in cars sold here. The U.S. Senate debated it the following year.

To blunt the threat of domestic content legislation, the Japanese automakers sought to curry as many votes as they could in the Senate. Hence the tidy geographic spread of their early siting choices, including midwestern states with lots of United Auto Workers: Honda in Marysville, Ohio (announced in 1980); Nissan in Smyrna, Tennessee (1980); Toyota (with General Motors) in Fremont, California (1983); Mazda in Flat Rock, Michigan (1984); Mitsubishi (with Chrysler) in Illinois (1985); Toyota in Georgetown, Kentucky (1985); Subaru-Isuzu in Lafayette, Indiana (1986); and Honda in East Liberty, Ohio (1987).[50]

Authors Martin and Susan Tolchin noted: "There was nothing secret about these strategies: The Japanese encouraged their companies to invest abroad as enlightened policy, designed to stave off protectionism and save jobs."[51] Yet all but one of these plants were subsidized to the tune of eight or nine figures, even though the Japanese had strong political and financial reasons for building them no matter what.[52] It was a marriage of mutual convenience. The recessions of 1982 to 1983 and 1986 humbled the Rust Belt; governors planning to get reelected had to look aggressive on jobs. And the Japanese needed to quiet calls for a domestic content law and cushion themselves from the high relative labor costs created by the strong yen.

However, when the threat of protectionism passed—evinced by Bill Clinton's election in 1992 and the passage of NAFTA in 1993—foreign automakers largely steered clear of the Midwest—with all of its United Auto Workers members—and headed for "right to work" states: BMW in Spartanburg, South Carolina (1992); Mercedes-Benz in Vance, Alabama (1993); Toyota in Princeton, Indiana (1995); Honda in Lincoln, Alabama (1999); Nissan in Canton, Mississippi (2000); Hyundai in Montgomery, Alabama (2002); and Toyota in San Antonio, Texas (2003). All of these assembly plants received nine-figure subsidy packages. And that doesn't begin to count the 450-plus so-called subplants or foreign-owned auto parts plants, which have also been routinely subsidized.

My point here is not to bash Japan. In 2003, the United States ran automotive trade deficits with 11 countries, and our total auto trade deficit far exceeds its level in 1983 when the House passed a domestic content bill. Asian and German companies, with the help of U.S. site location consultants, have played our state-eat-state system like a fiddle, the same way General Motors played 30 states against each other in 1985 with the Saturn assembly plant it sited in Spring Hill, Tennessee.

My point *is* to say that we are nuts to allow this "war among the states" to be exploited in a way that influences our national trade policies. Our commodity trade deficit is now way over half a *trillion* dollars a year. U.S. taxpayers gave huge subsidies to foreign-owned factories that were instrumental in blunting trade reforms like domestic content requirements long before NAFTA.

And what became of Big Jim's vaunted Illinois "auto corridor"? Did Illinois capture oodles of ripple-effect jobs from Diamond-Star for its $249 million subsidy? Not quite. The auto corridor never developed. Since 1985, the Prairie State has *lost* auto parts jobs despite gaining the assembly plant.

Scam #6:
CAPCOs: Beaucoup Ventured, Little Gained

How'd you like to put your money into a special state-sponsored fund, packaged to look like a venture capital fund for start-up businesses, and get a handsome rate of return on your investment— even if the fund does a lousy job of helping small businesses? Or, on the other side of the table, how'd you like to collect management fees and financing charges from the fund—and lend only half the money to small businesses?

Welcome to the magical world of Certified Capital Companies, or CAPCOs—an outrageous subsidy gimmick cooked up by Louisiana insurance lobbyists in the early 1980s that has quietly mushroomed to a total cost of more than $1.5 billion in tax credits in nine states and the District of Columbia.[53]

The states' rules vary a bit, but here is how CAPCOs basically work. An insurance company invests money in a CAPCO. For doing that, it will get a dollar-for-dollar tax credit from the state worth 10 percent of its investment every year for 10 years. That credit reduces the tax the insurance company pays on the premiums for policies it sells in the state.

Then the insurance company negotiates with the CAPCO for a guaranteed rate of return on the cash it invests in the CAPCO. To ensure that return, the CAPCO typically puts a huge chunk of the money—say 40 percent—into low-risk investments like treasury bonds. That money is used to pay the insurance company an attractive return.

That leaves the CAPCO with half or more of the money, so it has every reason to play it safe as it invests in qualified small companies, while collecting management fees and finance charges. That means mostly low-risk, short-term loans, preferably to the largest, safest companies the rules allow—not to young, risky start-ups. Once the CAPCO has lent out 100 percent of the original amount (by re-lending money from repaid loans), it becomes deregulated and can pay out profits.[54]

There are no job-creation requirements on CAPCOs, just requirements that they invest certain percentages of the money in a certain number of years. Most only require CAPCOs to invest half the money in qualified small businesses. Unlike private-sector venture capital funds, whose investors are at risk and whose fund managers have fiduciary obligations to the investors, in a CAPCO the state basically absorbs all of the risk and the CAPCO operator has no comparable obligation to the state.

However, CAPCOs are lucrative for a select group of operators. As three academic researchers have documented, a small group of corporations has lobbied for CAPCO laws and benefited the most from the program.[55] *Governing* magazine's Christopher Swope traced $1 billion of the insurance company tax credits that states have given to CAPCOs so far. He found that more than half went to just three corporations: Advantage Capital Partners, at least $261 million; Newtek Business Services' subsidiary The Wilshire Group, at least $140 million; and Stonehenge Capital Corp., at least $226 million.[56]

Swope even found that one of these companies, Newtek/Wilshire, uses the CAPCO money to bankroll its own subsidiaries (they process credit-card transactions and provide other financial services). In 2002, CAPCOs provided 88 percent of Newtek's revenue.[57]

State reviews of CAPCOs have repeatedly found big problems. Studies in New York and Florida, which have authorized $580 million in tax credits, found that companies getting CAPCO loans actually lost jobs.[58] A Colorado audit found that out of $100 million, the CAPCO had invested almost half in low-risk vehicles such as treasury bonds, then spent $11 million setting up its offices and another $4 million on management fees—so that only about a third of the money went for the program's intended purposes.[59] CAPCOs have also provoked heated debates in Louisiana, Missouri, Florida, and Wisconsin.

Some analysts who have tracked CAPCOs for years have decided they are such a scandal that the analysts have actively opposed their proliferation. George Lipper, who studied Iowa legislation, calls them a "raid on state treasuries." Julia Sass Rubin, a Rutgers professor, says they are "a crummy deal for taxpayers." Colorado state treasurer Mike Coffman is more blunt: "It's a scam."[60]

Scam #7: Pirate Thy Neighbor's Jobs

The 1990 to 1991 recession lasted longer for parts of California, especially the Los Angeles basin, as the end of the cold war prompted aerospace-defense cutbacks. Then the City of Angels suffered further, from the civil disturbance following the Rodney King police-abuse acquittal verdict in 1992. Economic development officials in the West smelled blood: a dozen states and as many cities set up aggressive job-piracy efforts that especially targeted manufacturers, complete with recruitment fairs, "trade offices," and targeted mailings.[61] The piracy got so bad, the city's development director complained to the secretary of HUD that he suspected federal monies were involved in some of the recruitment offers.[62]

This episode of kicking one's neighbor when she is down is especially egregious, but it is hardly unique. Indiana, Ohio, and Michigan have had recurring job-flight episodes; South Dakota has had sporadic jobs wars with Iowa and Minnesota; New Jersey and Connecticut have eagerly enticed companies from New York City; New Hampshire has received many firms from Massachusetts; Kentucky likes to land companies from Ohio. This systematic use of taxpayer dollars to solicit or subsidize jobs from other states became institutionalized in the 1950s, with officials from southern states making recruitment trips to New York City, and it continues to this day.

Some economists point out that from a national perspective, this is all a zero-sum game; that is, there is no net gain for the U.S. economy, just a reshuffling of the deck. Some argue that it is even worse—that it is a net-loss game. That's because overall, with so many tax breaks given to "new" jobs that are actually just moved jobs, there are fewer tax revenues for education and infrastructure and other public goods that benefit all employers, not just the footloose ones.[63]

Scam #8:
Pay Poverty Wages; Stick Taxpayers with Hidden Costs

While good manufacturing jobs were being pirated from Los Angeles by other western states and cities in the 1990s, the City itself had an odd counter-strategy: subsidize poverty-wage retail and fast-food jobs and call it economic development. This terrible waste of resources occurred as Los Angeles suffered a rise in concentrated poverty on a scale beyond that of any other U.S. city.[64]

The Los Angeles Alliance for a New Economy (LAANE), a labor-community network organizing to reshape the city's development priorities, has documented the tragedy of this "low road" approach. Together with scholars at UCLA, it analyzed the Community Redevelopment Agency's track record. Between 1990 and 1997, the agency spent $193 million on commercial development deals, but two-thirds of the money went to retail projects dominated by poverty-wage jobs. For example, the Baldwin Hills Crenshaw Plaza got subsidies worth $53,725 per job, but front-line workers got paid an average of only $6.50 an hour.[65]

LAANE and UCLA also examined the track record of the mayor's Los Angeles Business Team (LABT), a sort of rapid-response unit created to help improve the city's "business climate" by cutting red tape on permits and location assistance. The LABT was supposed to target certain industries that create good jobs, but the research found that most of its assistance didn't go to the targeted sectors—and a fourth of the companies it helped were retailers, including 21 fast-food restaurants, many of which sought special waivers to allow for drive-through windows.[66]

The problem of governments subsidizing lousy jobs is hardly unique to Los Angeles, or to urban areas. An analysis of more than 500 deals all over Minnesota, a state that is not known to "shoot everything that flies and claim everything that drops" when it comes to job creation, found that almost two-thirds of the companies it had subsidized were paying wages so low a family of three would qualify for Medicaid, and more than a fourth paid so low the same family would qualify for food stamps.[67]

The Kentucky Economic Justice Alliance (KEJA) *is* in a state known for subsidizing any old job. In just one two-year period, KEJA found that the state had granted tax breaks to at least 31 companies that paid average wages below the federal poverty line for a family of four. In the same period, KEJA found 10 deals in which tax credits exceeded $100,000 per job.[68]

These findings could hardly have come as a surprise to Bluegrass State taxpayers. For years, Bill Bishop of the *Lexington Herald-Leader* had been documenting how the Kentucky Rural Economic Development Act and other subsidies were attracting poverty-wage jobs. When uniform maker Cintas announced a sewing plant in Hazard in 1993, it was given a $1.6 million building and $2 million of equipment, plus no corporate taxes, plus the company got to keep taxes deducted from the employees' paychecks. The pay: $5 an hour. Calling the strategy a "two-time loser," Bishop argued that poor wages create no tax base and that "low-wage industries, once settled in an area, work hard (and successfully) to keep high-wage businesses out." Kentucky, he noted, was following the path of Arkansas, where a retired economist who had studied the subsidies-for-low-wages strategy called it "rural ghettoization." Declining schools and roads drove prosperous people out, putting the economy and tax base into a downward spiral.[69]

Of course, the all-time poster child for hidden taxpayer costs must be Wal-Mart. As we'll discuss in chapter 6 on sprawl, the world's biggest retailer has benefited from more than $1 billion in bricks-and-mortar subsidies. Those are the front-door costs. The back-door costs are the safety-net expenses to help Wal-Mart workers and their families survive on everyday low wages. U.S. congressional staff have estimated that each Wal-Mart store with 200 employees costs federal taxpayers $420,750 a year. That's when you add up costs for programs such as State Children's Health Insurance Program, Section 8 housing assistance, free or reduced-price school lunches, the Earned Income Tax Credit, and low-income energy assistance.[70]

Scam #9: Exaggerate the "Ripple Effect" Benefits

When politicians announce lavish subsidy packages, they often justify them with claims that the new jobs will also create lots of "ripple effect" jobs; they may even cite a number based on a consultant's study, such as three ripple effect jobs for each direct job, or five; I once read a claim of eleven. Journalists usually repeat the numbers uncritically, and the costs of the deal become more acceptable to taxpayers because they think the benefits are huge.

Many such claims are exaggerated, however, and the way the numbers are stated is often misread. First the misreading: usually when ripple effects are estimated they include the original direct job, but that is not clearly stated. So a claim of three jobs is actually one direct job and two indirect jobs—not one plus three. But even a claim of three total jobs is very likely to be exaggerated; experts caution that any claim above two and a half should be viewed with suspicion—that is, more than one direct job and one and a half indirect jobs.[71] That would be a high-impact deal with lots of feeder jobs "upstream" plus lots of "downstream" jobs created by virtue of the direct jobs paying good wages.

Another common problem with rosy cost-benefit claims is that although they claim lots of indirect benefits, they often fail to include indirect taxpayer costs above and beyond the subsidies to the company. That is, if an area gets new jobs and people move in to fill the jobs, local governments will have to build more schools and roads, lay more water and sewer lines, hire more teachers and public safety officers, pick up more trash, and so on. There's no such thing as free growth.[72]

Illinois made a rosy jobs claim to justify a big subsidy package it assembled to attract the headquarters of Boeing Corp. in 2001. In an unusually public auction, the aerospace giant announced it was moving its head offices with five hundred jobs away from Seattle and was considering Chicago, Dallas-Fort Worth, and Denver. A bidding war ensued, with Chicago and Illinois offering about $56 million in subsidies, Denver $18 million, and Dallas-Fort Worth $14 million. Boeing chose Chicago, although evidence suggests that it was the city's many assets—financial, business-service, cultural, and quality of life—not the subsidies, that won the deal.[73]

To justify the big subsidy package, the Illinois Department of Commerce and Community Affairs (DCCA) cited a projection that for each new Boeing headquarters job, the region would gain five more "high end" jobs. The number came from a study DCCA commissioned from the consulting arm of the now-defunct accounting firm Arthur Andersen (of Enron infamy).

The one-plus-five claim was not only implausible on its face, it was also wildly different from the ripple-effect claims made by DCCA years earlier when it justified a big retention package for the headquarters of Sears. In that 1989 episode, DCCA projected that losing 5,400 Sears jobs would have cost another 2,200 indirect jobs; that is, about 0.4 indirect jobs lost for each direct job lost—a plausible figure. In other words, DCCA claimed a job *gain* 1,150 percent higher for Boeing than the job *loss* it forecast for Sears, even though both episodes involved corporate headquarters jobs.[74]

DCCA released only a brief executive summary of the Andersen study that did not disclose its methodology or assumptions. An Illinois taxpayer then filed a Freedom of Information request to get the whole study. DCCA refused to release it, claiming confidentiality and that it would make it hard for DCCA to obtain similar studies in the future. Illinois courts upheld that claim and the study was never released.[75]

Scam #10: Subsidize Privatization of Public Jobs

Perhaps the most controversial form of privatization in the United States involves imprisonment of human souls. Today, about 95,000 people in the nation's state and federal prisons—about 6 percent—generate incarceration fees for companies such as Corrections Corporation of America and the GEO Group (formerly Wackenhut Corrections Corporation).

An investigation of the 60 largest private prisons in the United States found that 44—or 73 percent—have received job creation subsidies. These included $628 million in tax-free bonds and government-issued securities for construction, plus property tax abatements, infrastructure and land subsidies, training grants, and enterprise zones. The study also found widespread use of two specialized devices called lease-revenue bonds and certificates of participation. These devices do not require a voter referendum, so taxpayers are denied the right to decide if they want to finance a private prison in their community. The study even found a dozen instances of federal subsidies from four different U.S. agencies.

Of course, many would argue that private prison companies have little need for such subsidies. They have raised billions on Wall

Street as tougher state and federal sentencing laws have doubled the nation's prison population. The daily rates the companies charge include profit margins. And as largely non-union employers, they pay lower wages and benefits than the public agencies whose work they displace.

Corrections Corporation of America (CCA) is the biggest private prison company, with about half the "market." It built one of its facilities in Youngstown, Ohio, a depressed steel town in the Mahoning Valley near the Pennsylvania state line. There, CCA held inmates from Washington, DC. The city gave CCA 100 acres of land for $1 and free water and sewer hookups valued at $500,000.

From the time it opened in 1997, CCA's Youngstown prison was plagued by severe management problems, resulting in violence. In 1998, six inmates, including four convicted murderers, escaped by cutting through a gate in broad daylight. The facility became embroiled in lawsuits and investigations. Washington, DC's corrections trustee found that more than half of the senior corrections officers at the Youngstown facility had no prior correctional experience of any kind before being hired. The District did not renew CCA's contract and the facility was closed in 2001. Youngstown's mayor, who helped recruit CCA, said: "It's been a nightmare. [CCA's] credibility is zero."

Finally, in an apparent effort to redefine the term "chutzpah," CCA filed a property tax appeal in 1998 with Leavenworth County, Kansas, seeking a lower tax rate for its detention center there. It claimed to be a "residential" rather than a commercial structure.[76]

Scam #11: Bust the Union

Many of the manufacturing companies that have relocated plants from the North to the South, taking subsidies to make that move ever since the 1930s (and especially since the 1950s), have done so to get away from unions. Textile plants from the Northeast, auto-parts facilities from the Midwest, and many others have moved to "right to work" states where, because of the 1947 Taft-Hartley Act, unions are weaker because contracts between companies and unions cannot require a worker to belong to the union, even though he or she enjoys union wages and benefits.

An internal staff memo of the United Auto Workers from 1953, entitled "State and Local Subsidies to Promote Industrial Migration," noted with alarm an advertisement in *U.S. News & World Report* magazine. The ad featured a pitch from Governor Hugh White of Mississippi, touting his "Balancing Agriculture with Industry" plan, complete with "friendly labor" and taxpayer-financed buildings. The memo stated: "Under this plan political subdivisions are authorized to vote bonds to finance the purchase of land and the construction of buildings for lease to new or expanding industries." The union memo suggested further investigation into how many companies were migrating and where.[77]

A very early client of industrial realtor Felix Fantus, White had pioneered state legislation in Mississippi that accelerated a trend already established in the South: communities subsidizing footloose factories. With this new bonding authority from the state, localities could float a tax-free, low-interest bond to build a plant, then lease it to the company. And since the facility was publicly owned, there were no property taxes (see more in chapter 3).[78]

Ever since this southern innovation, subsidies have been given to runaway shops, and the movements don't always involve "right to work" states. In 1994, small-engine maker Briggs & Stratton announced it was moving 2,000 union jobs from the Milwaukee area to five college towns in the South and border states. The Paperworkers Union, which represented the Milwaukee workers, investigated the five sites and revealed that in Missouri and Kentucky, the company was slated to benefit from Community Development Block Grant funds—federal monies from the U.S. Department of Housing and Urban Development (HUD). In other words, Uncle

Sam was going to help finance interstate job transfers—back then, that was actually *a legal use of federal HUD monies!*

Wisconsin taxpayers went ballistic, and the state's congressional delegation eventually succeeded in attaching anti-piracy language to the HUD program (the last federal development program to lack such a safeguard).[79] But the jobs were moved and, once they were no longer union, wages and benefits were slashed.

The story does not always end as you might imagine for the southern communities that land the runaway shops. Many of the factories have moved on again, to Mexico, the Caribbean, or China. For example, auto-parts maker Bendix escaped the Auto Workers in South Bend, Indiana, in 1982 for Sumter, South Carolina. But in 2004, the company announced it would lay off 400 workers and move the work to Mexico.[80]

Scam #12: Soak the Taxpayer

Some subsidy programs and deals have become so astronomically expensive, they can only be fairly described as "soak the taxpayer" scams: as evidence of how job subsidies have become pure and simple transfers of wealth to corporate shareholders—from the rest of us.

How else do you explain 251 property tax exemptions given to Exxon over a 10-year period in Louisiana—to create *zero* new permanent jobs![81] As we'll detail in chapter 5 on property taxes, the Pelican State gives out huge property tax exemptions that disproportionately benefit petrochemical and paper companies.[82]

Connecticut spends aggressively on "job creation," but a 2002 study of almost 1,200 subsidized companies there found that 41 percent of them had actually *lost* jobs. Companies getting subsidies from the largest program, the Connecticut Development Agency, had created only *9 percent* of the jobs they had forecast. The average subsidy for each new job: $367,910.[83]

Florida governor Jeb Bush decided to take federal money that had been sent to his state to help with budget shortfalls and use it instead for a pricey subsidy deal with Scripps Research Institute to create a new biomedical research facility. Combining $369 million from the state with $667 million from Palm Beach County, the deal is slated to create 545 jobs—a subsidy of more than $1.9 million each![84] (Scripps is a non-profit corporation and thus has no shareholders.)

North Carolina used to be a stingy state. For decades, a mix of fiscal and ideological conservatism prevailed in the Tarheel State, so that in essence it said: we have low taxes and low regulation; we are improving our schools, universities and training programs; we have a few cookie-cutter subsidies that any business can seek, but we don't do big sweetheart deals. That philosophy worked; the state enjoyed strong job creation and low unemployment. But after "losing" a few high-profile competitions with other states in the early 1990s, North Carolina slid onto the slippery slope in 1996 with a law called the William S. Lee Act.[85] The first two subsidy deals out of the tubes said it all: $115.5 million or $77,000 per job for a FedEx hub (where more than two thirds of the jobs were projected to be part-time), and $161 million or *$536,000 per job* for a Nucor steel mini-mill. Under its agreement, Nucor reportedly won't pay any state income tax for 25 years.[86]

Dell's Fabulous Deal in North Carolina

Dell, Inc. is another aggressive company when it comes to seeking subsidies. Its recent deal in North Carolina may be setting a record for the highest ratio of subsidy to private investment. Subsidies usually equal a small fraction of the cost of a facility; a high-impact deal like an auto plant might have a subsidy ratio as high as one-fourth, and some deals may exceed even that. But a subsidy far bigger than the company's cost of building a facility—now, *that's* rare.[87]

That's exactly what North Carolina governor Mike Easley's administration negotiated with Dell for a new computer-assembly plant and distribution center announced in late 2004. In exchange for investing at least $100 million (and perhaps eventually $115 million) and hiring at least 1,500 people within five years, Dell was promised state subsidies estimated at $242 to $267 million—*roughly two and half times the cost of the plant and warehouse!* It's the biggest subsidy package in Tarheel State history.[88]

How can this happen? The big bucks—$200 to $225 million—will come from an unusual subsidy that is tied to neither jobs nor investment. North Carolina will give Dell a tax credit of $15 for every computer or peripheral unit the factory produces in 2006 and a tax credit of $6.25 for each such product produced from 2007 to 2019. Other subsidies will include infrastructure aid, training grants, and a grant that will rebate three-fourths of the personal income taxes paid by Dell's employees back to the company for the first 12 years. In announcing the North Carolina subsidies, Governor Easley's aides said Dell would locate in the three-county Piedmont Triad but did not specify a site, saying the company would also seek local subsidies. That set off a bidding war among the three counties, and Dell got another $37.2 million in subsidies from Forsyth County and Winston-Salem. So the whole package may eventually exceed $300 million.[89]

One of the few voices objecting to the Dell deal was that of Perri Morgan, then North Carolina state director of the National Federation of Independent Business (NFIB), the state's main advocate for small and independent businesses. She noted that legislators only received the Dell legislation on the day of the vote and were repeatedly told it could not be amended in any way or else Dell would walk away. Legislators in both the House and Senate tried to attach some safeguards, such as disclosure, but were defeated. "It's just an insult to the other business owners in North Carolina," Morgan said later. She said some NFIB members are beginning to see a link between tax hikes on small businesses and deals like Dell's. "I think with every deal, a few more people wake up," she said.[90]

Indeed, since the deal was announced, revelations about Dell's aggressive bargaining have inflamed public debate there. The North

Carolina Press Association and the John Locke Foundation sued for the disclosure of state files, and about 4,000 pages were released. They reveal that Dell officials sought to avoid paying any income tax (citing the fact that Dell's headquarters state, Texas, does not have a corporate income tax) and that they also wanted numerous other big subsidies.

"Here's what it'll take," Dell vice president Kip Thompson told Commerce Secretary Jim Fain in May 2004, according to Fain's notes. "1) free land; 2) free bldg.; 3) no taxes; 4) training at $5m; 5) participation in creation of future value in the community." The following month, Thompson said to Fain: "[I am] not wowed here—not sure the state's stepping up here . . . If a state like N.C. can't get after this, I'm worried for our country—there's a certain amount of patriotism here." Later in June, Thompson told Fain: "20-year program of no tax . . . 'That's my line in the sand.'" In early July, after the state had upped its offer again, Thompson said to Fain: "I'm personally disappointed. I was shocked when we ran the numbers. Unless I can get that income tax resolved, it's best we moved on." And days later: "Here's what's most disconcerting. 2,000 jobs—shouldn't you be happy with no revenue?"[91]

At least some of the state negotiators realized what a ruinous precedent the Dell deal was setting. As one official wrote: "Politically dangerous. Probably overestimated impacts. Is it economically feasible in the long run? Do we give a zero-tax package to IBM, Merck, GD, Bayer, Glaxo, Cisco? Who will pay the taxes?"[92]

Dell has used its high profile to get big subsidy commitments; one estimate put them at $429 million just between 1999 and 2004. In Nashville, it got a multiple-subsidy package that includes a property tax abatement—*for 40 years!* (This is the longest tax holiday I've ever encountered.) An official in West Chester, Ohio, said a Dell warehouse got a subsidy there that 20 other companies had been denied. "If you've got a good name, then you can play a good game," he said.[93]

Scam #13: Threaten to Leave New York City

New York City is in a class by itself as the "job blackmail" capital of the United States. The game of creating an appearance that you are interested in leaving Manhattan is simple and cheap. Go to one or two cities in neighboring New Jersey or Connecticut. Talk to local officials, look at some space, let the mayor pitch a deal, and don't make a secret of it. Then go back and threaten New York. Jersey City, which has landed quite a few companies that really did want to move, makes for an especially effective blackmail threat. As Jersey City developer Richard LeFrak put it: "A lot of people come out and kick the tires and then go back to New York and negotiate a deal. It's part of the process of getting subsidies out of New York."[94]

Numerous banks, stock exchanges, TV networks, and insurance companies cashed in on subsidies from the Big Apple in the late 1980s and early 1990s. Consider some of the eight- and nine-figure deals, shown in table 1.1, that had already unfolded by 1993:[95]

Table 1.1. New York City "Retention" Subsidies, 1988–1993

NBC (package #1)	1988	$72.0 million
Chase Manhattan Bank (now JPMorgan Chase)	1989	$211.8 million
Citicorp (now Citibank; multiple recipient)	1989	$90.0 million
Bear Stearns & Company (package #1)	1991	$30.7 million
CBS (package #1)	1993	$49.3 million
New York Times (package #1)	1993	$28.7 million
Kidder Peabody	1993	$31.0 million

But the pace of giveaways greatly escalated under Mayor Rudolph Giuliani. In his first 18 months on the job, *CFO* magazine estimated, he "cut 11 deals worth about $350 million in long-term tax breaks."[96] Consider the parade of major deals from 1994 to 2001 shown in table 1.2.

Table 1.2. New York City "Retention" Subsidies, 1994–2001

Capital Cities/ABC Inc.	1994	$26.0 million
New York Mercantile Exchange	1994	$183.9 million
BankAmerica (now Bank of America; package #1, terminated 1998)	1994	$18.0 million
Prudential Securities	1995	$122.9 million
Morgan Stanley	1995	$70.8 million
Donaldson, Lufkin & Jenrette, Inc.	1995	$28.0 million
Credit Suisse First Boston	1995	$63.0 million
Viacom Inc. (multiple recipient)	1996	$15.0 million
Depository Trust Co.	1996	$18.5 million
Equitable Companies/ Equitable Life Assurance Society	1996	$10.3 million
Cotton Exchange and Coffee, Sugar, and Cocoa Exchange (never used)	1996	$98.8 million
Mutual of New York (MONY)	1996	$5.7 million
Conde Nast	1996	$10.8 million
News America (package #1)	1996	$20.7 million
Fidelity Investments/ National Financial Services Corp.	1996	$3.6 million
Empire Insurance Group (package #1)	1996	$8.7 million
American International Group (AIG)	1996	$58.9 million

Table 1.2. (continued)

NBC (package #2)	1996	$7.0 million
Price Waterhouse	1997	$3.1 million
Merrill Lynch	1997	$28.6 million
Bear Stearns (package #2)	1997	$75.0 million
PaineWebber (multiple recipient)	1997	$14.5 million
Ziff-Davis Publishing	1997	$4.3 million
Guardian Life Insurance	1998	$11.3 million
ING Barings	1998	$7.5 million
McGraw-Hill/ Standard & Poor's	1998	$52.5 million
Reuters	1998	$26.0 million
News America/New York Post (package #2)	1998	$24.4 million
Murray Feiss Import Corp.	1998	$6.4 million
New York Stock Exchange (terminated)	1998	$940.0 million
Barnes & Noble	1999	$2.1 million
Bertelsmann AG (package #2, never used)	1999	$28.0 million
CBS (package #2)	1999	$10.0 million
Time Warner Inc./ Home Box Office (package #1)	1999	$10.0 million
New York Board of Trade	1999	$31.0 million
VNU USA Company	1999	$10.6 million
Time Warner Inc./ Time Inc. (package #2)	1999	$28.0 million
Quick and Reilly/ Fleet Securities	2000	$4.8 million
Federated Department Stores Inc.	2000	$2.3 million
Liz Claiborne	2000	$8.0 million

Table 1.2. *(continued)*

Bloomberg (renounced by mayor-elect Bloomberg 11/02)	2000	$14.0 million
Arthur Andersen	2000	$4.5 million
NASDAQ/AMEX	2000	$52.0 million
Reed Elsevier	2000	$29.0 million
Canadian Imperial Bank of Commerce (CIBC)	2001	$16.0 million
New York Times (package #2)	2001	$18.7 million
Met Life	2001	$20.8 million

The deal to end all deals was Giuliani's 1998 announcement of a package worth *$940 million* to retain 1,500 jobs at the New York Stock Exchange. The NYSE made the implausible threat of relocating to Jersey City. I say implausible because by then many of its major member firms had been subsidized to stay in Manhattan. As well, financial "clusters" benefit from physical proximity: deal makers like to have lunch together, and Wall Street thrives on face-to-face gossip.

Nonetheless, Giuliani announced the lavish deal in an event full of telegenic sound bites. The City's giddy press release quoted three different officials as saying the deal clinched New York City as "The Financial Capital of the World."[97]

As the details unfolded, the deal appeared ever more piggish. The Exchange demanded a huge, sprawling footprint for the main trading floor of 600,000 square feet, requiring that three or four large buildings on its block be demolished. Industry observers noted that the NYSE's plans contradicted the international trend toward more trading being done by computers, not by hand-signaling traders. In the ensuing years after 1998, the deal's projected costs mounted, yet Giuliani stayed the course, so that at one point the subsidies were estimated at $1.1 billion—or $733,000 per job.[98] The deal eventually collapsed, but not before buildings were acquired and tenants evicted. Research by Good Jobs New York and the *New York Post* indicates that taxpayers have still been stuck with bills totaling at least $145 million to buy land and buildings, move tenants out, and pay bond and architectural fees for the aborted project. The NYSE stayed put.[99]

The Giuliani administration was also very secretive about the dozens of big subsidy deals it did; except for occasional, upbeat press releases, it told the public very little about what the deals cost or what the companies actually promised in exchange. Mayor Bloomberg's administration has been more forthcoming. Although it took a Freedom of Information Law request and an appeal filed after a six-month delay, his Economic Development Corporation finally released reams of data about many deals.

The fine print reveals that some of the contracts (such as those with PaineWebber, ING Financial Holdings, NASDAQ/AMEX, and Credit Suisse First Boston) allow companies to lay off as much as 8 percent of their workforce before suffering any penalties. But some contracts also set the bar artificially low to begin with. For example, Merrill Lynch had 9,693 employees when it signed its deal with Giuliani's administration, but the contract set the number at 9,000 and then allowed another 8 percent of layoffs beyond that before any penalties would apply. In other words, the company could actually lay off 1,413 people—a seventh of its staff—before losing any of the subsidy. Company and city officials publicized the deal as a 2,000-job creator, but that figure does not appear in the contract.[100]

Generally, the New York contracts are soft. Besides the layoff leniency, some of the contracts gave the city's development agency discretion whether or not to apply a penalty. Two of the contracts said companies could even *relocate* as much as 15 percent of their workforce out of the City before a deal would be terminated.[101] The contracts typically do not require a company to repay the subsidies even if they have large-scale layoffs.

This from a man who first became famous as a federal prosecutor. Rudolph Giuliani may have been *Time* magazine's 2001 Person of the Year for his leadership on September 11, but he also gets my vote for Giveaway King of the Late Twentieth Century.

Mayor Bloomberg has been less profligate than Giuliani was—in part, no doubt, because of the financial crisis he inherited, including so much tax revenue lost to "job retention" deals. He has also tried to walk the talk. Upon his election, he actually renounced a $14 million package that had been granted to Bloomberg LP, his financial data firm, saying: "Any company that makes a decision as to where they are going to be based on the tax rate is a company that won't be around very long . . . If you're down to that incremental margin you don't have a business."[102]

Scam #14: Ride Enron's Coattails

Enron! Where is Enron in the Great American Jobs Scam, you ask? Surely, Ken Lay must have something to do with it.

Not to disappoint! In 1985, Lay was the chairman and CEO of a small pipeline firm, Houston Natural Gas Company. He and his board agreed that year to merge the company into the much larger InterNorth, Inc., a pipeline company long based in Omaha. InterNorth's chairman saw the merger as a defensive measure to make his company less vulnerable to a hostile takeover. Given that Lay was from Houston, Omaha civic leaders feared he might relocate the headquarters, but he did some things that made it appear he would stay in Omaha: the company started to buy a luxury condo for him; he was elected to the board of the Greater Omaha Chamber of Commerce; and he even became a governor of another powerful business group, the Knights of Ak-Sar-Ben (that's "Nebraska" reversed).

But by spring 1986 Lay had become InterNorth's chairman, and pro-Houston board members prevailed; they renamed the company Enron and announced a move to Houston. Omaha's mayor had tried to persuade Lay to stay, meeting him for lunch at the high-rise Petroleum Club in downtown Houston. After hearing the mayor's pitch, Lay walked him to a window and pointed to a sleek office tower. Houston was giving the building to Enron free of rent for three years, Lay said, even renaming it Enron Tower. Over the next two years, Omaha would lose 2,000 Enron headquarters jobs to Houston.[103]

The loss of Enron jobs shook Nebraska's leaders, making them especially vulnerable to new job blackmail threats. Sure enough, just months later in 1986, agribusiness giant ConAgra said it was considering relocating its Omaha headquarters to Knoxville unless it got big tax breaks. Haunted by memories of InterNorth/Enron and urged on by Governor Kay Orr, the state legislature in early 1987 began debating three tax-break bills favoring large companies and high-income individuals, including income, sales, and property tax breaks, plus Single Sales Factor—the income-tax windfall that Raytheon would later demand in Massachusetts.

The Nebraska debate got ugly. Although the tax breaks benefited many companies, they were publicly identified with the agribusiness giant, and some of the specifics were enacted at ConAgra's insistence, such as a property tax exemption on mainframe computers and corporate jets. Some state senators balked on the jets and computers, and Senator Ernie Chambers of Omaha even filibustered, offering dozens of amendments, such as requiring that the ConAgra corporate logo "be tastefully added" to the state flag. ConAgra issued a press release that it had "terminated its site selection activities in the Omaha area," "decided to solicit proposals from interested states" for its headquarters and a new product laboratory, and would "begin funding a new program for employee moving allowances."

Then-governor of Missouri John Ashcroft telephoned ConAgra's CEO to launch a bid for the company's headquarters. "To Nebraska's dismay, we will aggressively pursue that company," said a Missouri spokesperson.[104]

Less than two weeks later, the Employment and Investment Growth Act—better known as LB 775—passed the Cornhusker

State's unicameral legislature, with all of ConAgra's wish list intact. In addition to the corporate tax breaks, the package cut the state's top personal income tax rate from 9.5 percent to 5.9 percent. "If tax giveaways were fast food, there'd be an arch over this chamber," one senator lamented. Senator Vard Johnson, the main backer of the tax cuts, was blunt about the power dynamic: "This can be justified as an open acknowledgment of the ability of the affluent to vote with their feet," he said.[105]

Very quickly, it became evident that the main tax-cut law, LB 775, was going to cost far more than legislators expected, and that many companies were going to get tax breaks even if they created no new jobs—or even if they laid people off. Within six months, 75 companies had already applied for LB 775 tax credits, which had no cap. A fourth of the applicant companies said they would not create any jobs at all; one option under the law allows that. One company, Mutual of Omaha, applied for a tax credit on a new computer system even though it had announced it was *eliminating* 1,000 headquarters jobs. The tax cut's price tag? During the 1987 debate, the legislative fiscal office estimated that LB 775 would cost the state $5.3 million in lost tax revenue in its second year in effect. But the Nebraska Department of Revenue now reports that through 2003 companies have garnered $1.88 billion in LB 775 investment tax credits and used $1.02 billion of them (the entitlement period is seven years, plus up to eight years of carry-forwards if a company has any left over). Plus, companies have received sales and use tax refunds from the state of $534 million.[106]

In other words, the state has been incurring tax credits and paying tax refunds to the tune of *more than $150 million a year*—a far cry from the $5.3 million annual cost originally forecast.

With accounting like that, who needs Enron?

"This is Nebraska's corporate accounting scandal," says Tim Rinne of Nebraskans for Peace. A coalition of 20 groups seeks to repeal LB 775, citing the law's ruinous costs and inflated job claims. More than a dozen legislative efforts to reform the law have failed, mostly in committee. Reform advocates are concerned by state budget deficits that have forced the legislature to cut funding for K-12, higher education, and other state programs.[107]

But the Nebraska Chamber of Commerce and Industry suggests it wants more. "Business is different today than it was in 1987," says the chamber's chief executive. "It shows we need to be looking at the next generation of economic incentives."[108]

Chapter Two

Site Location 101: How Companies Decide Where to Expand or Relocate

[As a businessman] I never made an investment decision based on the Tax Code . . . [I]f you are giving money away I will take it. If you want to give me inducements for something I am going to do anyway, I will take it. But good business people do not do things because of inducements, they do it because they can see that they are going to be able to earn the cost of capital out of their own intelligence and organization of resources.

—*Paul O'Neill, former CEO of Alcoa and President George W. Bush's first Secretary of the Treasury* [1]

How companies decide where to expand or relocate is not rocket science. Their decision-making process is driven by business basics; subsidies rarely make a difference. The trouble is, the way the system is rigged, companies are getting huge subsidies to go where they would go anyway.

Here's a typical search process. A company of substantial size will usually hire a site location consultant to perform the research on new locations. If the company doesn't use a consultant, it will assign lead duties to one of its divisions, usually real estate or finance. In either case, a management team will coordinate with the consultant or internal lead, providing input about what the company needs, from operations, sales, and other departments.

The company—let's call it Acme Widget—says to the consultant: to make widgets, we need a location that has plenty of workers who know how to make widgets or who have comparable skills and can be readily trained. We also need a location with plenty of access to the main ingredients of widgets. And we don't want to be far from our widget customers or from transportation systems to reach them.

Business Basics: What Really Drives Site Location

The factors that drive site location—access to key inputs, suppliers, and customers—vary depending on the nature of the company's products or services. Three-gigabyte widgets are cutting-edge high-tech, so they need to be close to a research university or government lab, in a large metro area with cultural amenities. Titanium widgets require a lot of electricity, so they need a place with cheap (probably hydro) power. Software widgets require a lot of code writers, so they'll go to a city with similar companies, a labor market with code writers. Commodity widgets are low-margin, so they need a place where labor is cheap. Chemical widgets require a lot of oil, so they need to be in an oil patch, or on the coast where imports arrive. Paper widgets need to be near forests and fresh water. Fresh-caught widgets get put on ice and delivered rapidly to customers, so that widget-packing plant needs to be close to a freight airport hub.[2]

You get the idea. Companies base their decisions on business basics—affordable supply of key inputs and proximity to suppliers and customers. Key inputs vary and so do linkages. Boeing built up in the Seattle area because of the cheap hydro power from the Bonneville Power Administration for its complex metallurgy. Food processing companies locate facilities close to the farms and ranches that supply them and close to interstate highways and railheads to get product to market. Emerging high-technology companies need engineering schools and venture capital; Silicon Valley had both. Financial wheeler-dealers thrive on gossip and face-to-face meetings, so New York's Wall Street zoomed in the 1980s and 1990s. Lobbyists want to be on K Street in Washington, DC, where the power-lunch crowds throng. Sports franchises want the fattest TV contracts, so they go to the biggest metro area that is not already taken.

There are, of course, further complexities to the process. Different kinds of companies and facilities have different needs, even within the same industry. Headquarters are very different from branch plants. Headquarters usually need to be close to centers of finance or marketing; they need major airport hubs, cultural amenities, and a high quality of life to attract and retain key executives. Manufacturing companies' issues are different from those of service-sector companies or retailers.

Another factor is where the company is in its "life cycle." Newly emerging companies (as in Silicon Valley in the 1980s) are more likely to cluster together, sharing talent pools and capital sources; mature companies may be more concerned about costs and so are more willing to disperse geographically. Some companies, like utilities and hospitals, are tied to their markets, so they rarely move (except perhaps to change offices within a metro area). Companies facing a lot of technological change have special concerns—in particular, maintaining access to highly skilled workers. All of these industry-specific and facility-specific issues drive the location criteria.

Increasingly, the supply of skilled labor is a key issue, and the work of site location consultants often involves detailed analyses of labor markets. This became true in the tight labor market of the late 1990s, and it remains true today in many cases. As the Baby Boom generation approaches mass retirement, skilled labor supply will become a huge, chronic site location issue (see chapter 9).

At the early stages of screening, companies look at major cost issues, such as labor, transportation, and occupancy. At this first cut, companies may ask the consultant to weigh lots of factors. Some consultants claim they'll handle their clients' laundry list of 50 to 100 issues; other consultants say they have software packages that can account for as many as 200 variables. But there is usually a much smaller number of make-or-break issues. For example, if the company needs to be close to a university laboratory with a life sciences specialty, a labor market with a lot of web-software code writers, a major airport hub serving national markets because its sales representatives travel a lot, or a place with a lot of fresh water to make steel or paper, then many locations will be eliminated right off the bat.

Taxes: The Least Important Factor

The company and its consultant will also look at major kinds of taxes, but only to see if there are big differences that might be unfavorable to a site. Since corporate taxes have been cut in so many ways in so many states, and because subsidies reduce them even further, that is not often an issue.

Robert Ady, a longtime Fantus Company executive and now the head of his own company, Ady International, is said to have assisted more site locations than any living person. Here is what he says, based on hundreds of face-to-face dealings with companies deciding where to go: "[I]n the facility location process, taxes are not relatively important when compared with other cost factors such as labor, transportation and utility and occupancy costs. . . . In summary, site selection data do not suggest any correlation between low taxes and positive economic growth, or between high taxes and slow growth. The location requirements are too many, the process too complicated, and other factors too important to justify a strong relationship."[3]

Ady's finding is consistent with those of others: tax-rate differences and tax incentives are too small to make a difference. Subsidies cannot make a bad place a good place. Good places are competitive because they have the long-term business basics that a company needs to produce supply to meet demand. So if cities and states want to grow good jobs, instead of cooking up more tax breaks, they should focus on improving their business basics—the valuable inputs and linkages they have.[4]

There are other screening issues. Some companies, mostly manufacturers, seek to avoid unions, so they may seek either rural areas with few unions or locations in "right to work" states. This is a smaller issue now than in past decades, and less often an issue in non-manufacturing industries that are less unionized. (Today, 13.5 percent of factory workers belong to a union, and the overall rate of unionization in the private sector is 8.2 percent.)[5] Of course, for industries that are tied to specific markets—such as utilities, transportation, construction, and many parts of the service sector— moving to avoid unions is a moot issue.

There are often personal factors in location decisions. Executives especially like to create a short commute for themselves. They may also locate for amenities such as golf courses or good schools for their children. The smaller the company, the more likely it is that such factors will come into play, but they are sometimes evident at bigger companies, too. For example, a study of 38 companies that left New York City found that 31 moved closer to their chief executive's home, reducing the average CEO commute to eight miles.[6] When the founder of Kinko's sold the company to a group of New York investors, the company moved its headquarters in 2000 from Ventura, California, to Dallas, where the new CEO lived.[7]

At the next cut, the consultant provides a more detailed list, with information about communities within a chosen area that could be as big as a multistate region or as small as a metro area (with the explosion of web-based data, the early-cut research is increasingly an armchair exercise). Ady has written that the list at this stage could include as few as 15 communities or as many as 100, but other sources rarely mention such high numbers. The bigger the project, the wider the search is likely to be. For a medium-sized project, the list might narrow to half a dozen sites. For each site, the consultant develops a cost model; Ady says his models project 15 or 20 years out.[8]

Bruce Maus, a veteran site location consultant based in the Twin Cities with Corporate Real Estate, Inc., says he uses a 10-year spreadsheet model for the client, factoring in all of the company's projected costs in each competing space. He cautions his clients not to give economic development subsidies too much weight, because on a 10-year basis, they wash out; that is, they are dwarfed by the business basics—the big-ticket items that really drive the decisions.[9]

As a weighted cost factor of importance, Ady rates taxes a distant fifth—and last (see table 2.1).[10]

Table 2.1. Site Location Cost Factors, According to Robert Ady

Factor	Manufacturing Project	Office Project
Labor	36%	72%
Transportation	35%	0%
Utilities	17%	8%
Occupancy	8%	15%
Taxes	4%	5%

Federal tax statistics suggest that even Ady's low ranking of taxes is overweighted. They provide even stronger evidence on why taxes—and therefore tax breaks—can rarely influence corporate location decisions. Internal Revenue Service statistics show that all state and local taxes make up only 1.2 percent of the typical company's cost of doing business, far less than labor, materials, marketing, overhead, transportation—the business basics. And then companies get to deduct those state and local taxes when they file their federal tax returns, so Uncle Sam actually foots up to 35 percent of the bill. The bottom line: after federal deductibility, state and local taxes make up only 0.8 percent of the average company's costs.[11] (And whatever companies pay in taxes, it does not all come out of their profits. To the extent that market forces allow, companies pass on their taxes in the form of higher prices to customers and lower wages to their employees.)

But back to our example company's site search. The list is narrowed again, based on feedback from the company, including subjective issues as well as other factors that might not be obvious to the consultant. The company may eliminate a location because a competitor is located there, for example, or because it thinks the quality of life is not good enough. Taxes remain in the spreadsheet analysis, but may matter even less. For example, if the company is looking at different suburbs in the same metro area, many tax rates (corporate and personal income, sales and excise, utility) are going to be identical, though property taxes may vary.

So now the decision is down to the finalists—say, three to five places. Then the consultant goes on site to gather more data and knocks on the door of the local economic development agency. He probably won't even identify his client but will describe the proposed facility only in broad terms of jobs and dollars and physical specifications. And he will almost certainly start asking about subsidies available for the deal.

How Public Perceptions Get Distorted

Pause the tape! Freeze the frame! What just happened here? Notice how the development officials' perspective just got incredibly distorted. Someone just appeared at their door and said, "We might have a bunch of jobs for you, but first we need to talk about subsidies." The development officials—and their bosses, the politicians—haven't seen all that happened before that knock on the door. They don't see that the only reason the consultant is spending any time with them is because their community is an inherently profitable location for the company—*it has the business basics!* Any subsidies are icing on the cake, but the cake is already baked.

This system leads the public officials to believe that if they do the subsidy dance just right—and if they behave in ways that consultants like to describe as "sending business-friendly signals"—they will land the deal.

This "business-friendly signal" stuff is mostly about speed. Consultants and their clients like to see localities compete not only on subsidies, but also on how quickly they can snap to attention, keep the project secret, produce customized data overnight (not next week!), and expedite application paperwork. Part of this dynamic, frankly, seems to be about groveling; some companies want to see who will suck up the most, to see which community has the most "pro-business attitude." In fairness, though, a lot of it seems to reflect the fact that companies feel driven to make site location decisions faster than they used to, reflecting the accelerated pace of business life in general.[12]

Site location consultants don't even have to raise the issue of subsidies when they come knocking. Public officials have gotten so used to subsidy demands, they roll them out voluntarily. In one breath, the development officials brag about their schools and roads and workers and quality of life and other public goods that rely on taxpayer support. And in the next breath, they tout all the ways the company can dodge paying its fair share for those public goods. All the while sending those business-friendly signals. It's one twisted dance.

But back to the finalists. Chances are the company has already pretty much decided where it wants to go. In fact, it may have made its mind up before the consultant even went on site. Absent some big surprise when the consultant kicks the tires, City A is going to get the deal.

So why bother with Cities B through E? To maximize the subsidies! You need straw men with which to "whipsaw" City A.

Putting Public Officials in the "Prisoners' Dilemma"

Dennis Donovan is a nationally prominent site location consultant with the Wadley-Donovan Group, a big firm that was founded in 1975. In an obscure magazine called *Expansion Management,* he laid out a 30-point checklist in "Trade Secrets Revealed: An Insider's Look at Incentives Negotiations." Point #3 advises: "Negotiate incentives for the new project in two or three finalist locations, preferably in different states. Generally speaking, spend the most time negotiating in the preferred location. Use offers from the alternate areas for leverage." In Point #4 he further recommends pitting two cities against each other in the same metro area: "In the preferred area, tie incentive negotiations to a couple of sites, ideally in separate communities."[13]

Game theorists call this the "prisoners' dilemma." In such a dilemma, two people who ought to cooperate—crime suspects who acted together, but who have now been captured and separated—fail to cooperate, because each is being promised more lenient treatment in return for confessing and ratting on the other prisoner. For the individual caught in such a trap, the expedient course is to confess, to try to save your own skin. But if both confess, both go up the river. Applying this dilemma to our hapless public officials in competing locations, if all of them capitulate to the site location consultant's manipulation, the outcome is worse than zero-sum; it is lose-lose.[14]

Cities competing for deals are living this game. The consultant doesn't tell any of the finalist cities who they are competing against. Even if the deal is so high-profile that the news media identify the competing places, it is clearly understood that the cities (or states) will not compare notes or cooperate in any way. That leaves the consultant and the company in info-control—especially about competing subsidy bids—as they play the sites against each other to up the ante. But if the public officials stood fast and didn't accede to the consultants' game, they could both spend less on subsidies and gain more market power.

Given how this system is rigged, all the power rests with the site location consultants and their corporate clients. No wonder there have been recurring grumbles that consultants sometimes exaggerate the subsidy bids from one place to coax higher sums from another.

This is where corporate control of the system really pays off in outrageous returns on investment (ROIs). For the cost of a one-time fee to a consultant (or a lobbyist if special legislation is necessary) and depending on the size or prestige of the deal, a company may be able to extract a huge multiyear subsidy, producing an ROI greater than it might get from developing a new product or investing in new equipment. This is why companies are so willing to say or do almost anything to preserve the practice of lavish company-specific deals. Considered in isolation, they can be fantastically lucrative.

These prisoners' dilemma games also enable companies to create fictions about cause and effect. These fictions can be used to create public versions of how deals happened that no one can credibly contradict, because the company's real decision-making process will never be revealed. The most important fiction to maintain, of course, is that subsidies matter in deciding where a company expands or relocates. For example, being able to send secret signals to competing cities means companies can tell contradictory stories to different cities and have no fear of being exposed. If a company really has its heart set on City A, it can tell that city that it is in the hunt, but needs to do better. Meanwhile, it can send less urgent signals to Cities B and C, even if they offered bigger packages at first. Eventually, City A offers the biggest package, and the company announces its decision to go there.

This system can also be used to soften up a state, although exact corporate motives rarely get revealed. Consider the Boeing story. As described in chapter 1, Scam #9, the aerospace giant announced in 2001 that it would relocate its corporate headquarters from Seattle. It proceeded to conduct an unusually public auction between Chicago, Dallas, and Denver. It got a package estimated at $56 million from Chicago and Illinois. The episode sent chills through the Puget Sound region; leaders there feared that by reducing its civic profile in Seattle, the company was signaling its intention to disinvest production as well. That fear of disinvestment likely softened up Washington state for the company's next auction. Two years later, Boeing launched a 20-state bidding war for its next-generation passenger jet, the 7E7 "Dreamliner" project. The Evergreen State enacted a $3.2 billion aerospace-industry subsidy package to "win" the sweepstakes.[15]

Consultants, Commissions, Correlations, and Objectivity

Besides fantastic ROIs for the companies, there is an even darker motive afoot here: some site location consultants work on commission; that is, they get paid largely or in part by a percentage of the subsidies they negotiate for the company—*as much as 30 percent of the subsidy package!* And the industry trend is that pay by commission is becoming increasingly common. So of course, the consultants are highly self-interested in maintaining the fiction that subsidies matter, so they can run up the subsidy tab and get bigger fees.[16]

Commissions also raise the issue of the consultants' objectivity. As veteran site location consultant Bruce Maus puts it, "When the deal is incentive-driven, we lose our objectivity. I wish I had a nickel for every time a broker said she won't show the client the property unless he agrees to the commission. That means the client doesn't get to see all the options. The same is true with consultants paid by incentives. They only show the sites with high incentives. They lose the objectivity in the deal and may steer the client to the wrong place or not the best place."[17]

What does this all really mean for subsidies and jobs? Candid site location consultants will admit that the only time subsidies can actually tilt the scales is when a company has two equally compelling choices. But that rarely happens. So subsidies are a really crude tool that can only affect a really tiny percentage of deals. All the other times, the subsidies are just wasted windfalls, paying companies to do what they would have done anyway. That means less money for things that really do help create jobs, like skills and infrastructure.

Long-term statistical studies of the relationship between taxes and growth confirm this. Large "metasurveys" have looked at dozens of such studies on what economists call "elasticity," or how much the differences in taxes among states affect growth. They conclude that the correlation between taxes and growth is about −0.2 percent.[18]

Professor Peter Fisher of the University of Iowa explains what this statistic means. The coauthor of two books and numerous studies and articles on economic development incentives, he is one of the nation's foremost experts on the issue, especially on multiple-subsidy enterprise zones. During the 1990s, he says, for every 100 business establishments in the United States, about 10 new ones were born every year. If the elasticity rate is −0.2 percent, this means that if a state enacted a subsidy for new investment that reduced companies' corporate tax rate by a whopping 20 percent, the state could expect its growth rate to increase by 4 percent (20 times 0.2). In other words, instead of getting 10 new establishments per 100 each year, it would get 10.4 new ones. The trouble is, by lowering your tax rate for all newly arriving corporations, you just gave a tax break to 10 establishments to gain the additional 0.4. In other words, 96 percent of the businesses that benefited from the tax break just got a windfall for doing what they would have done anyway.[19]

I think of it like using dynamite to catch fish, or using a chainsaw to cut butter. We're talking *bad* technology.

Fisher and other experts also caution taxpayers to watch out for common flaws in studies that look at the relationship between taxes and growth. Many of them assume that even though corporate taxes go down, the quality of public services stays the same. That, of course, is not a realistic assumption, and it makes such studies questionable on their face. If corporate tax revenue goes down, the state has to either reduce the quality of public services or raise the revenue from other sources, and both of those options could also affect jobs. Cutbacks in education or infrastructure would be especially harmful. They also warn that studies often fail to factor in whether a state has lucrative tax loopholes, such as those that allow companies to hide their profits in Delaware or Nevada (see chapter 4). Some studies suggest that such loopholes can be just as profitable to a company (and just as harmful to public revenues) as development subsidies.[20]

Additional Evidence That Subsidies Don't Matter

In his autobiography, former Idaho governor Cecil Andrus recounted how he dealt with a knee-jerk subsidy demand from a high-tech company:

> Hewlett-Packard was pondering whether to put a plant in Boise or pick a site in Medford, Oregon. I had David Packard visit my office. He was a remarkable guy, a computer entrepreneur, Silicon Valley pioneer, deputy defense secretary—and somebody who spent years trying to persuade California's Republican Party to put up competent moderate candidates instead of right-wing ideologues.
>
> While no one had made this discovery yet, went my spiel, Idaho was an excellent place to make computers. We had low taxes, and we had a workforce with many people who were first-generation off the farm. They were willing to deliver a full day's work for a day's pay.
>
> Packard listened politely and then asked in a level voice, "What type of tax concessions is the state willing to give?" He was obviously alluding to inducements offered by Oregon. I took a deep breath and set out to sell him on a difficult argument. "We don't believe in existing businesses subsidizing new businesses," I told him. "When you come to Idaho you become a citizen, and we all play by the same rules. A few years down the line and you'll be an old-timer. Do you want to subsidize the next guy who comes along?"
>
> It was a nervous moment. After a brief pause, Packard grunted: "Makes sense. That's the way to go." He moved on to other questions. We captured the computer plant and gained a top-notch corporate citizen. Hewlett-Packard put up front-end money on a sewage treatment plant, practiced recycling, and was an innovator in heavy metals extraction.[21]

Besides such recollections, there is lots of other case-specific evidence that subsidies don't determine where companies choose to locate. Privately, economic development officials often speak of deals in which things happened that made it clear subsidies weren't the deciding factor. Perhaps the most damning systemic evidence comes from state auditors, who have repeatedly found either that subsidies do not cause companies to invest or that it is impossible to establish any cause-and-effect relationship. A survey of state audits in the 1990s found that in at least a dozen program investigations, the green-eyeshade folks found or opined that companies would have invested without the subsidies.[22]

An especially contentious series of audits has taken place in Vermont. In 1999 and 2000 there, the state auditor and a legislative oversight committee found massive problems with the Vermont Economic Progress Council (VEPC), a group of nine business people appointed by Governor Howard Dean to give out tax credits. The legislative report questioned the validity of VEPC's claim that none of its deals would have occurred "but for" the tax break. Most of the money intended for small businesses went to four of the largest companies in the state, and most of the subsidies went to the most prosperous counties of the state. VEPC hunkered down and tried to stonewall the auditor on his request to see the books; he sued and, after a great brouhaha, the attorney general backed the auditor. The final report found that VEPC made no effort to verify any information from the companies when they claimed "but for." It also found that VEPC had been issuing tax credits for investments *before companies even applied for them!* When asked by the *Wall Street Journal*, only 2 out of 21 subsidized companies would say the credits were decisive for their expansions.[23]

A third Vermont audit, issued in December 2004, still found the same kinds of problems. The 21 companies examined had gotten $20.9 million in tax credits—but created fewer than 7 percent of the jobs they promised. The audit also found that the VEPC was still not looking hard at the "but for" claims. "The Council does not review financial statements, business plans, or tax records to assess the financial necessity of a tax credit authorization," the auditor found.[24]

In 2003, Toyota chose San Antonio for its new pickup truck assembly plant, getting a subsidy package estimated at $133 million. It chose the Alamo City even though it had higher subsidy offers from Alabama, Arkansas, Mississippi, and Tennessee, one of which was reported to be $500 million—almost four times the amount of the Texas deal. Local reports at the time stressed business basics, such as the fact that Texas is the nation's #1 market for trucks, and local officials agreed to install a second rail line (in other words, San Antonio offered proximity to markets and access to competitive shipping). The company even volunteered to pay $34 million in taxes to the school district and didn't seek abatements from other taxing districts.[25]

In a refreshing moment of civic-minded candor, Toyota's senior vice president in charge of site selection in North America said, "If you pull too many incentives out of the community in the beginning, you pay the price down the road. It's a pennywise but dollar-foolish thing to do. We believe it is in our best business interest to be a good corporate citizen and contribute to the community right away."[26]

Even a company staying in Lower Manhattan after the attacks of September 11 admitted this. Upon receiving a $25 million grant for staying put, an American Express spokesman said: "Our decision to return downtown, which has been our home for more than 150 years, was not predicated on financial incentives." But then he hastened to add backside coverage, as if to say: we're no fools if people are going to throw money around. "Once those financial incentives became available, we chose to participate, as did other companies," he said.[27]

In other cases, deals get explained and companies cite the business basics that drove their decision—without mentioning subsidies.

In 2004, Citgo (which is 100 percent owned by the nation of Venezuela) got $35 million in subsidies to relocate 700 headquarters jobs from Tulsa to Houston. But the company readily admitted that the subsidies didn't matter. Citgo CEO Luis Marin said that strategic and operational concerns outweighed the incentives from Texas.

"The energy business is the cornerstone in the state of Texas and the city of Houston," Marin said. (Translation: we want to be in the nation's biggest petrocluster.) "This decision was not based on [subsidy] economics," Marin said.[28]

In 1999, America Online announced it would build a half-billion-dollar technology center in Prince William County, Virginia, even though Cobb County, Georgia, had offered a subsidy package almost twice as large (over $40 million versus $22 to $24 million). Cobb County officials were ticked off: half a year earlier, they had announced AOL was coming there. As *Site Selection* magazine saw it, "In the end, AOL's decision seemed to come down to proximity . . . Anxious to avoid the cyberspace hell it hit in 1996 when lack of capacity threw its network for a loop, AOL now seems intent on keeping its critical knowledge workers close to one another."[29]

Money Left on the Table:
More Evidence That Subsidies Are Irrelevant

Perhaps the most damning evidence that subsidies don't matter comes from site location consultants, some of whom pitch their wares by pointing out that companies routinely leave subsidy dollars on the table. In other words, subsidies have become so numerous, and companies making rational decisions pay them so little attention, that they routinely go unclaimed. Of course, that creates a market niche for consultants to help companies scour the public trough—for a fee, of course; preferably a commission.

Location Management Services, founded by James Renzas, bills itself as "a world-class leader in incentive negotiations for corporate America." In a 2003 press release announcing its web-based Incentives Management System to help companies get all the giveaways they have coming to them, the company claims that "the U.S. government has noted that over $10 billion of available tax credits and incentives go unused annually."[30]

Renzas made a gut-level appeal in a magazine article:

A majority of CFOs recently polled reported that they experience a sinking feeling when they consider whether their company is receiving all of the tax benefits that it is eligible to receive. Many will spend their entire career with a lingering fear they are missing something important, or perhaps not getting all that is due their corporation.

I'd love to see that polling question! Was it multiple choice?

When considering whether your company will receive all the financial incentives and tax credits it is entitled to, do you:

a) Have a sinking feeling?
b) Worry that your boss will cut your annual bonus if he finds out you missed a giveaway?
c) Fret about private school tuition bills because the schools at the new location will be so underfunded?

Location Management Services also said:

Corporate America typically leaves millions of dollars on the table when it expands, relocates, or finds new sites . . .

LMS has offices in 31 communities nationwide . . . Each LMS staff member has more than 17 years average service and has realized greater than a billion dollars in incentives for clients.

Unless you have an expert on your team to handle negotiation and collection of financial incentives and tax credits for your new company location, you may be leaving millions of dollars on the table.

Location Management Services . . . has helped hundreds of companies gain millions of dollars through strategic site selection. Its proprietary Incentives Management System ensures that all available financial incentives and tax credits are reviewed and capture[d] prior to making a facility investment.

A check with your name on it could be waiting . . .

It's like the Publishers' Clearinghouse Sweepstakes! Is that Ed McMahon at the door?

Without naming names, Location Management Services posted brief case studies that unwittingly suggested that subsidies are windfalls, not determinants. It said it helped a "Fortune 500 big box retailer with hundreds of locations around the country" to "collect more than five million dollars in credits and incentives that went directly to the company's bottom line." In another case, a "major national retailer was planning on expanding its California distribution center. It had already budgeted $1.5 million to acquire the 147-acre parcel next door." After Location Management Services got done, "the client received the entire 147-acre parcel for $1 per acre as well as other infrastructure construction grants. The benefit to the company was over $6.5 million." Finally, "a major national bank was consolidating multiple operations in its downtown core," and Location Management Services "was able to obtain Enterprise Zone status for the new development, resulting in over $6 million in state and local tax benefits without e[v]er relocating a single seat."[32]

Finally, the company's website suggested it works on commission: ". . . we are compensated based on the results we deliver."

Renzas, the company's founder, was not always so gung-ho about subsidies. In a 1995 talk, he said he strongly disapproved of the trend toward more subsidies. "If it were up to me and if it were a perfect world, I would pass a law prohibiting it," he said.[33]

Cabela's: Subsidies Increase Our Profits

Occasionally, companies admit the truth: subsidies rarely affect where they locate, but they *do* increase profits. Of course, the truth comes out more readily if the document in question is a shareholder filing with the Securities and Exchange Commission. Falsify an SEC statement, and you could get into serious legal trouble.

Cabela's is the nation's largest direct marketer of outdoor sporting goods. It sells by catalog and Internet and in nine megastores as big as or bigger than many Wal-Mart outlets. It competes with other chains like Bass Pro and Gander Mountain. It touts its megastores as economic development "destinations," like Disney World or Six Flags. The stores feature "museum-quality wildlife displays" and "large aquariums." "Our destination retail stores . . . reinforce our outdoor lifestyle image . . . and provide exciting tourist and entertainment shopping experiences for the entire family," it gushes.[34] The stores also feature "gun libraries, restaurants and educational centers." With an average of 4.4 million visitors per store per year, "our Kansas City, Kansas and Owatonna, Minnesota destination retail stores rank among the top two tourist attractions in their respective states."[35]

And here I thought Dodge City and the Boundary Waters were the places to see.

In 2004, Cabela's filed an Initial Public Offering (IPO) prospectus with the SEC as it prepared to convert from being privately held to being publicly traded on the stock market. In an IPO prospectus, a company must disclose a great deal about its business plan, so that potential investors are fully informed about both the opportunities and the risks. Because subsidies are integral to Cabela's strategy, the prospectus discusses them several times. Cabela's makes extensive use of tax increment financing (TIF), so that increased property and/or sales tax—revenue that would normally go to schools and other local services—is instead used to pay back bonds that subsidize the megastores.

The company's overall message is clear: subsidies give us higher profits.

> Historically, we have been able to negotiate economic development arrangements relating to the construction of a number of our new destination retail stores, including free land, monetary grants and the recapture of incremental sales, property or other taxes through economic development bonds [i.e., TIF], with many local and state governments.
>
> The government grants have been recorded as deferred grant income and have been classified as a reduction to the cost basis of the applicable property and equipment. The deferred grant income is amortized to earnings, as a reduction of depreciation expense . . .[36]

In other words, Cabela's is saying, subsidies make our stores cheaper to build and therefore more profitable. In its cautions to investors, Cabela's says it plainly:

> We may not be able to obtain similar economic development packages in the future. The failure to [do so] could cause us to significantly alter our destination retail store strategy or format. As a result, we could be forced to invest less capital in our stores which could have an adverse effect on our ability to construct the stores as attractive tourist and entertainment shopping destinations, possibly leading to a decrease in revenues or revenue growth. In addition, the failure to obtain similar economic development packages for stores built in the future would have an adverse impact on our cash flows and on the return on investment in these stores.[37]

In other words, without subsidies, Cabela's would have lower profits. And America might experience slower growth in museum-quality shopping destinations. Imagine!

Do the Cabela's packages pay off for taxpayers? Well, to justify subsidizing a tourist destination, you have to attract shoppers from outside the state, so you capture new sales tax revenue plus new hotel and restaurant business. If you only draw local dollars, that would mean you are merely shuffling those dollars among local vendors. (Of course, on a multistate level, shuffling is exactly what you are doing.)

The *Allentown Morning Call* set out to determine if the $32 million package for the Cabela's in Hamburg, Pennsylvania, is paying off. It opened in 2003, has 247,000 square feet—the company's biggest yet—and employs 600 people, mostly at low pay. The newspaper went back to the state and local agencies that had bragged about the taxpayer benefits of the original deal. But the Pennsylvania Department of Economic and Community Development said it was not tracking sales tax revenue. And Tilden Township said it had no data on local property tax revenues. So no one knows whether the deal is stimulating other new development. None of the public officials could provide any specific numbers about the deal's outcome.[38]

And what about that tourism strategy, with the store projected to attract six to seven million visits a year? (That's a lot of road wear and air pollution!) Merchants in downtown Hamburg said they are not getting much spillover traffic. Reporter Sam Kennedy counted license plates in the parking lot, finding more than two-thirds were in-state. Cabela's responded by claiming that by dollar volume, less than a third of the store's sales go to Pennsylvanians. A few competing sporting-goods merchants said the deal is hurting them. One, located nearby on the Appalachian Trail, said it is losing business, especially because Cabela's sends a courtesy van to the trailhead. Another store owner reported losing a fourth of his sales.[39]

Ultimately, the *Call* couldn't make a call. "The impact of Cabela's is nearly impossible to assess because Pennsylvania, like many states, doesn't pay close attention to such projects after the ribbon-cutting ceremonies have ended, the news cameras have stopped rolling and the politicians have gone home," it concluded.[40]

Clearly, the public officials who take credit for high-profile deals are not about to go back and look to see if they are wasting taxpayers' money. By failing to keep records, they also make it hard for others to discover the truth.

Finally, a truly weird footnote: in some cases, the stuffed animals and dioramas—*the visual centerpieces of Cabela's stores*—are actually owned by state or local government as part of the subsidy deals. ". . . in connection with some of the economic development packages received from state or local governments where our stores are located, we have entered into agreements granting ownership of the taxidermy, diorama, or other portions of our stores to these state and local governments."[41]

Can you say "taxpayers' taxidermy," five times, really fast?

★ Chapter Three ★

Fantus and the Rise of the Economic War Among the States

We're familiar with the needs of industry. We have a wealth of information on what particular industries want. We know the real reasons they move, not the phony baloney reasons they sometimes give out.

—*Maurice Fulton, manager, Fantus Company, Chicago (the long-dominant site location consulting firm)* [1]

Site consultants think about states the way 17-year-old boys think about 17-year-old girls.

—*Jay Hancock, Baltimore Sun* [2]

In the depths of the Great Depression, a young Chicago industrial real estate salesman named Leonard Yaseen grew impatient with his father-in-law and boss, Felix Fantus. The old man was doing a lot more for his corporate clients than helping them buy and sell real estate. He was giving companies that sought to relocate their factories information not just about land and buildings, but also about transportation and utilities, local wages and taxes. He had been doing this since 1919, when he performed his own site location search to move his chair-manufacturing plant from Chicago to Indiana. Fantus was giving all this valuable information away for free, and Yaseen thought they should be charging for it.

Unable to convince Fantus that his insights could be commodified into a business, in 1934 Yaseen left Chicago for New York, with his father-in-law's blessing. For a year and a half, he immersed himself in data about rail service, labor skills and wages, utilities, raw materials, and taxes. Then he sent a pitch letter to lots of Manhattan-based manufacturing companies, and one hired him.[3]

Thus was born the Fantus Factory Locating Service, one of the most powerful yet obscure consulting firms in U.S. history. Yaseen's fledgling business slowly took root through the rest of the Depression and World War II, and then boomed after the war. It prospered so much, he was able to buy a major stake in the Fantus real estate company in Chicago and immediately converted it to site location consulting as well. Another son-in-law of Felix Fantus, Maurice Fulton, would come to head that office.

For the next four decades, Fantus dominated the site location consulting industry, playing a central role in the relocation of thousands of workplaces, most of them factories moving out of the Northeast and Midwest to the South. By its own count, Fantus had helped engineer more than 4,000 relocations by the time Yaseen retired in 1977, and it shepherded 2,000 more in the next decade.[4] Fantus also did extensive work overseas as early as the 1950s, working for U.S. companies seeking sites in at least a dozen other countries.

Fantus survives today as a Chicago-based consulting affiliate of the Big Four accounting firm Deloitte & Touche. Although the industry is now more fragmented and its work more computerized, site locators still use the basic system Fantus created. The identity of corporate clients is still held confidential until late in the process. The real reasons a company chooses a place are not revealed. Cities and states are still "whipsawed" against each other to maximize subsidies, and when that happens, cities and states are often not told the places they are competing against, so there is no way for City A to know that what the consultant says Cities B and C are offering is true. Many of the consultants work for both private and public-sector clients, claiming no conflict of interest. Many of the profession's most influential players—including Robert Ady, Gene DePrez, and Dennis Donovan—are Fantus alumni.

It's not just the Fantus process that lives on, but also its philosophy that influenced the shape of the nation's economic geography and our belief system about what constitutes a good "business climate." Although obviously Fantus did not tell its clients what to do, the net result of the relocations it aided was anti–Rust Belt, anti-city, anti–corporate tax share, and anti-union. And although Fantus discontinued rating states on their "business climates" after issuing one study, succeeding studies by another firm played a major role in accelerating the state-versus-state subsidy wars and reducing corporate taxes in the name of jobs.[5]

Site location consultants are among the most powerful yet least regulated consulting industries in America. Most avoid publicity like the plague, yet they are in the middle of the majority of high-profile deals. Their methods have raised serious questions about conflict of interest, because many work for both sides of the street: for companies looking for places and for places looking for companies. This dual role gives them inordinate power, and they are central figures in the creation and escalation of the subsidy-bidding wars for jobs. They have a monetary self-interest in this escalation, because it makes their work more valuable and because they sometimes work on commission, taking a cut of the subsidies they help companies negotiate. They are the rock stars in expensive suits at economic development conferences, before whom public officials line up to give their cards. They are the shock troops of the corporate-orchestrated "economic war among the states" that is slashing corporate tax rates and manipulating state and local governments everywhere.

Fantus and the Birth of State-Sponsored Subsidies[6]

Fantus and Yaseen were pioneers in the science of business relocation, and one of their clients helped create the first state-sponsored economic development subsidy to benefit individual companies. Before Yaseen went to New York, Fantus had developed relationships with public officials in the South during the years he gave away free advice. One of them was Hugh Lawson White, the ambitious mayor of Columbia, Mississippi. In 1929, Fantus helped White land the Reliance Manufacturing Company, which made shirts and pajamas. Reliance agreed to move to Marion County if $85,000 could be raised to pay for the plant. Mayor White called a public meeting at the city's theater, made what must have been an impassioned appeal, and solicited promissory notes that he parlayed into a bank loan to land the deal.[7]

Six years later, White was elected governor of Mississippi, running on the fame he had gained as an aggressive recruiter, and pledging to "Balance Agriculture with Industry," to diversify the state's economy. Although localities in the South then routinely subsidized new plants, White soon proposed a more ambitious plan, a real breakthrough in state-sponsored job subsidies that is now called the Industrial Revenue Bond. IRBs are government-issued, tax-free, low-interest "private activity bonds" that subsidize private companies. They are deemed tax exempt because they serve the public purpose of economic development. Purported to address an "acute economic emergency" and wrapped in a great deal of New Deal–flavored language about the general welfare, the Mississippi Industrial Act enabling IRBs was passed by a special session of the state's legislature in 1936.[8]

The Mississippi Industrial Act set forth a system whereby counties and cities could issue bonds to build factories. Because the bonds were government-sponsored, the interest was exempt from federal income taxes in the same way a school or sewer bond would be, so the interest rates were lower than if the bond were a private issue. Once constructed, a facility would be leased to a company, with the lease covering the bond repayment. Since the facility was publicly owned, it would not owe any property taxes. When the bond was paid off, typically in ten years, the building would be deeded to the company.

Southern states already had cheap labor to offer; now they also had cheap capital. Tennessee and Kentucky soon copied Mississippi's IRB scheme, as did Alabama. They were criticized by governors in both North and South, challenged by the investment banking industry as creeping socialism, blamed by labor leaders for subsidizing anti-union runaway shops, and targeted by proposed federal legislation and by federal banking regulators. In the same years, southern states also began to popularize the use of long-term property tax abatements. Low-margin industries such as textiles and apparel that were already sensitive to labor costs began migrating wholesale; Textron moved 15 plants out of the Northeast between 1954 and 1957. The issue of southern states using subsidies to help lure factories became a heated issue in the 1950s, the subject of a 1952 American Federation of Labor resolution and much agitation among northeastern politicians.

Perhaps the most outspoken early opponent against this southern "raiding" was Massachusetts senator John F. Kennedy. But southern congressional leaders used their seniority—and the chairman of the House Ways and Means Committee, where federal tax legislation originates, was Wilbur Mills of Arkansas, a big IRB-using state. So IRBs survived—even though they had never been explicitly authorized by Congress and no one knew how much revenue the federal government was losing on the tax-free interest, because many, if not most, of the bonds were sold privately. IRBs spread within the South in the 1950s and early 1960s and then mushroomed, growing sixfold in dollar volume between 1965 and 1967. Congress did not regulate them until 1968 and didn't crack down on abuses of them until 1986.[9]

In other words, the financing scheme created by Mississippi governor White to help him lure jobs from the North was basically an unregulated free lunch at the expense of U.S. taxpayers. This problem—one level of government cooking up a gimmick that takes revenue away from another level of government—is a recurring theme in economic development subsidies. Tax increment financing (TIF) in some states is a current example: TIF districts get created by city governments (as allowed by state law), but other bodies of government, such as school districts and counties, lose property tax revenue. Property tax abatements awarded by cities or counties can reduce school district revenue as well (see chapter 5). It's easy to give money away to corporations when it is not your own. And as these spending schemes become more convoluted and confusing, they also become less accountable.

IRBs were more than just a free lunch—they were moneymakers. As historian James C. Cobb explains in his seminal book *The Selling of the South*, companies figured out that IRBs could enable them to actually make a profit on their buildings. Companies would buy their own bonds and receive the tax-free interest. And the lease payments were deductible as business expenses on their federal income taxes. So, for example, on a factory bond of $500,000 a company might pay $32,000 a year for the lease/debt payment. But then it would get back $23,750 in interest income, plus a federal income tax cut of $16,640 by deducting the expense of the lease. That's a net profit of $8,390 a year.[10]

Cobb chronicles the entrepreneurial zeal of many southern leaders as they created and honed various subsidies, but he draws very mixed conclusions about the long-term outcome. Subsidies may have boosted the region's industrial growth (although surveys at the time suggested most companies would have come anyway), but "they also helped to reinforce the region's attraction for competitive, low-wage manufacturers because these were the firms most in need of the extra savings afforded by subsidies or concessions." Such deals left the region "[s]hackled with poorly paying, slowly growing industries," so that "[i]n the long run, subsidies helped to perpetuate the deficiencies that in turn, appeared to justify the continued use of subsidies."[11]

Southern politicians gained political capital by taking credit when companies relocated,[12] but a lot of that really amounted to parade-jumping; that is, they took credit for things that would have happened anyway. The kinds of companies that were most likely to come were wage-sensitive and able to move. The construction of the interstate highway system, air conditioning, and the South's population growth made relocations all the more likely.

It wasn't just that the South originally attracted low-wage companies; public officials there sometimes kept better-paying companies out, to help the companies who got there first keep wages down. In 1978, in a rare disclosure of an aborted deal, it was revealed that Brockway Glass Company of Brockway, Pennsylvania, was blocked from relocating 300 jobs to Roxboro, North Carolina, because the Roxboro city fathers disapproved that the company accepted a union and paid good wages. People in Roxboro were ticked to lose the good jobs, and the county commissioners resigned en masse.[13]

The story prompted Fantus to disclose, approvingly, that there were "literally scores of companies that had been turned away from Southern towns because of their wage rates or their union policies." And as Maurice Fulton, the other son-in-law of Felix Fantus who now chaired the company, pointed out, "After all, if Brockway came in with a union and high wages, who would want to come to Roxboro?" Another unnamed site locator told the *Wall Street Journal* that in Gastonia, North Carolina, "You tell 'em you got a union, and boom—they'll flat run you out of town on the next plane."[14]

Working Both Sides of the Street

Many site location consultants today work both sides of the street: for companies looking for places and places looking for companies. At least a few firms work only one side of the street because they believe that working both sides is a conflict of interest. This is one ethical issue sometimes raised about the profession (along with the issue of commissions, discussed in chapter 2).

When site location consultants represent companies, they may both have a direct financial self-interest in getting the maximum subsidies they can from state and local governments. Then on other occasions, the consultants also work for states, cities, and regions, advising them on how best to attract companies. That advice sometimes includes suggestions for changing or creating subsidies. The consultants would claim this is not a conflict of interest because they do not work for the public and private sector on the same deal. Others would argue that because the consultants go back and forth at will (without waiting periods, such as those imposed upon former public officials before they may lobby), the possibilities for abuse abound.

At the very least, it's an irregular situation that is inconsistent with the way our whole adversarial American system of professional advocacy has evolved. Can you imagine a lawyer who represents cancer victims in a suit against chemical companies also getting a job representing a chemical company against cancer victims? Or a lawyer negotiating for a union one week and for management the next?

The fact that the consultants are allowed to work both sides is also a sad reflection of how disorganized the public sector is, how the corporate divide-and-conquer strategy has left public officials in a weak position. If public officials were more unified, they could command loyalty from consultants, the same way other constituencies do.

As early as 1953, Yaseen realized that the expertise Fantus was developing while working for companies could be parlayed into a new consulting niche: advising cities, states, regional organizations, utility companies, and railroads on how to attract businesses. He formed a wholly owned subsidiary called Fantus Area Research. When asked if this was not a conflict of interest, he defended his impartiality. "We are just making double use of our extensive library and files," he said. Six years after forming this subsidiary, he even claimed that he had never placed a company in a city that had employed Fantus Area Research.[15]

Little is known about this early Fantus work for the public sector (the company has never been the subject of a book or dissertation), but a 1956 account in the *Wall Street Journal* suggests that those who had concerns about the company's power were justified. The *Journal* reported that Fantus's first Area Study client was York, Pennsylvania, "a city that had failed to attract a new plant in 10 years. Within 18 months after the study was completed, York wooed and won five large factories." Did York gain influence with Fantus? Given how secretively the company operated with its corporate clients, there is no way to know. Within two years, Fantus Area Research had jobs with at least four more cities, two states, two railroads, and a 20-county region.[16]

Fantus's prominent role in the migration of hundreds of plants out of the Northeast and Midwest in the 1960s and 1970s drew criticism from some public officials, especially in New York. But eventually, many governments in those regions became Fantus Area Research clients as well. In a 1986 study for the state of Illinois, Fantus made nine subsidy recommendations, including new corporate income tax credits for research and development, job creation, and retooling. It also recommended that Illinois "reduce the proportion of state tax revenues generated by the corporate income tax to a level competitive with contiguous states."[17] In other words, shift the tax burden away from corporations.

When site location consultants work for government, reported prices for a community study range to $100,000 and state studies as much as $400,000.[18] Given the prevailing power dynamics, when a state or city hires a site location consultant for a business climate study, at least part of what's really going on is that the government agency is trying to gain influence with the consultant, hoping to land some of his future clients. Because there will always be future deals, and given how secretively the consultants operate, getting their personal attention matters. Of course, working in mysterious ways is good for business; it means more people have to court you. That's why site location consultants get taken on junkets to events like the Super Bowl, the Kentucky Derby, the Indianapolis 500, and the Masters golf tournament. As one state development director put it in 2001, "Having a good relationship with one site-location consultant is like having a good relationship with 50 or 100 companies."[19]

Leonard Yaseen's War on Urban America —and New York City

Yaseen had another dispute: with urban America. It played out most dramatically in the tortured relationship he had with his adopted work city of New York. Early in his career, he became convinced that manufacturers should get out of cities and move at least to the suburbs, but preferably to rural areas. Similarly, he disliked taxes and wage laws and disagreed with unions. How many of these opinions were originally his own and how many were those of his clients that he embraced is unknowable, but given his power, Yaseen's biases made news and certainly influenced many companies.[20]

During World War II, he noted with approval that the federal government was assisting some companies to get out of cities to make them less vulnerable to air attacks. During the Korean War, he criticized the Truman administration for not pushing contractors to disperse geographically. At the height of the cold war with the Soviet Union, he urged that core industries like steel, aircraft, oil refining, and machine tools be taken out of major population centers and scattered to rural areas so that a nuclear attack could not disable critical sectors. Putting such plants even on the outskirts of a metropolitan area "does nothing to protect our productive capacity," he said. The Soviet Union's "attack will be concentrated on war-making facilities themselves. Under these circumstances, space offers our greatest protection."[21]

In studies and pronouncements in the 1950s and 1960s, Yaseen tracked and boosted the flight of manufacturing jobs from urban areas. "In the next decade, it will be the very rare exception when a manufacturer decides to build a factory in a big city area," he declared in 1962, citing these lures of less-populated areas: lower wages, friendlier governments, cheaper land, and lower taxes.

Whether he saw it coming or not, the job flight from cities that Yaseen had promoted was disastrous for urban communities, particularly in the Northeast and Midwest. Together with other postwar trends that hurt U.S. cities (see chapter 6 on sprawl), the exodus of factory jobs was a major reason for the rising concentration of urban poverty and the racial and social tensions that arose.[22]

No city bore the brunt of Yaseen's bias more than New York, the city where he worked. As early as 1939, Yaseen was quoted in New

York newspapers about the city's loss of factory jobs, and by the mid-1970s, when the city entered its most dire financial crisis, he claimed to have helped more than 300 companies leave the city.[23] The city's loss of factory jobs hurt its tax base and swelled the welfare rolls.

Fantus also gained many clients involving white-collar jobs in New York, including corporate headquarters. In the mid-1960s, when the city was hemorrhaging jobs of every kind, Yaseen once disclosed that a third of his business was companies looking to move white-collar jobs out of New York; at another time he said he was working for 14 New York City companies with a total of 11,500 employees that were considering moving their headquarters out of the city, and he predicted that he might have 40 such jobs in 1967. Saying that headquarters moves often involve "social factors," he blamed "the commutation problem, the rising crime rate, swollen welfare rolls and the subway strike." Another time, he blamed labor-management tension as the biggest problem. "New York is not a happy place," he said, admitting he was considering a move himself.[24]

Finally, in 1969, Yaseen took his own advice and announced that most of the Fantus Company's headquarters operations would move from Manhattan to suburban New Jersey. Exchanging bitter words with city officials and calling the city's costs "exorbitant," Yaseen forecast that by 1980, New York City employers should expect to be providing 18 paid holidays, 32-hour work weeks, pensions pegged to inflation, more vacation days—and sabbaticals. For Yaseen, living in American cities was becoming impossible, between "a hopelessly snarled traffic system" and "fear of physical attack, air pollution and overpowering noise levels, coupled with high living costs and economic anxiety."[25]

In 1974, Yaseen publicly castigated New York City for failing to take "drastic action" to stop the loss of industry (others said Yaseen should just stop helping companies leave). Specifically, he urged that New York adopt a master redevelopment plan that would move all of the quarter-million blue-collar manufacturing jobs still in Manhattan to large industrial parks created in the outer boroughs. These would be more suitable to the large-footprint, single-story layouts that were increasingly required by factories. He recommended a "superagency" with powers like the Port Authority of New York and New Jersey to parcel land, do zoning, and even oversee workforce training.[26]

In 1977, Yaseen capped off his war with New York by obtaining a $280,000 consulting contract with a group of foundations and banks and the Port Authority of New York and New Jersey to identify industries that could be attracted to the city. At the same time, the company said, it was working for six companies that might be leaving New York. City officials denied they were trying to "buy off" Fantus, but Yaseen said that the company agreed "that we wouldn't issue any negative propaganda or negative reports" about New York for the four-month duration of the study.[27] Besides, Yaseen was retiring, going out on top.

Within months of Yaseen's departure, other Fantus executives began saying favorable things about cities and the North. Besides its New York "image and development strategy report," it had worked for Detroit, Cleveland, and New Bedford. "The big cities are beginning to fight back," said one Fantus executive. There are "excellent opportunities" outside the Sun Belt, said another. "We give the facts to counteract problem images," said a third. A few years later, the consultants were even saying there was bargain-priced labor to be had in New York City: immigrants. AFTER HELPING FIRMS GO, FANTUS LURES THEM BACK, read the *Wall Street Journal* headline.[28]

"Business Climatology" and the Second War Among the States

By the time Yaseen retired in 1977, a new term—"business climate"—had started to take root, and Fantus helped define it to serve corporate financial interests. The term was often invoked in ways that reflected rising regional tensions. The Rust Belt was beginning to show its tarnish and the Sun Belt was booming. In the early 1970s, the populations of some states in the South and Southwest grew at six to ten times the rate of those in the Northeast and Midwest.

Business Week declared "The Second War Among the States." "The nation's disparate economic growth is pushing the regions towards a sharp conflict" that "will take the form of a political and economic maneuver," it warned. Major articles also ran in *Fortune* and the *National Journal;* the latter suggested that federal spending was also biased against the Rust Belt. A new Northeast-Midwest Congressional caucus was formed to address regional injustices.[29]

Public officials were looking for explanations about the growth disparities, and Fantus supplied one, shaped to serve corporate lobbyists. In 1975, Fantus authored the first 48-state "business climate" study, commissioned by the Illinois Manufacturers' Association. Copies of the study itself may not survive, but a business publication reproduced the study's key data: Fantus rated Texas #1, followed by Alabama, Virginia, South Dakota, and the Carolinas. Only one northern state, Indiana, made the top 10. New York, Yaseen's nemesis, came in last.[30]

The very term "business climate" is brilliantly vague. Because the needs of different businesses vary so much, one size cannot fit all. And technology changes how work is structured, so the concept is always evolving. But the publicly understood version of "business climate" that was first established by corporate interests was a selective, politicized one. It remains an ambiguous, malleable term readily available for corporate use. Are we talking about the corporate income tax rate here, or is it how "business-friendly" people are, or how loose environmental enforcement is, or how generous the property tax abatements are? Companies and their lobbyists can always decide which part of the "climate" matters most today and whale away on it, insisting that if companies don't get their way, the area has a "bad business climate." Since the real decision-making process remains a black box, public officials have no way to judge such claims.

The Fantus/Illinois Manufacturers' Association study was a highly political document. In both the way it was structured and the way it was reported, it apparently exaggerated the importance of taxes and unions. It actually ranked the states based on three groups of criteria: "population characteristics," with 8 underlying factors; "quality of life," with 10 factors; and "business legislative climate," with 15 factors. However, the business legislative climate rating got the most attention; it included various corporate and personal taxes, per-capita debt, union regulation (whether a state was a "right to work" state or had a state labor relations board) and other factors (not reported). So even though Minnesota came in #1 for quality of life and #5 for population characteristics, it was rated #41 for business climate. And Alabama, ranked #47 on quality of life and #42 on population, was rated #2 for business climate.[31]

Fantus declined to perform the business climate study again after issuing the 1975 report.[32] The Conference of State Manufacturers' Associations (COSMA) hired the Chicago-based accounting firm of Alexander Grant & Company (later named Grant Thornton) to pick up the job. Starting in 1979, Grant Thornton issued the ratings annually. Like the original Fantus study, the Grant Thornton studies generally rated states in the South and the Plains as having the best business climates. Despite profound methodological flaws and political biases, the studies received broad media attention.[33]

Even Fantus became an articulate, though seldom-quoted, critic of the COSMA/Grant Thornton studies. "These surveys do a lot of harm" and are not a good basis for changing public policies, said Fantus vice president Charles Harding. He called them "a Trojan horse for a certain ideological position" because they are based upon business executives' opinions, not economic statistics. "Is there any empirical evidence that a high level of welfare expenditures is inversely proportional to the business climate?" he asked. And a Fantus consulting report to a state referred to "the popular generic study that purports to rank state business climates" and a "poorly conceived generic study."[34]

Grant Thornton's business climate ratings system was finally dissected and demolished in 1986 by a major study authored by the

Corporation for Enterprise Development (CFED), a non-profit think tank, and two other groups. *Taken for Granted: How Grant Thornton's Business Climate Index Leads States Astray* cataloged a series of omissions and biases that made the studies misleading and largely invalid.[35]

For example, the CFED study explained, the index punished states that had good jobs. By giving negative weight to states with the best wages, Grant Thornton was penalizing every state that had lots of highly skilled factory jobs, since those pay well. So even though a state must have had the business basics that attract manufacturers to land a lot of good jobs, in the ratings that was a negative. Two of Grant Thornton's labor cost factors had to do with unions, but neither accounted for higher skills or lower turnover in union shops. A key factor used to measure productivity was botched; it measured capital intensity or low wages instead. The index over-weighted energy costs and ignored key issues such as access to capital and quality of life.

The index was also blatantly anti-tax and anti–social safety net. Despite the fact that state and local taxes are a tiny business expense, 5 of the 22 factors Grant Thornton used were tax and budget issues. However, only one of them measured what states did with their revenue and then did so only to give a negative weight to welfare spending. Nothing else that employers and taxpayers get for their money was counted: not the quality of infrastructure, education, training, recreation, public safety, or cultural amenities. Two more factors had to do with workers' compensation and two others concerned unemployment compensation, both among the smallest of business taxes, but are common hot-button issues for manufacturing lobbyists.

Not only did Grant Thornton use poorly chosen and biased data as the foundation of its ratings, CFED found, but it then put the numbers through a weighting process that made the results completely subjective and political. It sent the list of the 22 factors to the state manufacturing associations and allowed them to allocate 100 points among the factors, based on their beliefs about the relative importance of each. The responses were then averaged and weights assigned. So if a state association was in a big fight that year about workers' comp rates, it might assign high weights to those two factors—even though there was no evidence that workers' comp rates were having any effect on jobs.

Basically, CFED concluded, the Grant Thornton index was at best a very crude measure for a tiny share of companies: only manufacturers, and more specifically, only manufacturers in mature industries with low profit margins who are most sensitive to costs such as labor and are looking to site a branch plant. It didn't really apply to the much larger service sector, or to what we today call the New Economy: high technology, life sciences/biotechnology, and other knowledge-intensive industries.

Borrowing Oscar Wilde's witticism about cynics, the CFED study concluded that the "Grant Thornton index knows the price of everything, but the value of nothing. It emphasizes the costs of labor but not its productivity. It calculates the expense of government but not its benefits." In short, the Grant Thornton index that dominated public perceptions of the states' attractiveness to business from the late 1970s to the late 1980s (when it ceased) was anti-tax, anti–public goods, anti–social safety net, and anti-union. In addition to receiving national media coverage each year, the ratings were recycled in lobbyists' testimony, fact sheets, and newsletters. After the CFED study was issued, Grant Thornton revised its methodology, issued a few more reports, then ceased their publication.[36]

Since COSMA/Grant Thornton quit issuing their studies, there has been a flowering of state and metro-area ratings issued by more than a dozen organizations, including some of the site location trade magazines (see following text). Some of these ratings still seem to be grinding political axes for business interests, but others are really trying to measure new indicators, especially those assets key to the New Economy—especially clusters of human capital, or what Richard Florida has dubbed the "creative class"—that are critical to high technology and other New Economy sectors.[37]

But the period in which the COSMA/Grant Thornton studies ruled—from the late 1970s to the late 1980s—shaped the debate on what states should do about jobs, in ways that still haunt us today. Those were the years in which states enacted a raft of new subsidies, chasing the first wave for foreign auto plants, the GM Saturn factory, and other such trophy deals. Consider these trends between 1977 and 1988: from 20 states with Industrial Revenue Bond programs, to 44 such states; from only 7 states allowing cities or counties to make loans for equipment, to 32; from just 23 states allowing property tax abatements, to 35; from only 13 states making loans for equipment, to 37; from just 21 states with corporate income tax exemptions, to 31.[38]

The message from the site consultants and the business climatologists and their Old Economy corporate sponsors, especially to states in the Northeast and Midwest, was clear: competition is never-ending, and we will publicly judge you based upon how much of your tax base you are willing to surrender to corporations, and how much you are willing to help us suppress wages. To compete, you have to become more like the South.

The Site Location Consulting Industry Today: Fragmentation and Niches

Though the structure of the site location consulting industry has changed, the getting of subsidies is still part and parcel of its work. Today, scuttlebutt says that Fantus—now Deloitte & Touche LLP's Fantus Corporate Real Estate Solutions—is a shadow of its former self, though still a big player in a small field of consulting.[39]

The industry has fragmented since the early 1990s; missteps by later owners of Fantus caused defections, and the explosion of data available on the World Wide Web has lowered the barriers to entering the business. Some site location consultants work within market niches defined by industry or corporate function; this reflects the reality that some industries have increasingly specialized needs and that technology is making it easier for companies to pull functions apart and move them around. As well, there is apparently an elite stratum within the profession that works mostly for Fortune 500-sized firms, while others work for second-tier and medium-sized firms.[40]

It's hard to sketch the industry, both because it is fragmented and because firms within it seem to wax and wane. There is no trade association of site locators, nor are they licensed or regulated by the states. Some have alliances with various publications, websites, utility companies, and economic development associations. Besides Fantus, there are many other long-standing firms, such as Wadley-Donovan-Gutshaw Consulting (part of the Wadley-Donovan Group, which also includes Wadley-Donovan GrowthTech); McCallum Sweeney Consulting; Location Consultants International; A.T. Kearney, Inc.; Carter & Burgess; Fluor Global Location Strategies (part of engineering giant Fluor Corporation); and Moran, Stahl & Boyer.[41]

Two of the other Big Four accounting firms besides Deloitte & Touche have site location practices: KPMG Strategic Relocation and Expansion Services and Ernst & Young International Location Advisory Services. IBM purchased PriceWaterhouseCoopers' Plant Location International business in 2002; it is now IBM Business Consulting Services—Plant Location International. The National Association of Manufacturers runs a Site Selection Network that provides member companies free search help. Some industrial real estate firms also have site consulting divisions, such as CB Richard Ellis Corporate Advisory Services and even the Staubach Company (yes, the former Dallas Cowboys quarterback).[42]

The getting of subsidies remains integral to the work of many companies in the field. Along with consulting, some firms feature decision modeling software products such as Dealtek, which advises: "Do: Congratulate the other side upon the conclusion of the negotiations, even if your company got its way. Don't: Don't gloat about your company's results or what the other side's results could have been."[43] Grant Thornton touts its expertise in negotiating for subsidies. On its website, it says, "we were able to negotiate with a city to extend the boundaries of an enterprise zone to include the location of our client. This strategy resulted in approximately $15 million in savings over 20 years."[44] Writing in a site location magazine, a KPMG Strategic Relocation and Expansion Services partner reported that almost two-thirds of executives polled said they missed a fourth or more of their subsidies. She recommended that companies make "incentives and credits a priority within their corporate culture" and "[r]equire business units to seek incentives."[45]

Some law firms specialize in subsidies, such as Stadtmauer Bailkin Biggins, which cautions in a presentation: "Incentives require justification in a political forum. . . . Be ready to defend materiality of incentives at every turn. This is fundamental."[46] Not all of the firms named here do subsidy negotiations; for example, Wadley-Donovan-Gutshaw refers that work out to Stadtmauer Bailkin Biggins.[47] On the other hand, some of the consultants stress their expertise in maximizing subsidies and minimizing taxes; in chapter 2, I cited the example of Location Management Services, with its pitch about not leaving money on the table. Another firm with a zealous subsidy pitch ("Your guarantee of maximum state credits and incentives") is Mintax, which maintains a subsidy database and claims to represent half of the Fortune 1000:[48]

> What some executives fail to understand is that they can go back in time and recapture incentive opportunities from previous facility expansions. Plain and simple, expansion incentives have retroactive applications. Retroactive incentives are exciting. Consider the sheer wonderment of a young child, who upon taking down the Christmas tree, finds another present hidden under the boughs. It's the same with incentives. After all, a lucrative 'refund check' is just as exciting as negotiating a million dollar incentive package for a new business expansion.[49]

And in another advice article, the same Mintax executive suggests:

Government agencies are more likely to treat you properly when they feel like they are competing for your business and are cognizant that you are flirting with others. . . . Play hard to get, flirt, create a bidding war, and the sky is the limit. With billions of incentive dollars available, and global competition at an all-time high, the future belongs to the corporations that best compete for these monies.[50]

In contrast, a more temperate pitch comes from Moran, Stahl & Boyer:

"What role do incentives play in the location selection process? We advise our clients to first seek locations that fundamentally meet the strategic needs for the company and allow incentives to act as a tie-breaker. In time, the incentive package will run out and if the location does not have the inherently favorable characteristics and the operation is not embraced by the community, the company may not fare very well long term. We strive to build economic relationships between companies and communities that result in a win-win situation for both parties."[51]

Conflict Questions Persist: The Case of Boeing and Washington State

You would think that with more consultants to choose from, it would be easier nowadays to avoid questions of conflict of interest, but somehow they persist. I've already described Boeing's unusually public 2003 auction for its next-generation 7E7 "Dreamliner" project. At least 20 states entered the fray and Washington state eventually "won," after its legislature enacted a special subsidy package worth an estimated $3.2 billion for the company and related businesses over 20 years.[52]

But after Boeing announced its decision, a conservative think tank in Olympia, the Evergreen Freedom Foundation, sued to win the release of records from the state. These revealed that even though Deloitte & Touche had audited Boeing's books for many years, and even though Deloitte Consulting had until recent years done a lot of consulting for Boeing, Washington state just happened to hire Deloitte Consulting—for $715,000—to help it land the 7E7 project.* In a key presentation, Deloitte Consulting had urged Governor Gary Locke to mount "an extraordinary response to provide a competitive environment for the 7E7." The governor had then proposed the $3.2 billion package to the legislature.[53]

Pressed about the issue, Governor Locke's office said development officials cleared the Deloitte Consulting contract with the attorney general's office. The attorney general's office contradicted that claim, saying it had not reviewed the contract, that Deloitte Consulting was added on as a subcontractor.[54]

The "Cash Cow" Game Plan

Occasionally, documents leak out that expose the subsidy-grubbing game plan. In March 2004 the national director of Ernst & Young's Business Incentives Practice led a workshop together with a former Boeing government relations vice president at the annual meeting of the State Government Affairs Council—"the premier national association for multi-state government affairs professionals of over 120 major US corporations, trade associations and service providers." The title of their PowerPoint presentation says it all: "Turning Your State Government Relations Department from a Money Pit into a Cash Cow." The audience reportedly included officials from Wal-Mart, Proctor & Gamble, Bank of America, and Microsoft.[55]

---

*According to Deloitte's website: "Deloitte & Touche USA LLP is the U.S. member firm of Deloitte Touche Tohmatsu. In the U.S., services are provided by the subsidiaries of Deloitte & Touche USA LLP (Deloitte & Touche LLP, Deloitte Consulting LLP, Deloitte Tax LLP, and their subsidiaries), and not by Deloitte & Touche USA LLP."

After citing some big deals and cataloging the many kinds of subsidies available, the presentation offered these pointers and cautions, among others:

Public doesn't like "corporate welfare."

Control publicity.

Make the case for incentives. What are YOU bringing to the party?

Use local subs and vendors whenever possible . . . and brag about it.

Identify milestones and publicize them.

Involve elected officials in press announcements.

Thank everybody a zillion times.

Offer to be a "reference."

Be mindful of the election and legislative cycle.

Identify the REAL incentives. Don't settle for "off the shelf" but . . . Don't be greedy. [ellipses verbatim][56]

The presentation was leaked to the John Locke Foundation, a Libertarian think tank with a long history of activism on subsidies in North Carolina; it broke the story in its *Carolina Journal* online magazine. Said one Tarheel State representative: "Cash Cow? You got that right. They look at [government] as just turning on the spigots . . . They play state legislators like violins. They're treating us like a scam."[57]

Real Life as a Reality Game Show

The power of site location consultants and their subsidy game has become so entrenched that economic development officials can spoof it. The 2004 annual meeting of the International Economic Development Council, the largest professional association of state and local economic development officials, aptly entitled one session with site location consultants: "Negotiations—How to keep a smile on your face and your shirt on your back!" Attendees could "[l]earn some of the signals site selectors give over the course of a negotiation—how should these be interpreted, e.g., how can you 'read thru the lines' to see that you are about to be eliminated. Where do you really stand?"[58]

But life imitated art at the IEDC conference, as the consultants got to preside, like Donald Trump, over a "reality-show" plenary session entitled "The Project: Are You Smart Enough to Win?" Three site consultants pretended to be executives of "TechWear," a high-tech clothing company siting a customer service center. They heard competing pitches from Pittsburgh; Yuma, Arizona; and Genesee County, New York. All three public officials opened with their business basics: workforce, infrastructure, quality of life, and available sites. They closed with a menu of subsidies. The Genesee County presenter really laid it on thick about New York's "Empire Zones" and estimated they would be worth $20 million over 10 years.

As the "executives" deliberated, Robert Ady himself, the "godfather of site selection," said he "liked the payback" from the Empire Zones, but wondered if they were being used to obscure problems with the location. In the end, the consultants-cum-executives chose generous Genesee County. The audience, mostly public officials, using handheld polling devices, went for Pittsburgh.[59]

Such antics aside, there is no mistaking who rules at such meetings: the site location consultants. They are the speaker-bait that brings in hundreds of public officials who hang on their every word, seeking to gain some new insight, learn some new website trick, to get the attention of the consultants and their clients. The consultants seldom offer handouts, and if they use a PowerPoint presentation, it is brisk and breezy. At the end of each session, the public officials line up before them to present a business card and offer a few hasty words to tout the little-known advantages of Springfield.

This deferential ritual is a sad reminder of the prevailing ideology that plagues us today, a hangover from the meanest elements of the

Old Economy, echoes of Fantus and Grant Thornton and their politicized studies and pronouncements that shaped our beliefs about jobs and taxes. The lobbying agenda of footloose manufacturers looking for cheap labor in the South before skipping to Mexico or China had no value for the rest of the economy then, and it is antithetical to good jobs in the New Economy today.

★ Chapter Four ★

"Single Sales Factor" and the Corporate Assault on the Income Tax

Suppose you're a manufacturing company executive and you don't like paying corporate income tax to your home base state. How'd you like to get an 80 or 90 percent tax cut? All you have to do is file your tax return, using a special new formula. No conditions, no strings attached. Just file your return and pay a tiny fraction of what you used to pay. Oh, just one more thing: be sure your state manufacturers' association keeps saying over and over again that this gigantic tax cut will create jobs, jobs, jobs. Maybe have it rent an economist to issue a rosy study. Remember, you're for jobs, so anyone who opposes this giveaway scheme must be against jobs.

Welcome to the magical world of "Single Sales Factor" (SSF), in which manufacturing lobbyists have gotten some state legislatures to radically rewrite their corporate income tax codes, sometimes under the threat of losing a major employer. The fact that several states have considered SSF in the past decade reflects the mutation of subsidies from their originally stated purpose—of job attraction and multistate competitions for specific projects—to job retention and multistate rewriting of entire corporate tax codes.

SSF is the special deal, recounted in chapter 1, that Raytheon and other manufacturers won in Massachusetts. As we learned, rewriting the formula that multistate corporations use to allocate their taxable income among the states can radically cut their income tax bills. To date, ten states have enacted SSF. Iowa and Missouri have had it for decades, plus Connecticut, Illinois, Maryland, Massachusetts, Nebraska, and Texas. Wisconsin will start in 2006 and Oregon is phasing it in. (In some of these states, the formula applies only to manufacturers.)[1]

Here is how Single Sales Factor works. Historically, the states agreed upon a system using three factors to divvy up—the technical word is "apportion"—the taxable income of multistate corporations among different states. One factor is the share of its payroll that the company has in a state; another is the share of its property in a state; and the third is the share of its sales that occur in a state.

Here's a quick hypothetical to show how it works. Imagine you own the Rapid Razor Company and you sell your razors in all 50 states. Your company is headquartered in a medium-sized state, and you have half your payroll and 40 percent of your property in that state, since your main office and biggest factory are there. But you sell only 2 percent of your products there, since a medium-sized state has only 2 percent of the population. Your annual profits are $10 million.

Before your headquarters state adopts SSF, your state corporate income tax computation would be as follows:

$$\$10,000,000 \times \frac{0.5 \text{ (payroll)} + 0.4 \text{ (property)} + 0.02 \text{ (sales)}}{3} = \$3,066,667$$

So about $3.07 million of your income would be apportioned to that state for tax purposes.

But after your state enacts SSF for manufacturers, you use only one factor, sales, to determine how much of your income gets taxed there. So your new calculation looks like this:

$$\$10,000,000 \times 0.02 \text{ (sales)} = \$200,000$$

So now only $200,000 of your income gets taxed by your head-quarters state. Assuming the same tax rate, your tax bill just shrank by *more than 93 percent.*

Can you say "windfall with no strings attached"?

Theory versus Reality

The theory behind SSF says that if your state adopts a tax formula based on the single factor of sales that gives manufacturers like Rapid Razor a big tax cut for having a lot of payroll and property but not a lot of sales in your state, and competing states do not adopt the same tax formula, such companies will relocate to or grow in your state.

In the real world, this theory presents many problems, including the slippery slope (that's a scientific term) and what economists call "declining marginal utility." The pro-SSF theory assumes that SSF will give your state an advantage because it creates a difference between your state's tax formula and those of the states you compete with. But then comes the slippery slope. If you accept the (implausible) argument that Wisconsin needed to enact SSF because Illinois did it after Iowa did it (a really long time ago), then the only logical thing for Indiana to do is follow suit, and then Minnesota, and so forth down the slippery slope. Every time this happens, for every state that went to SSF the earliest, the value gets diluted, because a competing state has the same tax break.

Declining marginal utility means that every time you do something again, it becomes less useful or effective or enjoyable. If Indiana or Minnesota goes to SSF, from day one the state will never enjoy as big a theoretical advantage as Iowa used to, because so many states it competes with already have SSF. So for every state that goes to SSF later on, the initial value also keeps shrinking.

As the *Wall Street Journal* put it, it's "a classic race to the bottom, in which states compete with tit-for-tat responses until nearly all impose the same low level of tax liability. At that point, the economic advantage of lowering corporate taxes vanishes, leaving as the ultimate winner the companies that pocketed millions in tax breaks."[2]

The pro-SSF theory also ignores the reality of why companies pay taxes. Using a tax formula that ignores payroll and property is like saying the company doesn't physically *exist* in a state. If a company has a lot of payroll in a state, that means the state has a lot of families with future workers to educate, a lot of roads to maintain, a lot of public safety and sanitation services to provide. Likewise, if a company has a lot of property in a state, that indicates it has a lot of activity there and creates a lot of both wear and tear on infrastructure and demand for public services there. Property may also relate to how much pollution or other costs the company generates. On the other hand, it is fair to include sales as one of three factors, because it reflects the value of markets; that is, sales reflect where the buying power came from to create the profits being taxed.

Basing taxes only on sales is also unfair because it punishes most small companies and those that only sell in-state, while favoring manufacturers and other kinds of companies that "export" most of their sales to other states. If you own a small bakery in Baltimore, 100 percent of your payroll, property, and sales were in-state before Maryland enacted SSF. And they still are now, so your tax bill didn't change a bit. If you own an oyster-canning company headquartered in Delaware and you sell a third of your oysters in Maryland but only have a fifth of your payroll and property in Maryland, under SSF your Maryland tax bill goes *up*.

The theory justifying SSF also has a big problem with results: there is little compelling evidence that it works in the real world. For example, eight states had SSF fully in effect by fall 2001, when the rebound from the most recent recession began. The U.S. economy has continued to bleed manufacturing jobs since then, and SSF states have been among the hardest hit. Five of the eight SSF states had worse than average manufacturing job losses between November 2001 and November 2004; only three did better than average. Ironically, Massachusetts—whose 1995 enactment of SSF to benefit

Raytheon set off the latest wave of SSF adoptions—had the steepest manufacturing job loss of the eight SSF states in this period.[3]

That's not scientific proof that the formula doesn't stimulate job creation, but it does suggest that other forces—especially globalization—are the real issue in manufacturing today. Occasionally, a company will say as much. The year after Maryland enacted SSF, one of its major manufacturers, Black & Decker, announced it would lay off 450 workers in Easton, moving production to Mexico. Pressed by a *Baltimore Sun* columnist about why SSF didn't work its promised magic of saving the jobs, a company spokesperson said the move was "part of a comprehensive restructuring of our entire global manufacturing network, and, thus, is based on a range of considerations well beyond Maryland tax law." That's exactly the point for manufacturing jobs today: as a location issue, state taxes are more microscopic than ever. *The* issue is globalization.[4]

More Corporate Losers Than Winners

Besides being ineffective, SSF is unfair to most companies. At least six states have estimated how many winners and losers there would be if SSF were adopted. In every single case, the states concluded that more companies—in some cases almost twice as many— would pay higher taxes than would get tax cuts. Winners get bigger tax cuts than the tax hikes suffered by the losers, so overall revenue goes down.[5]

In Pennsylvania, for example, the average winner would get a tax cut almost three times bigger than the tax hike imposed on the average loser, so the state would be out $63 million overall. Big companies would get the lion's share: those with more than $10 million in capital stock value would get the vast majority of the tax cuts.[6]

The Pennsylvania study included another ominous finding that suggests SSF could cause even worse damage—to both jobs and revenue. It finds that those companies with a very small physical presence in the state—just 4 percent or less of their property and payroll—would get stuck with more than 80 percent of the tax hikes. These are "national corporations primarily engaged in shipping products into Pennsylvania," such as, say, a national food company with a warehouse or a couple of sales offices in the state.[7]

If SSF were enacted, such a company would have a tax incentive to close the warehouse or sales offices, get rid of its Pennsylvania property, lay off those workers, and either truck its products in from surrounding states or contract out the sales work. They would still be able to sell as much and make as many profits in Pennsylvania, but they would no longer have nexus; that is, they would have so little physical presence in Pennsylvania, the state could no longer legally tax those profits. So instead of getting stuck with higher tax bills, these companies would avoid income tax altogether.

More than 8,300 taxpaying companies fit this profile of having a very small physical presence in the Keystone State. If they all restructured to dodge the tax hike, it would cost the state at least another $108 million in lost revenue—and untold thousands of jobs. Of course, SSF would also give these same companies a disincentive against ever investing in future job creation in Pennsylvania.[8]

Such distortions mean that some multistate companies would prefer to have it both ways: to have SSF in some states, but not in others. Usually they don't talk about it publicly. But Kraft Foods lobbied for SSF in Illinois (where it is headquartered) and then opposed it in Maryland. Ford Motor Company led a campaign for SSF in Michigan (where it is based) but then opposed it in Illinois.[9] And AT&T backed SSF in New Jersey but opposed it in Oregon.[10]

Flunking Every Measure of Accountability

It's not just the size of the Single Sales Factor tax cut that big manufacturers love; it's also the process. Cutting corporate income taxes by changing the *definition of taxable income* is the manufacturing lobbyists' coveted prize, because it flunks every measure of accountability. SSF includes no obligations such as job creation or decent wages; it is not at all transparent; and it does not provide for any kind of "clawback," or money-back guarantee if a company that gets a big tax break fails to deliver job creation benefits. Changing to SSF doesn't require a company to fill out any messy application paperwork, saying it is going to invest a certain number of dollars or create a specific number of jobs. It doesn't require any involvement at all by state or local economic development officials, so they have no clue about costs or benefits.

Indeed, Single Sales Factor does not create any paper trail for taxpayers to review—no records about outcomes at any specific company or industry at all. So no one has any way to see if specific companies are living up to the rhetoric of "jobs, jobs, jobs." And no one can see how big a tax windfall any specific company got. That's because state corporate income tax returns, like personal returns, are confidential. Once Single Sales Factor gets enacted into law, it becomes a secret matter between each corporation and the state revenue department.

In the end, the only thing the states can be sure of is that they will have less revenue for the public goods—like roads and education— that benefit all employers.

Massachusetts: The Slippery Slope on Steroids

For a prime example of the SSF slippery slope in action, we return to Massachusetts, where the original proposal had been SSF for defense contractors, which morphed into SSF for all manufacturers, and would soon become SSF for all mutual fund companies as well.

The financial press was impressed by Raytheon's 1995 tax coup. *CFO* magazine's January 1996 cover story blared: "There's No Place Like Home: How Companies Are Cashing in by Staying Put." Naively, the magazine claimed that the day of huge packages for multistate competitions was over. "Instead, the focus now is on retaining current businesses," it said. "As the Raytheon case illustrates, companies can force states to focus on retention. . . . Who can blame them? After years of seeing the goody bag opened for incoming businesses, in-state companies are asking 'What about us?'"[11]

Indeed, Boston-based mutual fund giant Fidelity Investments had started asking that very question in the summer of 1995 as the Raytheon battle heated up. Creating leverage on Massachusetts, Fidelity won SSF for mutual fund companies in Rhode Island in August 1995 and hinted that it was considering moving its fixed-income group to Providence.[12]

Massachusetts's Governor Weld proposed extending SSF to all corporations in September, but the legislature balked and proceeded only on the Raytheon/manufacturing part. After all, Fidelity was a growing, profitable company. And multibillionaire Ned Johnson and his family owned about half of the company. Through the fall, it was reported that the company was negotiating to buy property in New Hampshire and looking at space in Rhode Island. In December 1995, Fidelity announced that it planned to move as many as 900 Boston jobs to the two sites. The Rhode Island site might grow to 2,500 jobs, it said, and the New Hampshire facility might grow to 2,000. A Fidelity executive called the news "a kind of wake-up call" to Massachusetts.[13]

The mutual fund tax-break campaign reignited in April 1996 and succeeded by August. As in Raytheon's campaign, a study was commissioned, this one by Coopers & Lybrand, that made robust predictions for both jobs and tax benefits. In releasing the study, the Massachusetts Business Roundtable pointed out lower tax rates on mutual fund companies in Rhode Island and New Hampshire and quoted a Coopers & Lybrand partner: "Massachusetts is becoming an island relative to the surrounding New England states that are competing for this growth . . ." The study kicked off a lobbying campaign aided by Governor Weld. "If you think the textile industry moved south in a hurry over a weekend in the 1950s, watch what can happen in other industries," he told a legislative hearing.[14]

After wrangling between Massachusetts House and Senate versions, by August the mutual fund companies won both tax breaks they sought: the Single Sales Factor formula and a "destination test" that exempted sales to people outside of the state even though the sales were handled in-state. Together, a legislator had estimated, the cuts would reduce Fidelity's tax bill by nearly 90 percent. (Boston is also home to Putnam, Scudder, MFS, Pioneer, Wellington, State Street, Eaton Vance, and other funds.)[15]

Stung by layoffs that were already starting at Raytheon by the spring of 1996, Bay State legislators negotiated for jobs language in the mutual fund tax cut that was better than the language in the manufacturing law. It required a company to expand Massachusetts employment 5 percent a year for five years through 2001 and then maintain that many jobs in 2002, with the requirements expiring as of 2003. That was a modest goal, given that the industry had been growing by 19 percent a year in Massachusetts in recent years. The law allowed for exceptions in the event of adverse economic conditions, and Fidelity did have layoffs in 2001 and 2002 as U.S. stock markets declined. Despite the layoffs, the company exceeded the 25-percent job-creation requirement, reportedly growing jobs by 35 percent in the Bay State from 1996 through 2003.[16]

However, now that the job requirements have expired, mutual fund companies have no obligations to keep jobs in Massachusetts, even though they still get the big tax break. Who knows whether the industry will continue to grow jobs there? Fidelity did begin outsourcing to India in 2003 and rapidly became one of the largest customers of Mastek, a company in Mumbai that specializes in financial services. A securities trade journal cites Fidelity as an industry leader, along with Morgan Stanley, in offshore outsourcing of *front office* functions, not just processing.[17]

High Costs in Lost Revenues, Public Service Cuts

The DRI/McGraw-Hill study commissioned by Raytheon also made state revenue and spending forecasts about the SSF tax cuts for manufacturing.[18] Starting again from that dire assumption of 50,000 prime defense contractor jobs lost *without* the tax cuts and retention of all of those jobs *with* the cuts, it forecast only a one-year net budget loss for the state and cumulative gains of $534 million in 10 years. Even from the less dire "10,000 jobs saved" scenario, it forecast a $112 million net budget gain for the state "because it eliminates the need for defense industry relocation and stimulates job growth and new sources of tax revenue."[19]

But the state's revenue department makes it clear that no such thing ever happened. By FY 2005, the Raytheon and Fidelity SSF tax cuts for defense contractors, manufacturers, and mutual funds had cost the Bay State's treasury about *$1.5 billion* in reduced corporate taxes, with about two-thirds of that going to mutual fund companies.[20]

The Bay State has enacted so many tax breaks (and stayed linked to federal cuts) that for every $5 it collects in corporate income taxes, it forgoes $4 more in tax breaks.[21] It also enacted a raft of personal income tax cuts. With less revenue, between FY 2001 and FY 2005, the Commonwealth cut funding for higher education by 21 percent and for public health by 24 percent in real terms. Between FY 2002 and FY 2004, Massachusetts cut state aid per school pupil by a greater share than any other state.[22]

The bottom line: in less than one year between 1995 and 1996, under the duress of job threats, dire studies, and intense lobbying, Massachusetts radically rewrote its corporate income tax code in ways that would not ensure long-term job creation or even job security, but *would* cost the state treasury a billion and a half dollars over the following decade and shift the burden for public services away from a few favored industries and onto working families and small businesses.

Illinois: Losing Factory Jobs *and* State Revenue[23]

Illinois enacted SSF in 1998 at the insistence of the Illinois Manufacturers' Association and some of its biggest members. It was reportedly backed by Ameritech, Abbot Laboratories, Deere & Company, Duchossois Industries, Kraft USA, Nalco Chemical, and Quaker Oats. Caterpillar and Motorola were likely major beneficiaries, along with Archer Daniels Midland, RR Donnelley, and Amoco.

It was no secret that the deal would heavily favor a small number of big boys. During the debate on an early version of the bill, the Illinois Department of Revenue estimated that just five companies, unnamed, would receive 63 percent of the tax-cut dollars. That's five companies out of 133,769 that file income tax returns in Illinois.[24]

Of course, given how completely unaccountable SSF is, none of the companies getting the huge windfalls would ever be required to create—or even retain—one single job in Illinois. In fact, many did just the opposite. Since SSF began taking effect there, Abbott, SBC Ameritech, Kraft, Motorola, Nalco, Deere, and BP/Amoco have announced layoffs totaling more than 9,900 workers.[25]

As part of its campaign for SSF, the Illinois Manufacturers' Association hired two University of Chicago economists to perform a study. The study predicted that SSF would cause Illinois to gain 155,000 factory jobs and 130,000 other jobs within three years.[26] Officials at the Illinois Department of Revenue called the forecast "so absurd it's laughable"—but of course it was the rosy forecast, not the sober expertise of career state economists, that got the most attention.[27]

So did the hired guns' forecast pan out? Not quite. The Bureau of Labor Statistics reports that the Prairie State has *lost* a whopping 188,000 of its factory jobs—more than one in five—in the five and a half years since SSF began taking effect there. In other words, so far the lobbyists' economists are 343,000 jobs short of the promised factory jobs.[28]

The hired economists also made a rosy forecast for tax revenues. They predicted that all those new manufacturing and ripple-effect jobs were going to generate $200 million a year in new revenue— in the form of *personal* income taxes. They did not predict the impact on corporate tax revenues.[29]

Given that Illinois has lost 188,000 factory jobs instead of gaining 155,000 (not to mention lost ripple-effect jobs), the state has obviously *lost* a lot of personal income tax revenue. Dislocated factory workers, when they can find new jobs, take overall pay cuts. And on the *corporate* income tax side, SSF has also become a huge drain on the Illinois treasury. From FY 1999 through FY 2004, it cost the state an estimated $462 million in revenue and now costs the state about $90 million a year, according to the Illinois Department of Revenue. The share of state revenue from the corporate income tax has plummeted as a result. In FY 1998, before SSF, corporate income taxes supplied 7.3 percent of the state's revenues. By FY 2004, they had plunged to just 3.4 percent. The FY 2005 projection: just 3.0 percent.[30]

Given the weight of the evidence, the state's leaders considered repealing SSF, but the business lobby went to the mat over the issue. In one of the most bizarre statements ever made in defense of a giveaway, the Illinois Chamber of Commerce said that SSF "encourages job creation and capital investment," but that opponents "focus instead on estimates of state revenue loss that do not take into account increased economic investment and that cannot be backed up with actual data."[31]

In other words, trust us.

Georgia: Have It Your Way

Georgia came up with a unique answer to the apportionment issue: let companies choose their own formula! No kidding. In a low-profile bill that flew from legislative filing to Governor Zell Miller's desk in barely three weeks in 1998, the Peach State said to newly arriving or expanding companies: let's make a deal. The state revenue director is authorized to negotiate customized apportionment deals for your income tax. You get to propose you own formula; that is, you can use SSF or you can use property, payroll, and sales one third each, or variations thereof. Just tell us why you want it, and satisfy a few criteria— including the conveniently vague "significant beneficial economic effect" requirement—and we will slate it to run for an unspecified "limited period" of years. Then it will be reviewed for approval by a three-person board whose members are also appointed or nominated by the governor. It's a nice brief law, too; it doesn't set out any kind of monitoring or compliance systems.[32]

Subsequent press reports revealed that the deal was initiated to encourage General Electric to relocate 500 Power Systems jobs from Schenectady, New York. But in 2000 and 2001, when *State Tax Notes* magazine and the *Atlanta Business Chronicle* filed Open Records Act requests to get the names of all the companies that got the special deal, the revenue commissioner refused to divulge them, and the attorney general ruled in favor of keeping them secret.[33]

The *Business Chronicle* responded with a blizzard of investigative articles by reporter Meredith Jordan through fall 2001 and winter 2002, revealing that six companies had gotten tax breaks worth $98 million. The debate grew ugly, with aides to then-governor Roy Barnes (a self-described "open records" governor) stonewalling on the records requests, while the *Business Chronicle* ridiculed them for their outrageous position. Finally, in early 2002, the state legislature amended the law to provide some disclosure—of company names and their projected investments, jobs, and wages.[34]

Armed with the names of the other five companies, the *Business Chronicle* investigated and reported that Alltel Corp., a telecom company, had fallen far short of its job creation pledge. The company repaid $11.5 million to the state and agreed to forgo its special deal for the remaining three years, saving taxpayers an estimated $17.2 million more.[35]

The Long-Term Corporate Assault on State Corporate Income Taxes

How did we get into this chaotic mess with all these gimmicks? Why don't the states agree on a standard tax system? There is actually a little-known history to it all: the corporate lobbying drive to enact Single Sales Factor is just one part of a broad, multidecade campaign by multistate corporations to gut state corporate income taxes.

The story boils down to this: since the 1950s, the states have been trying to cooperate and set up a simple, uniform system so that all profits of multistate corporations are taxed somewhere, somehow. And since the 1950s, corporations have been relentlessly attacking the states' effort to cooperate—with litigation, lobbying, and creative accounting.

I have to get wonky for a few pages here. Stick with me. It's important.

Between 1955 and 1957, the tax commissioners of the states advised a committee of the American Bar Association on a model state tax law. Issued in 1957, it was called the Uniform Division of Income for Tax Purposes Act, or UDITPA ("you-DIT-puh").[36] This model law included the three-factor formula for apportioning corporate income already described: one third based on the share of payroll a company has in a state, one third on its property, and one third on its sales.

Some state commissioners sought this model law because companies had been complaining and even suing some states over allegedly unfair rules. Because states used different rules about how to apportion income, companies had to literally keep different records for different states. The only reasonable and fair solution was to devise a system that, if adopted by all the states, would make sure 100 percent of corporate income got taxed. That is the genius of UDITPA.[37]

A few states had already adopted the three-factor formula, most notably Massachusetts. In their deliberations, the commissioners sometimes referred to the "Massachusetts formula" when discussing the three-factor model.[38] It's especially tragic, then, that the Bay State was later one of the early states to abandon this fair system, in the Raytheon and Fidelity episodes.

Although this carefully negotiated system did not make everybody happy, it was about as close to a corporate-government consensus as there has ever been on the issue. But UDITPA failed to address one big issue: nexus. At what point does a state have the right to say a company has enough of a presence in the state to owe income taxes on profits it makes in the state? Many companies refused to pay taxes in states even though they solicited and made sales there.

In 1959, a U.S. Supreme Court decision threatened to expand the definition of nexus. In *Northwestern States Portland Cement Co. v. Minnesota,* the Court ruled that a state could tax an out-of-state company's profits even if the company's only activity in the state consisted of sales representatives soliciting business in the state.[39]

Corporate lobbyists, led by the Pennsylvania Manufacturers' Association, rushed to Congress in 1959 and within six months won Public Law 86-272. This obscure law restricts how the states can define nexus; that is, it enables companies to have certain activities in a state yet avoid paying income taxes there. Basically, it says a corporation can avoid being taxed on the profits it makes selling goods in a state if it does not also manufacture or warehouse the goods in that state. Public Law 86-272 says that if a company solicits sales using the U.S. mail, or telephones, or the Internet—or even traveling salespeople—and then delivers the product from a warehouse outside the state, the company has not established nexus. Therefore the state where those sales occurred cannot tax the profits.[40]

Congress also created a special select committee that held a series of hearings between 1959 and 1965 to explore how unfairly and unevenly states were taxing corporations. It recommended drastic federal controls on how states and cities could tax corporations.

In response to the threat of restrictive federal legislation, in 1966 a group of states convened as a committee of the Council of State Governments to create the Multistate Tax Compact—and the Multistate Tax Commission (MTC) to administer it. The Compact gathered steam through 1967; by the end of 1968 there were a dozen member states.

The MTC's main purpose was to help the states proactively address the issue of tax uniformity. It promoted the adoption of the model law, UDITPA, so that more states would use the three-factor formula, but whether a state did so was voluntary. UDITPA was one of 12 articles of the Multistate Tax Compact—the formal agreement among the states that guided the work of the Commission.

Besides pushing UDITPA, in the early 1970s the MTC also began performing multistate corporate income tax audits. Companies hated this. Before the MTC started these audits, state officials had widely suspected that companies gave different numbers to different states, creating "nowhere income," or profits that never got taxed anywhere (I'll have more to say about this soon). The MTC's first executive director, Eugene Corrigan, recalled how a company could no longer deal separately with State A and then State B; instead, the company heard the MTC say: "We are here for your figures on States A *and* B."[41] No longer could a company get away with telling different stories to different states.

Corrigan recalled one audit the MTC performed for several states. The auditor asked the company's tax manager for a 50-states-and-DC breakdown so he could verify that the corporation was attributing all of its income somewhere among the states. The tax manager denied that he had any such document or had ever prepared one. A couple of days later, the auditor was working in one of the corporation's offices when he needed a paper clip. When he opened the desk drawer, he noticed a piece of paper: the company's "nonexistent" fifty-one-state breakdown. It revealed that the corporation was systematically attributing to each state only a set percentage of the sales that it was actually making in the state. The auditor left the document in the drawer and diplomatically avoided mentioning it while he proceeded to perform the audit armed with the knowledge that he had inadvertently acquired.[42]

Seventeen of the nations' largest corporations sued in 1972, seeking to shut down the MTC and its multistate audits. The case is known as *U.S. Steel v. Multistate Tax Commission,* and the plaintiffs were United States Steel Corp., Standard Brands Inc., General Mills,

Inc., Procter & Gamble Distributing Co., Bethlehem Steel Corp., Bristol Myers Co., Eltra Corp., Goodyear Tire & Rubber Co., Green Giant Co., International Business Machines Corp., International Harvester Co., International Paper Co., International Telephone & Telegraph Corp., McGraw-Hill, Inc., NL Industries, Inc., Union Carbide Corp., and Xerox Corp. (IBM and Xerox withdrew as intervenor plaintiffs before the decision.) The corporations alleged that, in creating the MTC, the states violated the Compact Clause of the U.S. Constitution.[43]

Corrigan described the companies' aggressive legal tactics. "The high-powered law firm of White & Case represented the plaintiffs, which were 16 of the nation's most powerful corporations. They inundated us with interrogatories," he said, referring to questionnaires each party in a lawsuit is allowed to serve upon its adversaries during the pretrial phase known as discovery. "One interrogatory might consist of as many as 200 questions. It would be served not only upon the MTC but upon each of our 17 member income tax states. We had to get each question answered and coordinate all the states' answers for accuracy. As soon as we finished one set, we would receive another. It amounted to nothing more nor less than harassment."

The case dragged on for three years, with no progress.[44] Determined to fight back, Corrigan and the MTC brought on new counsel, William Dexter, a former assistant attorney general in both Michigan and Washington state. Dexter quickly brought the case to a head. He filed a motion for summary judgment, asking the U.S. District Court in New York (where the case had been brought) to promptly rule in favor of the MTC, based on the evidence, and end the case without spending time on a trial. The Court granted the summary judgment for the MTC. Because the case involved many states, it went directly to the U.S. Supreme Court. In a landmark ruling for the states, the Supreme Court in 1978 saved the MTC, ruling that states are free to form compacts, even without specific federal approval, so long as they don't interfere with or reduce federal powers.[45]

The business lobby, unable to kill the MTC through federal litigation, responded to the *U.S. Steel* decision by centralizing its efforts through the Council on State Taxation (COST), the obscure but powerful coalition of multistate corporations that had been founded in 1969 (the year after the Multistate Tax Compact took root) for the apparent purpose of killing or at least thwarting the MTC. As COST's website says, its birth was "precipitated by the need of corporate taxpayers to be represented by a united voice on state tax issues—to counterbalance a number of organizations of state tax authorities."[46] Indeed, as Corrigan explains, the Multistate Tax Commission was COST's raison d'être. A colleague told Corrigan that more than two decades after the *U.S. Steel* decision, COST meetings still included lengthy sessions devoted to ranting against the MTC about that case and other long-ago events.

The 1970s were heady times for the MTC staff. Said Corrigan, "We felt we were on the frontier of effective auditing of the major corporations, of effective tax administration. We felt we were breaking new ground, that we would end up making the corporations admit their tax liability as it should have been."[47]

The MTC's multistate audits uncovered another kind of tax dodge. Some companies would game the system by creating multiple subsidiaries, to avoid nexus. An auditor for State A might be assigned to audit a business that had 12 closely related corporate subsidiaries. But if only three had nexus in the state, the audit would cover only those three corporations. An auditor for State B would be allowed to audit only the three or four subsidiaries that had nexus in State B. Neither auditor would see the entire picture, even though all 12 subsidiaries were actively helping to create income from both states. The solution was to take into account the activities of all 12 subsidiaries in determining the taxable income for States A and B. Looking at the companies in their "unitary" relationship in a "combination" auditing procedure meant treating all the entities as if they were one company. The MTC led the way in performing such audits and in encouraging member states to adopt what is now called "combined reporting."[48]

Corrigan's MTC also promoted the extension of combined reporting to foreign corporations; that is, requiring companies to include their foreign subsidiaries in their income statements. Corrigan cites this as "the first attempt in this country to cope with what has become a national scandal—the exporting of jobs and income to foreign nations so that businesses pay little or no income tax to either the federal government or the states."[49]

Worldwide combined reporting—also called the "unitary tax"—stood as a major threat to offshore tax dodges. COST went so far as to try to ban it through a tax treaty between the U.S. and the United Kingdom that was being renewed. The states blocked Senate ratification of the treaty. Finally, in 1983 in *Container Corp. vs. California Tax Board,* the U.S. Supreme Court upheld the states' right to require combined reporting—including worldwide reporting.[50]

Frustrated by *Container* and its failure to win a federal ban on worldwide combined reporting, COST turned its lobbying fire upon state legislatures. Claiming that combined reporting would jeopardize jobs, the corporate lobby succeeded in getting many states to prohibit or limit its use.[51]

Today, COST claims about 570 corporate members and continues to spearhead opposition to many state efforts to bolster their corporate income taxes. Besides orchestrating legislative action, it issues studies, files amicus briefs, keeps a database of tax regulations, and provides referrals to attorneys and consultants. COST often uses a series of studies it has commissioned from the Big Four accounting firm of Ernst & Young; these purport to show that corporations' state and local tax burden are unfairly high or rising. And it holds conferences, including the Fall Audit Session, with "optimal time to share tips, ideas and strategies for handling difficult state audits." In 2004 testimony, a COST official said combined reporting is "poorly defined" and "subject to endless litigation."[52]

At the federal level, corporate lobbyists keep trying to get the federal government to limit states' taxing rights. They seek to extend the federal restrictions on state nexus for physical goods (the notorious Public Law 86-272) to the entire *service economy*. The proposed "Business Activity Tax Simplification Act of 2003" would narrow the definition of nexus so that lots more corporate profit would never be taxed in any state. As Michael Mazerov of the Center on Budget and Policy Priorities explains, it would mean that "a television network would not be taxable in a state even if it had affiliate stations within the state relaying its programming and regularly sent employees into the state to cover sporting events and to solicit advertising purchases from in-state corporations . . . A restaurant franchisor like Subway or Dunkin' Donuts would not be taxable in a state no matter how many franchisees it had in the state and no matter how often its employees entered the state to solicit sales of supplies to the franchisees."[53]

By taxing companies for having employees and property in a state, the bill would create a perverse incentive that would be bad for jobs. The current chair of the MTC said it well: "If a company is subject to state and local taxes only when it creates jobs and facilities in a state, then many companies will choose not to create additional jobs and invest . . . Instead, many companies will choose to make sales into and earn income from the states without investing in them."[54]

The bill would likely reduce the revenue of 45 states and the District of Columbia and create a new wave of corporate tax-dodging gimmicks. The so-called Coalition for Rational and Fair Taxation (CRAFT) pushing the bill has not disclosed its corporate membership since 2001, and even then it omitted the names of six large members. The named members included media companies such as Viacom/CBS and Walt Disney/ABC, high-tech giants Microsoft and Cisco, and retailers such as J.Crew and The Limited.[55]

Finally, corporate lobbyists have continued their defense of two other loopholes: "nowhere income" and Delaware Holding Companies. I know, I know, I just used two new terms. Read on for the goods on two more amazing tax dodges.

Two More Corporate Income Tax Loopholes[56]

"Nowhere income" and Delaware Holding Company loopholes are not sold as "job, jobs, jobs" subsidies the way Single Sales Factor has been. But they are active examples of the lengths to which corporations will go to dodge state income taxes.

Nowhere income. Let's say you produce corn dogs in Iowa and you sell them to a vendor at Wrigley Field in Chicago. Under Public Law 86-272, because you don't have a factory or a warehouse in Illinois, and you used a traveling salesman who works out of his home to market the dogs to the vendor, you did not establish nexus in Illinois. So the Prairie State has no right to tax your profits on the sale. Iowa doesn't either, since the sale didn't occur there. That means the profits are "nowhere income"—they are never taxed anywhere. States have one possible solution, the "throwback rule"; when applied to cases such as this, the profits get "thrown back" to Iowa as taxable income there. But 20 states still lack a throwback rule: Arizona, Connecticut, Delaware, Florida, Georgia, Iowa, Kentucky, Louisiana, Maryland, Massachusetts, Minnesota, Nebraska, New York, North Carolina, Ohio, Pennsylvania, Rhode Island, South Carolina, Tennessee, and Virginia. Corporations have actively fought efforts in recent years to enact throwback rules in states such as Arizona, Maryland, North Carolina, and Massachusetts.[57]

Delaware Holding Company loophole. Now let's say you own a chain of clothing stores, with outlets in 20 states that have not adopted combined reporting. Don't like paying income taxes on your profits in those 20 states? No problem! Doesn't your store have a valuable logo, slogan, and/or character associated with it? (Think of certain companies' use of cartoon figures, animals, mottos, and the like.) Well, make sure you have that "intangible" property trademarked. Then, in either Delaware or Nevada, set up a wholly owned subsidiary shell (called a Passive Investment Company, or PIC) that owns that trademark. Now, have that PIC bill all of your stores, charging them "royalties" for the use of that trademark. The size of the royalty bill might even equal the stores' profits. That's a good thing, because the stores will then show no profits and therefore owe no income taxes in the 20 states. When the royalty checks arrive in Delaware or Nevada—presto!—no income tax there, either, since the Diamond State does not tax this "passive income" and the Sagebrush State has no corporate income tax. You can even lend those tax-free profits back to your company—and deduct the interest! Is this a great country or what?

Neither Delaware nor Nevada even requires that holding companies *publicly disclose their existence,* so no one knows how many thousands there are. A Delaware official said his state had 6,000 at the end of 1998 and was gaining 600 to 800 more each year. Thanks to some lawsuits, we have a peek behind the curtain. Toys "R" Us set up its Geoffrey Inc. subsidiary in Delaware; it took in $55 million in 1990 for the use of the company's name, trademarks, and "merchandising skills." The retail giant The Limited/Victoria's Secret/Lane Bryant/Express set up a Delaware PIC that collected $949 million between 1992 and 1994 from trademark licenses. Kmart set up a PIC that took in $1.25 billion from 1991 to 1995. Multiply these figures times thousands of companies. Since no one knows how many PICs there are, there is no estimate on how many dollars in corporate profits are dodging state income tax due to this scam. But it's obviously a lot.

The *Wall Street Journal* compiled a list of 50 companies with PICs, made public by litigation. The list includes ADP, Inc., American Greetings Corp., Budget Rent-A-Car Corp., Burger King, CompUSA, ConAgra Foods, Inc., Gap, Inc., Home Depot USA, J.P. Stevens and Co., Kohl's, Long John Silver's, May Department Stores, Payless Shoesource, Inc., Radio Shack Corp., Sherwin Williams, Snap-on, Inc., Stanley Works, Staples, Syms, Tyson Foods, Inc., Urban Outfitters, and Yellow Freight System.[58]

What's the best solution to this massive sidestepping of state corporate income taxes? Combined reporting, whereby a state requires a company to file a tax return as if all of its subsidiaries are one company and then apportion the income. But only 16 states require that. Nine more states prohibit companies from deducting royalties or interest paid to a related company. That leaves 20 states prey to the PIC scam: Arkansas, Delaware (!), Florida, Georgia, Indiana, Iowa, Kentucky, Louisiana, Missouri, New Mexico, Oklahoma, Pennsylvania, Rhode Island, South Carolina, Tennessee, Texas, Vermont, Virginia, West Virginia, and Wisconsin.[59]

What do all these scams cost the rest of us? The Multistate Tax Commission has estimated that corporate tax sheltering such as nowhere income, Delaware Holding Companies, incorporating offshore, and offshoring of profits cost the states $12.3 billion in 2001.[60]

"Why do we have less uniformity in state tax laws than we did in the early 1980s?" asks the MTC's current executive director Dan Bucks. "Because businesses don't support it. They undermine uniformity whenever they see it because they have learned [that] the lack of uniformity creates opportunity for tax shelters." He concludes that "[t]he multistate tax system is becoming a Swiss cheese income tax system . . ."[61]

★ Chapter Five ★

Property Tax Abatements and Your Local School

For our clients, education has been found to be the single most important service, greatly exceeding the value of all other services combined. . . . The single most important factor in site selection today is the quality of the available workforce . . . in fact, a qualified workforce may be the single most important determinant in the economic development success of any community.

—Robert Ady, longtime Fantus executive,
said to be the nation's most experienced living site location consultant [1]

Companies love to locate in areas with good schools; they just don't like to pay for them. American families care a lot about their schools, too. They often move and accept higher housing costs to gain access to better schools. And they support bond issues for public schools at a greater rate than they do any other service except healthcare.[2] The trouble is, families don't get a 10-year holiday on their property tax for moving into their preferred school district, but companies often do.

When corporations seek to avoid paying their fair share for schools and other local services, the issue is bigger than who bears the burden. The corporate assumption that businesses are *entitled* to property tax abatements—or the related subsidy, tax increment financing (TIF)— is threatening our economic future by harming our schools.

Now that's a harsh thing to say; let me explain. First, property taxes are the largest tax many companies pay, so when a company gets a property tax break, it can be a very lucrative subsidy. This is especially true for companies with lots of land, buildings, or equipment.

Second, property taxes are also the largest single source of revenue for public education, providing on average almost a third of school funding. Schools used to be even more reliant on property taxes, but many states have changed their school-funding formulas because state supreme courts have found what author Jonathan Kozol called "savage inequalities" in funding levels between inner city schools and those in wealthy suburbs. So on average, state governments today provide almost half (49 percent) of school funding and local sources provide 43 percent, two-thirds of which is property taxes. These are national averages; in some states, property taxes are still far more important. (Despite all the brouhaha about No Child Left Behind, the feds only contribute 8 percent of K-12 budgets.)

Given these facts—property taxes matter a lot for schools, but they can also be a lucrative subsidy if a business gets an abatement—there's a direct collision between companies avoiding their property taxes and children having good schools. Along with suburban sprawl, harm to state budgets, and the problem of burden-shifting, the harm that subsidies do to public education is a prime example of the massive collateral damage subsidies are causing because they have grown so costly and unaccountable.

To be sure, school finance is complicated, and state formulas vary widely. Some states help school districts make up for revenue they lose to abatements or TIF; others don't, or they only cover part of the losses. The bottom line: when a company gets an abatement or a TIF, less money goes into the local hopper for schools.

There is a second bottom line here: at the state capitol. Since schools now get almost half their funding from the states, many other kinds of subsidies I discuss in this book that erode state revenue (such as income and sales tax breaks) mean less money is available for schools—from the state hopper. It's just a little less obvious because it involves sources of revenue that are not traditionally identified with schools, but are nonetheless a growing component of how schools are financed.

Giveaways That Keep on Giving: Abatements and TIF

Especially on new investments, companies routinely receive property tax abatements—that is, discounts or outright 100 percent exemptions—that run for years: 5, 7, 10, 20, even 40 years in Dell's case in Nashville. Some states restrict abatements to manufacturing or other heavy industries; other states restrict them to enterprise zones, or give extra kinds of abatements in zones. Some states give localities a lot of latitude about how much of an abatement or for how long; others have fixed rules. Forty-three states plus Washington, DC, allow abatements.

I spoke briefly about tax increment financing (TIF), another kind of subsidy that is usually based on property taxes, in chapters 2 and 3. When a TIF district gets redeveloped and property assessments go up, all of the resulting increase in tax revenues—the increment—is diverted away from schools and other local services. Instead, the increment is used to subsidize the redevelopment within the district. This diversion can last 15, 20, 23, even 30 years, depending on state rules. The traditional justification for allowing this diversion is that the property in the TIF district is "blighted" or "distressed." But as I explain in chapter 6 on sprawl, many states have loosened their rules so much those terms are meaningless. Forty-seven states and Washington, DC, have TIF.

These subsidies are often more than one-shot deals; many states allow abatements, TIF districts, or both to be extended for additional terms.

Despite the long duration and high cost of these subsidies, abated companies often fail to deliver, and cities often hesitate to seek repayment or simply fail to monitor outcomes. Fort Wayne and the surrounding Allen County, Indiana, have long used abatements as part of their aggressive recruitment strategy. But a 2003 investigation of almost two hundred abated companies by the *Fort Wayne Journal Gazette* found that more than half had fallen short of their job promises—yet no government body in the county has ever rescinded an abatement (or ever turned down a request for one). In the city of Fort Wayne itself, 89 out of 136 abated companies—65 percent—had fewer employees than promised. The paper estimated other taxpayers pay $3.5 million more than they would if abatements were not used. "It's the tax-bill version of five people splitting the check for a six-person meal at a restaurant," the paper concluded. "Those companies with tax abatements still get to eat, but their doing so raises the price for everyone else."[3]

After Sony announced the closure of its Springfield, Oregon, CD factory, which had enjoyed a five-year enterprise zone property tax break, the *Eugene Register-Guard* investigated 76 other abated companies—6 big firms that got 95 percent of the tax break dollars and 70 smaller ones. It found that three of the big companies— Hynix, Weyerhaeuser, and Symantec—had fallen short of their job projections but renegotiated deals to keep some or all of the breaks. The net outcomes with the smaller companies were far better. Although 11 had closed, the small companies as a group created almost as many new jobs as the six big companies did—with just 5 percent of the dollars. Cost per job at the small companies: about $2,100. At the big companies: $32,000.[4]

Harris County (Houston), Texas, got stingier after three high-profile abatement disputes, including the closure of an MCI call center. After the county took a hard line, two companies expanded in the area even though they got turned down for the tax break: Albertson's built a grocery warehouse, and Sonangol, the Angolan national oil company, built a new headquarters. As the *Houston Business Journal* editorialized: "Authorities also are starting to wise up after watching companies pit cities against each other in bids to obtain tax abatements, only to discover that many of the relocation decisions had already been made."[5]

Louisiana: Big Breaks for the Big Boys in Cancer Alley

The stretch of the Mississippi River between Baton Rouge and New Orleans has one of the nation's largest concentrations of oil refineries, chemical plants, and paper mills. The region suffers from extremely high rates of toxic emissions—hence its nickname, "Cancer Alley."

When these factories are rebuilt, expanded, or upgraded, the projects routinely get ten-year property tax exemptions. The decision whether to grant these exemptions is not controlled locally by a county board in the way most states do it. Instead, property tax breaks in Louisiana are initiated by the state's Board of Commerce and Industry, dominated by gubernatorial appointees and including the governor him- or herself.

The Louisiana Coalition for Tax Justice compiled all of the state's property tax exemption records for the 1980s and published a devastating set of findings. The exemptions had cost local governments $2.5 billion. The harm to schools, the most costly local service, was the greatest. The state ranked last in high-school graduation rates, while $941 million of the tax exemptions could have gone to improve the schools. Just nine big, profitable companies got more than half of the tax benefits: Louisiana Power & Light (Entergy), Gulf States Utilities, Cajun Electric Power, Shell Oil, Exxon, Texaco (Star Enterprise), International Paper, Dow Chemical, and Mobil Oil (Exxon and Mobil later merged).

Incredibly, almost three-fourths of the projects that got exempted created no new permanent jobs (some created temporary construction jobs). Most of the tax breaks went to the big toxin-emitting industries. Exxon, for example, got 282 exemptions over the 10 years—251 of which created no new permanent jobs! The Exxon deals cost taxpayers a total of $93.3 million, including $42 million lost for the schools. The subsidies also failed as overall job creators: the oil, chemical, and paper industries actually lost almost eight thousand jobs.

Louisiana also gave out enterprise zone rebates and credits; in just four years, these totaled another $188 million. One of the zone subsidies is a $2,500 tax credit for each new employee hired. Shell Oil collected seven such credits for hiring workers at its plant in Norco—to replace seven workers killed in a 1988 explosion. The tax credits far exceeded the $3,630 fine imposed by the Occupational Safety & Health Administration for the fatal tragedy.[6]

There was one brief, shining moment in Louisiana's property tax history. Dr. Paul Templet directed the state's environmental agency in 1991. He created a scorecard system that used the exemptions to give companies an incentive to comply with state environmental rules, reduce their toxic emissions, install recycling systems, and use recycled materials. In just one year, the system reduced toxic emissions by 8 percent, helped create 3,500 jobs (as companies spent on pollution-reduction systems) and even improved revenue to local governments.[7]

When Governor Edwin Edwards took office in January 1992, his first official act was to eliminate Templet's scorecard system.

Ohio: The Poor Pay More

Ohio is one of those states where property taxes still provide a very large share of school funding, about half. It has both TIF and property tax abatements. The abatements are especially generous in its 339 enterprise zones, where it also exempts personal property (machinery and inventory). One analysis found that in 1999, TIF and abatements cost $102 million per year for schools. Three years later, an *Akron Beacon Journal* investigation put the annual loss at $115 million.[8]

Indeed, the *Beacon Journal* found, by 2002 Ohio had exempted $3.9 billion of corporate real estate from property tax—more than "religious institutions, charities, private universities, or city, state, federal, or county governments." Fifteen years earlier, religious institutions had three times more real estate exempt than did companies. Back then, only 2 percent of corporate real estate was abated; by 2002, that figure was 10 percent.[9]

The largest revenue losses tend to be concentrated in the state's biggest urban areas with the highest numbers of poor people. For example, an audit found that abatements cost schools $13.7 million a year in Toledo, or 14 percent of their budget. Since the state changed its definitions due to the federal No Child Left Behind

Act, the Toledo School District is no longer in a state of "academic emergency." But it fails to meet 11 of 18 standards, and almost a third of its students don't graduate from high school. As the *Wall Street Journal* pointed out, Toledo businesses complain that the poor schools make it hard to find well-trained workers—at the same time those businesses are taking big property tax breaks.[10]

The state tax department found that Hamilton County (Cincinnati) loses more than $20 million a year. And an audit in 2001 found that more than a fifth of the abated companies in the county were falling short on jobs or investment. "They're a slippery slope," said the county auditor. "Once you start [abatements], they never end. Eventually, there'll be one little old guy in Price Hill paying all the taxes because everyone else will be abated."[11]

A state audit found schools in Cleveland losing $9.2 million a year—on just eight subsidized projects—at a time when the district was closing schools, cutting sports programs, and laying off teachers. The issue of lost school revenue got so hot in Cleveland, it went to a ballot initiative in 1997; the proposal to shield the school share from abatements failed, but the city has been more cautious about handing out abatements since the vote.[12]

The problem of funding disparities among school districts has been the subject of more than a decade of litigation and state supreme court rulings in Ohio. Among the court findings: K-12 overdependence on property taxes is a root cause of inequality. That overdependence also makes TIF and abatements especially harmful.

Illinois: TIF on Steroids

Schools in Illinois are also more dependent than average on property taxes, and the big problem there is TIF. The state now has more than 870 TIF districts diverting revenue away from schools and other public services—135 in Chicago alone.[13] TIF districts in the Prairie State typically last 23 years, and when a district expires, the increased tax revenues created by the redevelopment are supposed to finally start going to the schools and other local services. But already, more than 30 localities in the state have applied to extend their TIF districts—for 12 more years.[14]

In Chicago, the Neighborhood Capital Budget Group (NCBG) has documented the fact that properties in many of the city's TIF districts were growing in their assessed value before being designated (suggesting they were hardly "blighted"). That means that the TIF diversion is capturing a lot of tax-base growth that would have occurred naturally anyway—because once the TIF district is created, *all* increases get diverted away from schools and other public services, even if they aren't caused by the TIF-subsidized redevelopment. For just 36 of the city's TIF districts, NCBG estimates that this diversion—of revenue captured by TIF but not caused by it—will cost public services $1.3 billion over the 23-year life of the districts, including $632 million lost to the Chicago public schools and $53 million lost to the community college district.[15]

Sharon Patchak-Layman is an active parent and school board member in Oak Park, a diverse suburb on Chicago's western border that has extended its TIF after much debate produced some concessions. She spoke out at a national press conference about her frustrations with TIF and later told a reporter: "When the TIF was first formed, my children were very young. Now they are adults and living on their own, and they have yet to receive the [promised] benefits of that boon for education."[16]

Maine: Turning Property Taxes into Profits

Maine has created a perverse subsidy situation that can be twice as lucrative as an abatement. The state offers two different subsidies that reimburse companies for property taxes—*and some companies are eligible to claim both*. So instead of property taxes being a cost, they can become a profit source. The more you "pay," the more you profit!

The first reimbursement subsidy is TIF. In Maine, the property taxes a company owes on new machinery and equipment (the tax increment in TIF) can be paid back to a company via TIF; that is, from local property taxes. The second subsidy is called the Business Equipment Tax Reimbursement (BETR) program. Under BETR, a company gets a 100-percent refund on business equipment taxes from the state, even if those taxes have already been refunded under a TIF. For capital-intensive manufacturers located in a TIF district, this presents a lucrative "double dip" opportunity.

The Maine Citizen Leadership Fund reports that about 50 companies qualify for the TIF/BETR double-dip. It estimates that double-dippers cost BETR more than $15 million a year (over and above their first 100-percent reimbursement), including $3.4 million to National Semiconductor and $2.1 million to International Paper in 2001. The scandal has festered publicly for several years, while the state has cut funding for both schools and low-cost drugs for the elderly. The Leadership Fund finds that double-dipping is rising sharply and estimates that it will cost the state $256 million through 2012.[17]

"Free Growth"? Just Ask South Carolina

Finally, a common argument made in favor of abatements and TIF is that they are actually cost-free because the project would not occur "but for" the subsidy. Therefore, *any* tax revenue the project creates (aside from its unpaid property taxes) is a plus.

This argument has several fatal flaws. First, as I discuss in chapter 2, for the vast majority of companies, subsidies don't actually determine where they will expand or relocate, so the basic "but for" assumption is rarely valid. Second, there is no such thing as free growth. If a company does arrive and the community gains jobs, workers with their families are going to move to the area. That means local governments are going to have to build more classrooms, hire more teachers, widen some roads, hire more police and fire department personnel, pick up more trash, and so on. All of those things cost money. If the newly arriving companies are not paying their fair share of the costs for those services, government must either (1) raise everyone else's tax rates and fees, (2) reduce the quality of public services (increase classroom size, allow roads to stay congested, or the like); or (3) some of both.

Taxpayers in South Carolina understand this squeeze play. As Jay Hancock of the *Baltimore Sun* described in a 1999 investigation, the Palmetto State has been very aggressive in offering multiple subsidies to new companies, including property tax breaks, corporate income tax credits, and other subsidies. As a result, many of the shiny, outsider-owned facilities that dot the I-85 corridor are contributing very little directly to public services.[18]

Indeed, South Carolina has two other kinds of subsidies that reduce property tax revenue for schools and give school boards no say in the matter; both are controlled by county councils. Three tax scholars there estimated in 2000 that just one of these subsidies costs school districts $121 million a year.[19]

Instead of good new jobs, workers are getting low wages and taxpayers are getting poor public services. The South Carolina Department of Commerce brags, on its website, that the state has the lowest rate of unionization and that its manufacturing wages are almost 10 percent below the national average. But as jobs and population grow, public systems get strained and services suffer. With overcrowded roads, South Carolina has the nation's sixth highest rate of auto fatalities. With poorly funded public healthcare systems, its infants are the sixth most likely to die. With low school funding, its children fare poorly on SAT scores: lowest among the states in verbal and second lowest in math.[20]

As the three tax scholars put it: "Property tax incentives no doubt were put in place with the best of intentions. But so was kudzu."[21]

The Root Problem: School Boards Usually Have No Say

When one part of government gets a free lunch at the expense of another, that's a recipe for irresponsible behavior.

Like some other development subsidies, abatements and TIF really amount to an intergovernmental free lunch. School boards are legally charged with the duty of educating our children, and they are assigned certain sources of revenue, including property taxes, to fulfill that duty. But then other government bodies—such as county boards and city councils—mooch in and grant abatements and TIF that undermine the schools.

Can you imagine your local school board passing a resolution that allows a company to pay no property tax for the fire department and the police department—without those departments having any say in the matter? Of course not. But that is exactly what is happening to school boards in most states. This is terrible public policy, a telling sign of our collective disrespect for public education, at a time when education matters more than ever for our economy.

A study issued in 2003 surveyed the issue nationally, looking at states with abatements and TIF and whether they protect schools from them. In particular, it looked at what say—if any—the school boards have. It found that in the vast majority of states, school boards have nothing to say about the granting of abatements or TIF. They have no seats on the boards that make the decision; they don't even get consulted.[22]

Only five states—Kansas, Minnesota, Ohio (sort of), Pennsylvania, and Texas—say that school boards must approve the abatement of the school "increment"—the share of property taxes assigned to schools. Only seven states do the same for TIF, and two of those have only limited power; the seven are Colorado, Michigan (limited), Ohio (limited), Oklahoma, Pennsylvania, South Carolina, and Texas.

A handful of other states give school boards some sort of notice or advisory role, but no real power. And at least 14 states make it possible for school boards or localities to negotiate what is called a "Payment in Lieu of Taxes" or PILOT. However, the amount of money a company pays in a PILOT is often just a fraction of what it would pay if it did not get an abatement.

Only four states, by virtue of their subsidy and school funding rules, were found to shield schools from losing revenue to abatements and TIF: Alaska, Florida, Maryland, and South Dakota.

Even taking into account the fact that some states' school-funding formulas offset the losses school districts suffer to abatement or TIF, school board associations and other sources indicate that schools in at least two-thirds of the states—and perhaps as many as four-fifths—are vulnerable to lost funding due to abatements, TIF, or both.

Would the "business climate" suffer if school boards got to say whether or not their property taxes got abated? The experience in Texas clearly says no. Between 1993 and 2001, the state stopped reimbursing school districts for revenue they lost to abatements. School boards had the power to participate or not. In just two years, the share of school districts that participated in new abatements plunged, from 55 percent to 8 percent. Did the sky fall? Not at all. During those nine years, the Lone Star State gained about 2 million private-sector jobs, a one-third gain.[23]

There has been very little media coverage, but at least 21 states' school board associations have researched or lobbied on the issue of abatements or TIF hurting schools. Many have sought to convince their legislatures to protect school revenues from subsidies or to at least give school boards some say. Like many aspects of subsidy abuse, there is a tendency for people to think "this only happens to us."

Schools: A Key to Creating Good Jobs

Given the fundamental importance of public education for growing good jobs, it's especially tragic that so much property tax gets given away in the name of boosting the economy.

Veteran site location consultant Robert Ady said it well in the quotation that opens this chapter. When companies seek a place to relocate or expand to, the single most important thing they are looking for is an adequate supply of skilled labor. And the most important quality of life issue they look at is the schools. They look at data such as test scores, spending per pupil, and teacher salaries. And they will likely talk to local sources for more subjective impressions. Companies do this both for the employees they hope will agree to move to the new location *and* to make sure the location will be attractive to talented people they will seek to recruit in the future.[24]

A good education system boosts job creation not just because it helps attract employers, but also because it produces smart learners who grow up to become skilled workers, making companies more productive and the region more competitive. *Expansion Management*, one of several national site location magazines, publishes an annual "Education Quotient" survey rating secondary school districts, with an emphasis on results: test scores and graduation rates. It also publishes a "High Value Labor Quotient" survey of metro areas, analyzing college-educated workforces, and a "Quality of Life Quotient" that includes school quality.[25]

Education is also the key to individual success; as our economy has changed over the past 30 years, the long-term value of an education—in terms of a person's lifetime earnings and other measures of well-being—has greatly increased. College-educated men on average now earn about twice as much over their lifetime as men with a high school education.[26] As I'll argue in the closing chapter, those regions with the most skilled labor are destined now more than ever to be the job development winners of the twenty-first century.

These payoffs—an advantage for recruiting employers and a more productive workforce—explain why the quality of education, along with infrastructure, consistently shows up as a top predictor of an area's economic performance.[27] That's why I believe that slashing corporate property taxes in the name of job creation actually *harms* the business climate. It bears repeating: when big companies pay less, governments are forced to either raise the tax rates on homeowners and businesses that don't get the tax break, cut the quality of public services (with education often taking the biggest hit), or some of both.

★ Chapter Six ★

Subsidizing Sprawl, Subsidizing Wal-Mart

Subsidizing economic development in the suburbs is like paying
teenagers to think about sex.

—*Lyle Wray, Minneapolis Citizens League*[1]

Does your metro area suffer from suburban sprawl? Here's a checklist of diagnostic indicators to help you find out.[2]

- ❑ Do most commuters have any choice except the car to get to
  work? Are commutes getting longer and traffic delays becoming more common?
- ❑ Is the air quality getting worse? Do you know more people
  with asthma?
- ❑ Are there neighborhoods in older areas with large numbers of
  people of color who suffer high unemployment?
- ❑ Are older areas having trouble maintaining public services because they have lost a lot of their tax base? Are there many
  abandoned or contaminated properties in older areas?
- ❑ Are newly developing areas on the outer fringe suffering
  financial strains because they are growing too rapidly? Are
  there calls for growth slowdowns?
- ❑ Is there not enough affordable housing in the suburbs? Are
  there many suburbs that are poorly served by public transit?
- ❑ Do many residential areas lack sidewalks? Are more people
  becoming obese?

- Are big-box retail power centers and Wal-Marts opening up, undermining older malls and downtown retail districts?
- Are farms and natural spaces getting paved?

As was the case for the proverbial judge who couldn't define pornography but knew it when he saw it, sprawl means different things to different people. However you define it, sprawl is a very serious problem, a huge drag on our economy and our health. It worsens racial inequality and costs us thousands more acres of natural spaces every day. In most metro areas, our built environment has grown dysfunctional, and it's getting worse fast.[3]

As if all that weren't bad enough, you guessed it: taxpayers are often subsidizing sprawl—in the name of jobs. The economic war among the states is a serious problem, but so is the economic war among the suburbs.

Taxpayers pay for sprawl when they subsidize corporate relocations, many of which go from older core areas to newer fringe areas. Those are the most typical corporate moves—within the same metro area, so firms can retain their workforces and stay close to their suppliers and customers. But when companies move *outward*, that often means jobs move away from public transit, away from areas of high unemployment, maybe even away from areas with existing infrastructure into "greenfields"; that is, farmlands or natural space.

Taxpayers pay directly for sprawl through two kinds of job subsidies—enterprise zones (EZs) and tax increment financing (TIF). Ironically, both of these programs were created to revitalize older areas. But in many states, they have been perverted: their rules have been rewritten so that now they fuel sprawl that undermines older areas. The most outrageous cases are when TIF and other subsidies go to big-box retailers like Wal-Mart.

Taxpayers also pay for sprawl when they subsidize companies through the many other kinds of giveaways that are available no matter where a company goes. That's because, as I'll explain, not one single state coordinates any of its job subsidies with public transit.

Stay tuned as we investigate the real suburban issue today: is a mall "blighted" unless it has a Nordstrom? We report. You decide.

What Is Suburban Sprawl?

"Suburban sprawl" refers to development patterns with low density and no mixed uses (for example, no jobs or stores anywhere near homes), a lack of transportation options (forcing everyone to drive to work or shopping), and job growth in newer suburbs simultaneous with job decline in older areas (both the core city and older suburbs).

So, as the checklist of indicators suggests, sprawl makes people ever more dependent on cars. Commuting times get longer, air quality deteriorates, and natural spaces in outlying areas are rapidly lost. Older areas lose jobs and tax base, so central city infrastructure crumbles and services decline, even though there is a greater concentration of people who need help. Newly developing bedroom suburbs on the fringe struggle to pay for a lot of new roads, schools, and teachers, but they lack much commercial or industrial property to balance their tax base.

As jobs spread out from older areas, work becomes scarce for unemployed workers who are concentrated at the core. Many suburbs lack affordable housing (often because they enact exclusionary zoning that blocks the construction of apartment buildings and townhouses), and many suburban jobs are not accessible by public transit (either because a suburb opposes the entry of transit lines or because jobs are simply spread too thinly). So sprawl effectively cuts central city residents off from regional job markets. This means concentrated poverty in core areas, where residents are disproportionately people of color.

Meanwhile, out at the suburban fringe, thin, sprawling development consumes open space at an alarming rate. Every day, the United States loses 3,000 acres of productive farmland to sprawl: the equivalent of all the acreage in Delaware every year.[4] Americans hate this. That's why 75 to 80 percent of the time they approve ballot measures for smart growth, to improve mass transit and to preserve natural lands.[5]

Sprawl causes us to chew up land far faster than our numbers grow. Between 1982 and 1997, the U.S. population grew by 17 percent, but urbanized land area increased by *47 percent*. In the Northeast and Midwest, where population growth was slowest, the people-land trends are worse: land there is being consumed about five times faster than population growth. For example, in this period the Detroit metro area gained only 5 percent in population, but its urbanized land area grew by 29 percent.[6]

In the South, where population growth was higher, the trends are not so lopsided, but metro areas there were thinnest to begin with. Atlanta is arguably the worst-sprawling metro area, with a density of fewer than three people per acre; it's the only region to have its federal highway money held up because its air quality became so bad.[7] By contrast, many cities in the West have stopped sprawling so badly. For example, the Los Angeles-Anaheim-Riverside metro area was much more dense than Atlanta to begin with, and actually became slightly more dense, with more than eight people per acre.[8]

When metro areas thin out, tax systems become unjust and inefficient. Taxpayers in older areas get stuck with higher property tax *rates* as cities try to make up for the loss of the corporate property tax *base*. Taxpayers on the outer fringe also get socked, because their growth is thin and inefficient. And taxpayers in the region as a whole pay more, because on a per capita basis there are more miles of roads and sewers and water mains to build and maintain. Plus, police, fire, sanitation, and other public services cost more to deliver when the population is thinly distributed.

Sprawl is bad news for your health, too. The most obvious problem is air quality, since cars and trucks are the fastest-growing source of air pollution. The occurrence rate of asthma in the U.S. more than doubled between 1982 and 2002. Our children are the canaries in the coal mine here: their rate has always been higher and has also more than doubled.[9]

But it's not just bad air. Sprawl also makes you more likely to be fat and suffer from high blood pressure. No joke. Since people who live in sprawling areas really can't do much on foot, they tend to put on pounds. Indeed, many post-war suburbs even lack sidewalks for walking around the neighborhood, much less giving residents a choice about how to get to work, school, or shopping. A 2003 study in the *American Journal of Health Promotion* found that people living in counties rated as most sprawling are significantly more likely to be heavier, have a higher body mass index, or suffer high blood pressure, compared to people living in less sprawling counties.[10]

Do all these symptoms of sprawl sound like a recipe for a globally competitive U.S.A. of the twenty-first century? I don't think so.

What Causes Sprawl (Besides Job Subsidies)?

Urban experts say sprawl is caused by many factors, including

- Some people's preference for low-density housing
- White flight
- Lack of effective regional planning
- Cities competing for jobs and tax base instead of cooperating
- "Redlining" (geographic and racial discrimination in older areas by banks and insurance companies)
- Crime and perceptions of crime
- Declining quality of central city schools
- Contaminated land or "brownfields"
- Exclusionary suburban zoning
- Federal capital gains rules that used to encourage people to buy ever-larger homes
- The historically low price of gasoline
- Federal transportation spending that grossly favors highways over public transit

Don Chen, director of Smart Growth America, refers to all of these factors as a system of "mutually assured sprawl"; that is, they represent a post-war consensus that said sprawl is the way things ought to be. That consensus in turn created a system of mutually reinforcing systems to make sure we got what we thought we wanted.[11]

Another contributing factor to sprawl—overlooked until recently—is economic development subsidies. Sprawl happens when states allow subsidies to go anywhere (like a cornfield), and often pay companies to do what they would have done anyway (move outward). It happens because states fail to coordinate their job programs with land use planning—in particular, public transit planning. And it happens because subsidies that used to be targeted for urban revitalization, such as TIFs and EZs, have been perverted. Their rules have been changed so that newer and more affluent areas can give these lucrative subsidies away.

When newer suburbs are pitted against inner cities and older, inner-ring suburbs, it's a rigged fight. Newer suburbs have all kinds of advantages: more undeveloped and uncontaminated land, newer infrastructure, a more educated workforce, less dependency, and higher incomes. That's why many states enacted subsidies in the 1970s and early 1980s that were written to favor older areas, to try to level the playing field. But over time, many states have loosened the rules so that almost any locality can give away "anti-poverty" or "anti-blight" subsidies. Or pay teenagers to think about sex.

EZ subsidies are supposed to help poor areas attract new investment and jobs—in exchange for locating there to improve things, companies get one or more tax breaks (property, income, inventory, sales, utility, and so on). Therefore, all designated EZs are economically depressed areas—right? Well, that was the original idea, before states like Ohio started perverting the EZ theory. The Buckeye State now has a whopping 339 zones—many in areas that are not at all economically depressed. And it just happens to record corporate migrations into its zones, including where the company came from and how many jobs were affected. Want to guess the ratio of jobs moving *within the state* compared to those coming in from *other states?* It's 20 to 1.[12]

Policy Matters Ohio compared enterprise zones and found that very-high-income school districts received two times more EZ-subsidized jobs and five times more dollars of investment in zones than very-low-income school districts. "It's the wealthy areas that tend to land the most lucrative deals," the author wrote. Legislators "should not pretend that they're helping struggling communities. . . . Ohio's poorest communities have been zoned out."[13]

TIF is a little more complicated. A city designates a small area as a TIF district for redevelopment. New construction occurs, property values go up, and therefore property taxes also rise. When that happens, the tax revenue is split into two streams. The first stream, set at the "base value" before redevelopment, continues to go to schools, police, fire, and other local services. The second stream—made up of all the increase or "tax increment"—gets diverted back into the TIF district to subsidize the redevelopment. As I explained in chapter 5, this diversion can last 15, 20, 23, even 30 years, depending on each state's rules. It usually goes for infrastructure or other public improvements, but in some states, it may also be directly paid to developers to subsidize private construction costs.

Here's an example of TIF subsidizing sprawl. Anoka, Minnesota, is a suburb of the Twin Cities about 20 miles up the Mississippi River. (It's Garrison Keillor's hometown; yes, Lake Wobegon got engulfed in suburbia.) Anoka used TIF to give free land to 29 small manufacturing companies with about 1,600 jobs. Half of the companies relocated from Minneapolis or older, ailing suburbs on its edge; all the others came from other suburbs. Most of the companies were moving because they needed to expand, and only one of them even considered leaving the Twin Cities area.

By staying in the region, the companies got to retain their skilled workers and stay close to their suppliers and customers. But when you look at these 29 corporate relocations from a regional perspective, the maps are ugly. Jobs were moved away from the region's poorest neighborhoods and those with people of color, and away from areas with the most welfare households (at a time when welfare reform was forcing recipients into Work First programs). The moves also took job opportunities away from low-income families who cannot afford a car: more than 70 percent of the jobs had originally been accessible by public transit, but in Anoka they are not. The new job-takers likely came from rural areas farther north.[14]

Although TIF usually only diverts property tax, several states like Missouri also allow the local share of the *sales tax* increment to be "TIFed." Obviously, if a TIF project consists of paving a cornfield to build a sprawl-mart, all of the sales tax from the site is new, so all of the local share of the sales tax could go to subsidize the big box, instead of supporting public education or other services. So in addition to its potential for subsidizing the relocation of manufacturing or service-sector companies, TIF can become a super-subsidy for retail sprawl.[15]

Enterprise zones in Ohio and TIF in Anoka are far from isolated cases; several other studies and news investigations have linked development subsidies to sprawl:

- In the Chicago metro area, the Woodstock Institute examined the geographic distribution of loans made under the Small Business Administration's (SBA) 504 loan guarantee program and found that higher-income and outlying zip codes received more loans than lower-income and closer-in areas (where most minority entrepreneurs live).[16]
- Friends of the Earth and the Forest Conservation Council analyzed SBA loan guarantees in the Washington, DC, metro area. The map of deals looked like a donut; almost all of the loan aid had gone to companies in the outlying areas of the region. The two groups sued the SBA for failing to analyze the environmental impact of its loans, and the SBA agreed to start considering such impacts.[17]
- The New York state Comptroller found that over a 12-year period in the 1970s and 1980s, one-fourth of all the low-interest, tax-free business loans made by a state authority (usually packaged with property tax abatements) went to just one county on Long Island, "a boom area with rock bottom unemployment rates." Further, he found, "only 4 percent of the authority's

deals were in a depressed area of approximately the same population size — Buffalo and Erie County — with some of the highest unemployment rates in the nation. The result shows what is instinctively thought: tax abatement activity follows rather than leads economic development."[18]

- The *Kansas City Star* did a terrific investigative series citing several companies that received subsidies to leave core areas with high unemployment and relocate into prosperous suburbs. The paper found the deals particularly galling because the tools being used by the wealthy suburbs were originally intended to help central cities. "Created to combat sprawl, tax breaks now subsidize it," the *Star* moaned.[19]

- Illinois perverted its TIF program in 1989 as part of a subsidy package worth at least $178 million, given to Sears when the retailer threatened to move its headquarters out of state. The deal ripped 5,000 jobs out of the Sears Tower in the Loop — where it drew a racially diverse workforce coming to work aboard a century of magnificent public-transit investments — and whisked them away to a "campus" in the affluent white suburb of Hoffman Estates, 29 miles away and then without any transit service.[20] Today, thanks to loose program rules, Illinois has more than 870 TIF districts.[21] Even the wealthy Chicago suburb of Lake Forest (median 2000 family income: $165,512) has a TIF district — and a Ferrari dealership! (In a 1986 consulting report to Illinois, Fantus Company recommended TIF rules be changed to allow it to be used to develop raw land.)[22]

- The *Milwaukee Journal Sentinel* cited a mutual fund company in suburban Menomonee Falls that received a $3 million tax credit. The paper reported that the deal was justified because it was "close to Milwaukee County, which continues to have higher unemployment than the state average." A state senator was more blunt: "It's essentially a government subsidy to promote sprawl."[23]

- New York state's "Empire Zone" program is such a sprawling upstate mess, it's hard to pick just one example. How about $100 million in tax breaks for auto insurer GEICO to locate a regional service center in Amherst, a well-off suburb nine miles outside of struggling Buffalo? GEICO is largely owned by Warren Buffett — the second-wealthiest person in the world, with $42.9 billion.

Worshiping Competition, Subsidizing Sprawl

There is an ideological link between the economic war among the states and the wealthy suburbs' use of loose subsidies to pirate jobs from older areas. The link is the blind worship of competition—or at least the version that says corporations get to define the rules of the game and that government officials must always compete, never cooperate. Especially since the early 1980s, states have enacted hundreds of subsidies in the name of "staying competitive" with each other. In the same period, many states have also loosened programs such as TIF and EZs in ways that fuel the wars among cities and suburbs.

Some states, like Ohio and Idaho, even deformed their EZ rules with the explicitly stated purpose of fighting other states for jobs. For example, Ohio's enterprise zone program barely pays lip service anymore to fighting poverty or unemployment. Although it was enacted in 1981 to reduce blight in depressed areas, its rules were amended in the late 1980s and early 1990s so that its officially stated purpose now is to reduce business property taxes and protect Ohio against competition from other states.[24]

Others have loosened rules in ways that make the programs less targeted and therefore less likely to benefit poor areas. States do this in several ways:

- Lowering the required rate of poverty or unemployment or other eligibility factors — or even saying every county can have a zone
- Allowing zones to become huge or so numerous they cover areas that really don't need help
- Making it easier for cities to gerrymander the boundaries to favor special interests
- Making the criteria more subjective or giving officials case-by-case power to designate an EZ

States can even let companies outside the zones get EZ tax breaks. New York, Texas, Connecticut, Louisiana, Utah, Wisconsin, and Indiana have each made one or more of such changes.

Give Arkansas, Kansas, and South Carolina credit: each has decided to drop all pretense of aiding poor neighborhoods with EZs—and simply declared the entire state to be one big enterprise zone![25]

Other states embraced loose new TIF rules, basically saying an area that "is capable of being substantially improved" or is a "non-blighted economic development area" or "lacks proper utilization" can be TIFed. Alaska, Indiana, Iowa, North Dakota, Oregon, Virginia, and South Carolina fall into this category. Indeed, the Palmetto State extended TIF eligibility to "sprawl areas" to include those considered to be at risk of blight because they could be developed as a planned community! And Virginia just waved the white flag and said any city could designate any place as a TIF district to promote "commerce and prosperity."[26]

Loosening TIF rules is an invitation to the proliferation of sprawling giveaways. Before Iowa loosened its TIF rules in 1989, it had 185 TIF districts; ten years later, it had 2,473, funding such distressed projects as golf course developments, market-rate single-family homes, and car washes. TIF districts have become such a mess that everyone from the Farm Bureau to the teachers' union thinks they need reform. Minnesota has seven kinds of TIF districts and only two require blight, so the state grew more than 2,100 TIF districts before a school-finance reform curbed the craziness.[27]

Most of these bad state rule changes occurred in the late 1980s and early 1990s, when the state-eat-state sweepstakes—like those for auto assembly plants—got so hot. In other words, misguided reactions to interstate competition have caused many states to deregulate their subsidy rules in ways that grossly favor wealthy suburbs. Other states, like Missouri and Pennsylvania with their scandalous TIF programs, have had loose rules all along. We can't worry about saving the cities, the states are collectively saying; we are too busy bulking up to fight each other.

As a result, taxpayers are needlessly subsidizing inefficient and wasteful development that is creating huge long-term problems for our economy, our environment, and our health.

Sprawl Worsens Economic and Racial Inequality

Sprawl is also bad news if you care about racial and economic equality. Because poor people and people of color live disproportionately in big cities and older, inner-ring suburbs, job sprawl makes inequality worse. New suburban office parks, retail power centers, and industrial parks are routinely given development subsidies. They are also often poorly served by public transit, if at all, so they often deny job opportunities to people who cannot afford a car.

That is bad news for low-income families, and especially bad news for workers of color. Transportation (overwhelmingly automobile) costs are second only to housing expenses for the average U.S. household, at 18 percent versus 19 percent—and rising faster. For families in the lowest-fifth income bracket, transportation now consumes 36 percent of their after-tax income![28] Such high costs exclude one in ten families from owning a car, and they are disproportionately people of color. African-American households are more than three times as likely not to own a car as white households, and Latino households more than twice as likely.[29]

A huge national survey of job subsidies sought to find some positive examples of governments actually coordinating job creation with transit. This was no small task, given that the average state now has 30 different subsidy programs on the books. Despite scouring hundreds of sources, the survey could not find one single example of a subsidy program that even gives preference to projects that are transit-accessible—much less requires it. The title of that report: *Missing the Bus.*[30]

Let me repeat: despite the fact that the states collectively have more than 1,500 job subsidy programs, and despite the fact that everyone knows poor people and people of color are less likely to own cars, and despite all the pro-subsidy rhetoric politicians have used about reducing poverty and unemployment, not one single subsidy says to companies: "If you want this taxpayer money, the jobs have to be accessible by transit." Not one single subsidy even says "We'll give preference to transit-accessible deals."[31]

Another way sprawling jobs fuel inequality is through housing: rents and prices are higher in the suburbs, and so is the rate of racial discrimination. Many studies have shown that when jobs sprawl from central city to suburbs, workers of color and low-wage workers are disproportionately harmed because they face barriers finding suburban housing.[32]

The Hidden Taxpayer Costs of Subsidizing Big-Box Retail

America is awash in excess retail space. The National Trust for Historic Preservation estimates we have 38 square feet of store space for every man, woman, and child. Measures vary, but other industrialized nations report between 1.5 and 8 square feet per capita.[33] We are way out of whack with comparable economies—and with our own history. In 1960, we had about four square feet per capita, and by 1977, still only about eight.[34]

Despite the fact that retail is a truly lousy economic development investment, a lot of this excess retail space has been getting subsidized. The big dogs driving this trend are the "category killer," "power center" players like Wal-Mart, Home Depot, and Target. Of course, Wal-Mart is the alpha dog of department stores, since it is five times bigger than #2 Target. It's also apparently the alpha hog at the public trough, as I'll explain—benefiting from more than $1 billion in bricks-and-mortar subsidies for its stores and warehouses.

Retail rarely deserves to be subsidized, because it packs such a lousy bang for the buck compared to manufacturing or almost any other activity. To measure the ripple effects of a new business, you look "upstream" to see how many supplier jobs the region would gain, and then you look "downstream" to see how many jobs would be created by the buying power of the people who work at the business. The upstream of a big-box store does not create many jobs for the local economy (think of all those goods made in China), and the downstream ripple effects are terrible because retail jobs are overwhelmingly part-time and poverty-wage, with no healthcare. That means most retail workers have very small disposable incomes: after paying for bare necessities, they have nothing left with which to stimulate the local economy.

In short, retail is not economic development; it's what happens when people have disposable income. But you'd be surprised at the arguments I have had with newspaper business writers, trying to get across one simple concept: you and I do not have more money in our pockets because we have more places to shop. Building new retail space just moves sales and lousy jobs around. It doesn't grow the economy. (The only exception to the poverty-wage problem is unionized grocery stores. And I think there is one justifiable time to subsidize retail: to help revitalize a truly depressed inner-city neighborhood that lacks basic retail such as grocery, drug, and clothing stores.)

In almost every region, the plague of overbuilt retail is evident. The National Trust for Historic Preservation's Main Street Center has helped downtown retailers in more than 1,000 cities fight against big-box centers such as Wal-Mart. The program's director has testified that cities with too much retail space suffer all kinds of hidden costs—in addition to whatever subsidies they grant the big box. When just one Main Street store, with two floors of 2,000 square feet, goes from being occupied and busy to being vacant, the total cost to the local economy is almost $250,000 a year, she reported. That includes losses in property taxes, wages, bank deposits and loans, rent, sales, and profits.[35]

It's not just downtown retail areas that are suffering: malls are also getting cannibalized. Indeed, the U.S. is "de-malling," as the construction of windowless, inward-looking malls has almost stopped and the power-center format takes charge. A 2001 study by the Congress for the New Urbanism and PriceWaterhouseCoopers about "greyfields"—the euphemism for dead malls—found that 7 percent of regional malls were already greyfields and another 12 percent are "potentially moving towards greyfield status in the next five years." That would be 389 dead malls.[36]

Since vacant or underutilized properties usually get reassessed and pay much lower property taxes, dead malls mean big tax revenue drops. For example, Northridge Mall in Brown Deer, Wisconsin, went from an assessed value of $107 million in 1990 to a greyfield sale value of $3.5 million in 2001.[37]

This process costs taxpayers three ways: the bricks-and-mortar subsidies going to the new big boxes; the losses caused by abandonment of both Main Street and the mall; and the massive hidden costs in the form of public assistance to low-wage workers. When Wal-Mart and other poverty-wage retailers fail to provide a decent wage and full-time hours, many employees and their families qualify for safety-net help such as Medicaid, state children's health insurance programs, earned income tax credits, Section 8 housing assistance, low-income energy assistance, and free or discounted school lunches.

Indeed, U.S. congressional staff have tallied all of these hidden costs; they estimate that each Wal-Mart store with 200 employees costs federal taxpayers $420,750 a year in safety-net costs.[38] Multiply that by the 3,500 stores Wal-Mart already has in the U.S.—and by the 300 more stores it plans to open every year.

For years, runaway increases in Medicaid costs have been the states' biggest spending headache. Healthcare inflation is partly to blame. But it is becoming increasingly obvious—as more than one million Americans a year lose health insurance coverage—that corporate freeloading is also fueling the problem and that retailers are among the biggest hogs. A few states are so fed up with the problem that they are starting to release hard data. Some company-specific data has become available, but as of late 2004, only Massachusetts has enacted legislation requiring such disclosure; other revelations have come out thanks to investigative journalists and healthcare advocates.

In the data available so far, Wal-Mart stands out, but it is hardly alone. The retail giant had the greatest number of enrolled beneficiaries in state-sponsored healthcare programs for low-income families in Connecticut, Tennessee, and Washington and the greatest number of employee children on Medicaid or SCHIP in Georgia and West Virginia. Wal-Mart had the fifth-greatest number of Medicaid beneficiaries in Florida and the third-greatest number in two Massachusetts programs combined. Wal-Mart reportedly has 3,765 employee, spouse, or child beneficiaries in Wisconsin's BadgerCare program, but data on other companies has not been released there. McDonald's ranked high for use of various public healthcare programs in Florida, Massachusetts, Connecticut, and West Virginia. The grocery chain Publix ranked high for employee children on Medicaid in Florida and Georgia. Both the grocery chain Stop and Shop and fast-food provider Dunkin' Donuts ranked high for beneficiaries in Massachusetts and Connecticut.[39]

How did we come to such bad policy? Why are we paying to kill downtowns and shutter malls and subsidize companies through the back door for their poverty wages?

No, no, no, say the developers! You're asking the wrong questions! *We have to stay competitive.*

How Suburbs Compete for Taxes—and Fuel Sprawl

Most states have tax rules that force local governments to compete, rather than cooperate, for their tax base. These dumb state rules seriously warp how cities and suburbs regulate the use of land, causing them to embrace pro-sprawl policies that maximize their income and minimize their expenses. The policy term for this is "fiscalization of land use." It means cities let budget issues dictate how land will be used.

Specifically, this means localities adopt land uses that maximize property and sales tax revenue and minimize public-service expenses (such as for school-age children—K-12 is local government's biggest cost). Land use gets driven by local governments trying to balance their budgets, not by human needs or what's most efficient or what's best for public health—or what's good for jobs.

Our tax systems, by pitting local jurisdictions against each other, fail us in many ways. We live in a *region*. What matters is how *the region* is doing. Many of us live in one jurisdiction, work in another, shop and play and worship in still others. We live regionally, but a lot of our local tax dollars act like, well, Hatfields and McCoys.

On property taxes, fiscalization of land use means localities have every reason to use subsidies to pirate companies from each other. Large business facilities have high values and therefore generate substantial taxes (unless, of course, they get abatements). Plus, business parks don't have any homes housing those costly school-age children.

On avoiding expenses, fiscalization causes localities to enact exclusionary zoning ordinances (saying, for example, only one single-family home per acre). That means only one family's children to educate. The family that can afford such a house is most likely white, so that helps keep the school system racially segregated. Of course, large-lot zoning, which excludes apartments, duplexes, and townhouses (read: affordable housing), also permanently screws up a suburb's built environment. Most residents there will never have a transportation choice; they will always be forced to drive because jobs, groceries, and parks will always be too far away to walk to. Thin density means transit will never work there.

Dog-eat-dog also makes no sense if a region wants to be economically competitive. Regional cooperation can improve productivity by reducing time lost in traffic. It can give companies fuller access to a region's labor force. And it can enable areas to focus on improving their business basics that attract new companies.

First, traffic. The Texas Transportation Institute's annual survey of traffic congestion found that in 2002 U.S. commuters lost a total of 3.5 billion hours due to traffic delays—five times what they lost 20 years before—at a cost of $63.2 billion. The trends are worst in the thinnest metro areas with poor transit systems. So in sprawling Atlanta, hours lost per person per year jumped from 14 in 1982 to

60 in 2002.[40] And with more employers beginning to experience shortages of skilled labor (see chapter 9), they need workers from all over the region to fill vacancies; in large metro areas, that means reliable job access by transit is critical.

Regarding recruitment, when a company is considering where to expand or relocate, it evaluates a metro *region,* not an individual suburb. It knows it will have to draw workers from the whole region, and depend on the region's infrastructure, and trust the region's schools and universities and quality of life to attract and retain good workers. It *will* look at individual cities within a metro area once it decides it likes the region, but *only* after determining that the region has the right stuff. So if an individual suburb wants to thrive, the best thing it can do is organize with other cities to make *the region* attractive. Public officials in some areas have figured this out and are cooperating more on recruitment efforts (and they downplay the use of subsidies to attract companies because they know they rarely matter). Cities in some regions share some of their revenue. But the harsh reality is that most states' rules still make local governments fight each other for tax base.

But the tax-sprawl story gets really, truly ugly when it comes to sales taxes and retailing. Many states allow localities to add a "local sales tax increment" (usually capped at between a half and one percent) on top of the state sales tax. This "point of sale" tax often goes only to the city where the sale occurs, not to a regional pot. This gives local governments a perverse incentive to zone a lot of land for retail, subsidize retail construction, and pirate lots of retail sales from other cities in the region. Of course, from a regional perspective, that makes no sense, given the excess retail space and dead malls we already have. But from the narrow viewpoint of an individual suburb, the goal is to land lots of busy cash registers. And the biggest prizes, again, are the "category killer" national chains—such as Wal-Mart, Home Depot, Target, Circuit City, Borders, and Bed Bath & Beyond.

This perverse incentive goes on steroids if local governments have budget problems because of property tax caps (like California with its Proposition 13) or cutbacks in state revenue-sharing to cities. It goes on double steroids when states allow cities to use property tax-TIF to subsidize retail (like Pennsylvania). And it goes on triple steroids in states that also allow the local sales tax increment to get "TIFed" for retail (like Missouri).

You've heard the term "smokestack-chasing"? I call this cash-register chasing. By every measure I can imagine, it fails the definition of good jobs policy.

Missouri: "TIFing" for Nordstrom

Missouri, which allows sales taxes to be "TIFed," has had a raging four-year debate about how to reform its TIF program before it subsidizes any more unnecessary new stores. The problem is especially severe in the St. Louis area, where the East-West Gateway Council has documented that most TIF districts are for retail projects that are dominated by national chains and located in wealthier suburbs.[41]

Yet the Show-Me State apparently does not want to be shown any cost-benefit data. The TIF law has no accountability rules to measure outcomes, even though it is widely known that the St. Louis area is swimming in overbuilt taxpayer-subsidized retail space. The issue has brought together a bipartisan coalition of existing retailers, school boards, small business groups, the Food & Commercial Workers union, planning bodies, and elected officials.

Missouri state senator Wayne Goode, a Democrat who represents St. Louis County, has sponsored a reform bill. "Putting public money into retail in a big metropolitan area doesn't make any sense at all," Goode says. "It just moves retail sales around." About one-third of the 90 municipalities in St. Louis County keep "point of sale" sales tax, he explains. The other two-thirds pool their local increments. So the one-third of municipalities fight both among themselves and against the two-thirds—often using TIF. Meanwhile, the county schools alone suffer a diversion of more than $5.1 million a year.[42] Area developers have gone to great lengths to block reforms because the TIF is so lucrative; it has financed a fourth or more of the cost of numerous projects.

St. Charles County executive Joe Ortwerth, a self-described "Reagan Republican," is equally incensed about the situation. He sued to end TIF, based on the Missouri state constitution's ban on the use of public money for private interests. His county is growing rapidly as people move outward from St. Louis, and it has no quantifiable measure of blight, he argues. Premier malls are getting TIF dollars just to get spruced up, he says.[43]

As for claims about higher sales tax revenues, that is just a "total ruse," says Ortwerth. "It is just a change in the point of sale." Indeed, he argues that because of the taxes diverted into TIF, there is actually a net revenue loss. Job creation claims are just as bogus, claims Ortwerth. Not long after Home Depot got a TIF deal in the city of St. Charles, says Ortwerth, the HQ store in St. Peters closed down.[44]

In a letter endorsing Senator Goode's bill, the CEO of Schnuck's, a major grocery chain in Missouri, said: "Over time, the definition of 'blight' has become more or less meaningless. TIF has in many cases become just a subsidy offered to entice a developer for the benefit of enhancing a municipality's sales tax base." Acknowledging that his company has accepted TIF in the past, he concluded that "TIF has distorted the free market," and he urged reform.[45]

As the St. Louis *Post-Dispatch* editorialized: "With towns handing out TIF like bubble gum, St. Louis may be getting over-stored, while developments are under-taxed."[46]

Many of those stores are getting built in wealthy areas, and the developers want TIF to offset high land prices. Shopping-center giant Westfield America, a publicly traded real estate investment trust, bought West County Center in Des Peres, an upscale suburb of St. Louis (2000 median family income: $106,195). Announcing it wanted to redevelop the center to include Nordstrom and Lord & Taylor, Westfield asked for a $29 million TIF subsidy. The Des Peres

Board of Alderman dutifully declared West County Center to be "blighted," even though it was almost 100 percent occupied and grossing more than $100 million a year. Being "blighted" made it eligible for the TIF subsidy, and the aldermen also approved that. Angry Des Peres citizens, together with the owners of a rival mall, sued to block the deal, but lost at trial and before the Missouri Court of Appeals.[47]

Presumably, the neighborhood is stabilized now that residents have ready access to Nordstrom's 117 brands of shoes.

California: Proposition 13 Fuels Sprawl as Cities Chase Pennies

California's tax revolt, marked by the passage of Proposition 13 in 1978, has had many unintended consequences. It has harmed public education and other public services, contributed to a massive infrastructure deficit, and created unfair tax disparities among different companies—and it is also a major cause of sprawl.[48]

Prop 13 froze property tax assessments at 1975 values, and said assessments could be raised no more than 2 percent a year—unless a property changes hands. When a property is sold, it gets reassessed at full market value; then once again the assessment can only go up 2 percent a year. If a structure is improved, the building is partially reassessed, but not the land. The net effect of these rules has been to artificially depress business property assessments and thereby depress property tax revenue. That, in turn, makes local governments in the Golden State ever more dependent on sales taxes.

Cities or counties receive a penny and a quarter-cent of the sales tax on each dollar, based on where the sale occurs. That means localities have a perverse incentive to subsidize too much retail, to steal sales from each other to capture those pennies. Surveys of local development officials in California find that their #1 redevelopment concern is getting more sales tax revenue, so land-use decisions get horribly warped.[49] And who has the most undeveloped land available for power centers? The suburbs out on the fringe, of course.

California localities are allowed to charge development fees on new developments; that makes it easier for them to recover the costs of infrastructure, partially mitigating the impact of Prop 13. But since these fees are primarily levied on undeveloped land on the fringe, that means more sprawl, too.

Occasionally, large parcels become available in built-out areas of California, and cities will spend huge sums to get lots of busy cash registers. In 1995, I was asked to testify in a dispute between Long Beach and Lakewood. The U.S. Navy was handing over a property to Long Beach, and of course the city was proposing to reuse the site as a big-box power center. This property was right on the city line between the two cities, and Lakewood Center, a mature but healthy mall that had opened in 1951 (said to be the nation's second oldest regional shopping center), was just two miles away.

In my testimony, I questioned the wisdom of spending at least $37 million in various subsidies on the deal and turning it over to big-box retailers then paying workers an average of only $6.50 per hour, for only thirty one hours per week, or $10,478 a year—way below the family poverty line.[50] In Long Beach, the traditional cost-benefit balance sheet was missing in action. The quality of the jobs didn't matter. It was all about the sales-tax pennies. Today the Long Beach Town Center is a big, low-grade power center, a boring mix of unconnected boxes and chain retailers clustered around a multiplex theater and outdoor food court: Lowe's, Wal-Mart, Barnes & Noble, Linens & Things, Old Navy, and Bed Bath & Beyond.

Lakewood's mall didn't get cannibalized as the city had feared, but the area has grown thicker with retail. Lakewood also got a Wal-Mart. And the Lakewood Center mall has actually grown, landing one of the region's first Macy's, plus a new Target. Still, Lakewood's spokesman, D. J. Waldie, who chronicled the city's history in his lyrical book *Holy Land: A Suburban Memoir*,[51] says there is a troubling level of over-storing in the region. When more housing is so badly needed, he points out, "Do you actually need 136,000 square feet of Wal-Mart every two miles?"[52]

Prop 13 also has a loophole that enables corporations to dodge property reassessments. Again, it froze assessments at 1975 values, allowing only a 2 percent annual increase—unless the property changes hands. The trouble is, the ways in which investment properties are often owned—through publicly traded companies, limited partnerships, real estate investment trusts, and the like—means owners can come and go, but the same corporate entity still holds title, so there is no "change of ownership." The most common way this happens is through limited partnerships, which hold large amounts of California real estate such as office parks, shopping centers, and hotels. Partners may come and go, but the partnership retains title, so there is no "change of ownership," and therefore no reassessment.[53]

This system results in huge inequities. As the California Tax Reform Association has documented, in downtown San Francisco, the Hilton Tower Hotel paid 80 cents per square foot of land in property taxes in 2002 and 2003, while the Clift Hotel paid $16.55 a square foot—a difference of more than 20 times. The Hallidie Building paid $1.48, while the Bank of America building paid $15.90. In Silicon Valley's Santa Clara County, IBM paid a microscopic four-tenths of a cent, while Applied Signal Technology paid 67 cents—167 times more. In swank west Los Angeles County, the Luxe Summit Hotel in Bel Air paid 22 cents, while another Luxe, the Luxe Rodeo Drive, paid $3.35. In Orange County, large chunks of Disneyland's holdings were locked in at the 1975 assessment and paid just 1 to 5 cents, while more recently bought parcels paid 36 cents. In San Diego's pharmaceutical cluster, Dublin Medical paid 1 cent, while Amylin Pharmaceuticals paid 35 cents.[54]

"The law itself could be called loophole-ridden, except that it is all loophole and little else; the circumstances under which change of ownership takes place are fully subject to manipulation," writes Lenny Goldberg, the Association's president.[55]

Wal-Mart: More Than $1 Billion in Subsidies

It's hard to overstate Wal-Mart's role in making sprawl worse. A company with rural roots, it has a car-oriented format for stores that run as big as 220,000 square feet and Supercenters (that means groceries, too) of up to 261,000 square feet. Add about a thousand parking spaces, and you're talking about an enormous footprint.

No wonder it loves to site stores in greenfield locations near freeway off-ramps; such huge footprints rarely fit into existing urban areas. Among the big-box retailers, Wal-Mart has often been the most resistant to adapting its format to respect local communities' character. The trouble is, urban America is just about all that is left for Wal-Mart to saturate. It seems inevitable that "site fight" frictions will increase.[56]

That's why the National Trust for Historic Preservation named the entire state of Vermont an endangered historic place after Wal-Mart announced its intention of opening seven more stores there. "The likely result: degradation of the Green Mountain State's unique sense of place, economic disinvestment in historic downtowns, loss of locally-owned businesses, and an erosion of the sense of community that seems an inevitable by-product of big-box sprawl," said the Trust.[57]

Wal-Mart is also notorious for closing stores. It often closes a regular store upon opening a new, bigger Wal-Mart Supercenter nearby. In fact, Wal-Mart Realty's website in early 2005 listed about 350 properties available (mostly leased), with more than 27 million square feet of space![58] That's a lot of potential ghostboxes—the equivalent of 54 more dead malls. "Don't expect a long-term relationship with any superstore in your town," warns sprawl-buster Al Norman. "Wal-Mart arrives with its bags already packed."[59]

Despite the fact that Wal-Mart is the world's largest corporation; despite the fact that many public officials understand that it grows largely at the expense of existing retailers, causing abandonment and blight; despite its long-standing reputation as a land-chomping

"Sprawl-Mart"; and despite allegations concerning labor and discrimination and immigration-law violations—in spite of all this, Wal-Mart's phenomenal growth has been supported by taxpayers in many states through job subsidies.

Indeed, a company official once said the company seeks subsidies in about a third of its stores, suggesting that more than 1,100 of its U.S. stores are subsidized.[60] A national survey by Good Jobs First in 2004 found taxpayer subsidies of more than $1 billion benefiting Wal-Mart. Besides documenting subsidies to 160 stores, the study looked at all 91 of the company's distribution centers—*and found that more than 90 percent of them have been subsidized!* Altogether, 244 subsidized facilities in 35 states got taxpayer deals of more than $1 billion.[61]

The subsidies run the whole gamut: free or reduced-price land, infrastructure assistance, TIF, property tax abatements or discounts, state corporate income tax credits, sales tax rebates, enterprise zone tax breaks, job training funds, and low-interest tax-exempt loans. The most deals and dollars were found in Texas (30 deals worth $108 million) and Illinois (29 deals worth $102 million). And because of poor disclosure in most states, the authors concluded that this could be just the tip of the iceberg.[62]

The study even found outright cash grants totaling more than $30 million. For example, the state of Virginia gave cash grants to three Wal-Mart distribution centers totaling more than $2 million. The Old Dominion's "Governor's Opportunity Fund," like other such subsidies, gives the governor a lot of discretion to hand out cash grants as "deal closers."

Some Cities Just Say No

Of course, the real force driving Wal-Mart's site location behavior is its voracious appetite for more market share, not subsidies. So the study found cases in which the company sought subsidies, didn't get them, and still built. In Chula Vista, California, a $1.9 million subsidy deal was successfully challenged in court in 1998, after citizens complained that local redevelopment agencies were awarding state money to big-box retailers for projects with little benefit to the public. The Chula Vista Wal-Mart ended up being built without public assistance.

In 2001, voters in Galena, Illinois, rejected a $1.5 million sales tax rebate sought by the company for a planned Supercenter. Immediately after the vote, Wal-Mart said it would drop the plan, but it later decided to move forward after getting the private seller of the land to agree to a lower price.[63] Wal-Mart also proceeded with the construction of an unsubsidized Supercenter in Belvidere, Illinois, after its request for a $1.5 million sales tax rebate was opposed by local officials.[64]

Such events are especially controversial in TIF deals, because the governing law often requires that the beneficiary of TIF affirm that the project would not occur "but for" the subsidy. According to a report by 1000 Friends of Wisconsin, Wal-Mart admitted that the TIF funding provided to a project in Baraboo did not meet that requirement. The report also noted that the supposedly blighted area chosen for the project consisted of a cornfield and an apple orchard.[65]

Public opposition to subsidies for Wal-Mart has played a role in some successful "site fights":

- In 2000, voters in Olivette, Missouri, rejected a $36 million TIF proposal for an eighty-acre shopping center that was to be anchored by a Wal-Mart and a Sam's Club.[66]
- In 2002, Wal-Mart was rebuffed when it sought an $18 million subsidy in connection with a project that was to be located on the Near South Side of Chicago. According to a press report, Mayor Richard M. Daley "guffawed" when presented with the request. The project was abandoned.[67]
- Denver officials appeared to have dropped plans for a Supercenter project in 2004 that could have involved as much as $25 million in public money. The plan was controversial because of the subsidy and because it would have used eminent domain to displace a group of Asian-American small businesses.[68]

- Another Denver-area Wal-Mart controversy involving subsidies and eminent domain has been taking place in the city of Arvada. Wal-Mart has been seeking $7.5 million in TIF for a Supercenter. The project included a plan to condemn a lake so that it could be drained and partly filled with dirt and concrete to serve as part of the site.[69] The Colorado Supreme Court recently struck down this use of eminent domain, throwing the project into question.[70]
- In 2004, voters in Scottsdale, Arizona, voted resoundingly against a plan to give a developer up to $36 million in sales tax rebates for a complex that was to include a Supercenter and a Sam's Club.[71]

Some of the subsidies go to developers who build sites for Wal-Marts. When developers build for Wal-Mart, it is sometimes "all in the family." That's because THF Realty, which has been developing shopping centers anchored by Wal-Marts since 1991, was co-founded by E. Stanley Kroenke, the husband of Ann Walton, one of Sam Walton's nieces. By 2000, when Kroenke last had to disclose because he was a Wal-Mart board member, he was pulling down $23 million a year from rent on Wal-Mart stores.[72] Kroenke and his wife are estimated by *Forbes* magazine to be worth $4.4 billion.[73]

Costs and Benefits . . . or Costs and Costs?

When Good Jobs First released its study about subsidies for Wal-Mart, the company responded by saying it couldn't verify the figures, but that if they were correct, then "it looks like offering tax incentives to Wal-Mart is a jackpot investment for local governments." Specifically, the company claimed that over the past 10 years, it collected $52 billion in sales taxes, remitted $192 million in income taxes, wage withholdings, and unemployment insurance, and paid $4 billion in local property taxes. "Do the math and you will see that every dollar invested returned more than 30," the company summarized.[74]

Read those *verbs* very carefully. Of course Wal-Mart "collected" sales taxes—it's a retailer, it's required by law to do that. But that's *consumers' money,* not the company's. Wal-Mart is just a pass-through. And since much of its sales come at the expense of other retailers, any gain is obviously offset by lower sales taxes collected at competing stores—and by the taxpayer costs of abandoned downtowns and malls.

Of course Wal-Mart "remitted" income and payroll taxes—it's an employer, it's required to deduct taxes from its workers' paychecks. But income tax is not the company's money; it's *money from the workers' measly paychecks!* And since Wal-Mart jobs are largely shifted from other retailers, and Wal-Mart pays so poorly, the net revenue gain is unclear. And don't forget that estimate of $420,750 per year per store in hidden taxpayer costs for poverty-wage safety-net help like earned income tax credits, housing, and free school lunches.

Finally, of course Wal-Mart paid some property taxes—all property owners have to support local services. Unless, of course, they get an abatement; the study found more than 40 such instances. But Wal-Mart offered no disclosure on how much in property taxes it *hasn't* paid. And as economists point out, companies pass on the cost of property taxes to customers as much as market conditions allow.

So there you have it, folks: Wal-Mart's version of cost-benefit analysis. Taxpayer costs for job creation are balanced by "benefits" that mostly consist of, well, workers' costs, consumers' costs, and taxpayers' costs.

Can you say "other people's money"?

TOM the DANCING BUG PRESENTS:

BY RUBEN BOLLING
TOMBUG@AOL.COM

NEWS of the TIMES

Ned Balter To Remain In St. Louis

ST. LOUIS KINKO'S EMPLOYEE NED BALTER, 27, HAS ANNOUNCED THAT HE WILL **STAY IN THE ST. LOUIS AREA.**

I'M COMMITTED TO ST. LOUIS THROUGH 2015!

PARTY!

THE DEAL BETWEEN BALTER AND ST. LOUIS ENDED OVER A YEAR OF SPECULATION THAT BALTER WOULD MOVE TO CHICAGO.

ST. LOUIS TELEGRAPH
BALTER DECLARES ST. LOUIS "LAME"
Tells Friend He's "Out of Here"

AS PART OF THE INCENTIVE PLAN, BALTER WILL RECEIVE SIGNIFICANT TAX BREAKS, AND THE CITY WILL BUILD AND MAINTAIN THIS STATE-OF-THE-ART 50,000 SEAT SPORTS STADIUM FOR HIM.

IS THIS A COOL CRIB, OR WHAT!

ALTHOUGH BALTER IS TO PAY $400/mth FOR FULL EXCLUSIVE USE OF THE FACILITY, IT IS RENT-FREE IN ANY YEAR IN WHICH BALTER DOES NOT HAVE A GIRLFRIEND FOR MORE THAN 180 DAYS.

SO I'D SUGGEST THE ST. LOUIS LADIES GET WITH THE PROGRAM!

AHMET VARNU, MANAGER OF THE BUCKA-ROOSTERS THAT BALTER FREQUENTS, PRAISED THE PLAN.

I DON'T KNOW WHAT WOULD HAPPEN IF WE LOST BALTER'S TWICE-WEEKLY PURCHASE OF A BUCKA-MEAL.

NEVERTHELESS, ECONOMISTS SAY THAT THE PLAN WILL NOT BE FISCALLY VIABLE, AN ASSERTION THAT MAYORAL AIDE VINCE NELSEN DOWNPLAYED.

THIS GOES BEYOND DOLLARS AND CENTS. WE WERE **NOT** GOING TO BE THE ADMINISTRATION THAT LOST BALTER!

BEST OF ALL, TAXPAYERS DON'T HAVE TO FOOT THE BILL--THE COSTS WILL BE TAKEN SOLELY OUT OF PUBLIC SCHOOL FUNDS.

THIS DEAL WILL CERTAINLY BEAR ON THE NEGOTIATIONS WITH CYNTHIA'S FLORIST SHOP, WHICH HAS THREATENED TO MOVE TO ALTON.

I'D BETTER GET A RETRACTABLE DOME NOW.

★ Chapter Seven ★

Loot, Loot, Loot
for the Home Team

The pride and the presence of a professional football team is far more important than 30 libraries.

—*Art Modell, owner of the Cleveland Browns
(later the Baltimore Ravens) football team*[1]

Americans have a love affair with professional sports, and, as with other types of romance, we like to spend money on the relationship. Total outlays on big-league sports—tickets, advertising, broadcast rights, and so on—are well in excess of $100 billion a year.[2]

Yet not only private funds are involved. In cities across the country, taxpayer dollars have been used to help finance the construction of expensive new stadiums. Compilations prepared by the National Sports Law Institute of Marquette University Law School show that public funding has, in fact, become the norm. The Institute's profiles of the stadiums or arenas used by the 92 teams in the three major sports (football, baseball, and basketball) indicate that 83 of them— or more than 90 percent—were built to some degree with public money. Among those, the public paid a majority of the cost in 63 cases, including 32 instances in which taxpayers footed the entire bill.[3] The grand total of public money used in building the 83 sub-sidized stadiums has been roughly $10 billion.[4]

Politicians of all stripes are taken in by the assumption that the presence of a professional sports team is a leading contributor to the vitality of cities and thus presumably a generator of new jobs. So strong is this notion that public officials are willing to give team owners subsidies that go far beyond what other private-sector businesses can hope for. Companies are generally satisfied with tax breaks, low-cost financing, or some infrastructure improvements around their property. Team owners expect taxpayers to pay most—or *all*—of the cost of new stadiums, which these days cost several hundred million dollars apiece.

The Brooklyn Threat

How is it that scarce public resources came to be used to finance construction of new facilities for what are typically quite profitable local monopolies? The origins of the practice can be found in the 1950s. Until then, team owners paid for their own stadiums, with the exception of a few—such as the Los Angeles Coliseum and Chicago's Soldier Field—that were built with public funds as part of efforts to lure the Olympic Games. In 1953, in the first team relocation in major league baseball in half a century, the Boston Braves moved to Milwaukee, where a new stadium had been built for the team with public money.[5]

The Braves' move paved the way to an era of footloose franchises, but a more significant event came a few years later, in 1957, when Walter O'Malley, owner of the Brooklyn Dodgers, announced plans to move the baseball team to the West Coast. After having failed to strike a deal with public officials in New York for a new stadium to replace the cramped Ebbets Field, O'Malley decamped to Los Angeles, where he was greeted with open arms (and free land and infrastructure improvements).[6]

It's been said that Brooklyn never recovered—psychologically or economically—from the departure of the Dodgers. This image of a community crippled by the departure of a sports franchise has been put to good use by team owners around the country, who bully public officials with threats to move out of town. Whereas O'Malley himself was vilified for absconding with the Dodgers, these days local politicians worry that they will be held responsible for losing a popular team by failing to meet the owner's financial demands. In *Field of Schemes,* a compelling critique of stadium subsidies, Joanna Cagan and Neil deMause write: "It's difficult to find a major U.S. city that hasn't been cajoled, threatened or blackmailed into building a new sports palace."[7]

The dynamics of owner manipulation are perhaps best illustrated by a sequence of events that began in 1984, when Baltimore Colts owner Robert Irsay packed up the team and moved to Indianapolis, where a domed football stadium had been built with public money even before there was a tenant to use it.[8] Irsay, who had previously pressured Baltimore to spend $25 million on improvements to Memorial Stadium, turned his back on the city and signed a lucrative low-rent deal with Indianapolis.

Shaken by the loss of the Colts, officials in Maryland decided to give the Baltimore Orioles baseball team, which had shared Memorial Stadium with the Colts, just about anything it wanted. This turned out to be a $235 million new stadium devoted exclusively to baseball that opened in 1992. Yet the city fathers still yearned to fill the void that had been left by the Colts. They accomplished this by making a deal with Art Modell, owner of the Cleveland Browns, who agreed to come to Baltimore in exchange for a promise to build the team (which became known as the Ravens) a spanking new stadium adjacent to the Camden Yards baseball field. Modell became notorious for saying—in the quote that opens this chapter—that government should make retention of a sports team a greater priority than providing public access to books.

Cleveland, whose voters had been pressured in 1990 to approve a "sin tax" on alcoholic beverages and tobacco products to finance a new baseball stadium for the Indians, later won an expansion franchise for a new football team (which took the Browns name)—and, of course, the city agreed to pay some $240 million toward the cost of a stadium for its new gridiron heroes.

And so it goes. Time and again, cities have succumbed to implicit or explicit threats by team owners. In some cases public officials are the ones manipulating public opinion. In his 2000 book *Stadium Games,* Minneapolis *Star Tribune* reporter Jay Weiner quoted public officials as admitting that *they* had fabricated a threat by the Minnesota Twins to move to North Carolina, in an effort to get state legislators to vote on a publicly funded stadium for the team.[9]

These days, politicians are inclined to take it for granted that public money will play a central role in new stadium projects and that this will somehow result in additional jobs. Washington, DC, mayor Anthony Williams, for example, did not hesitate to offer up a stadium funded mostly with public dollars as part of the 2004 deal with major league baseball to relocate the struggling Montreal Expos to the nation's capital. Some members of the DC council balked at the obligations being taken on by the city in the project, whose estimated costs ranged up to nearly $600 million, but in the end they, too, ended up approving a plan that would use tax revenues to pay for a large portion of the costs.[10]

Faith-Based Stadium Economics

Public officials' fear that they will be held responsible for losing a team is not the only motivation for stadium deals. Subsidies to sports franchises are also justified in terms of job creation. As with other forms of government-assisted investment, proponents of publicly funded stadiums have tried to make the case that these sports palaces are job generators.

This is a difficult case to make. A professional sports team does not operate on a continuous, year-round basis. Each sport is limited to its season, and half the games are played out of town. The most egregious example is football, with games played only once a week for five months. A stadium devoted exclusively to professional football will be in use for the game only about ten days a year.

Then there's the question of the quality of the jobs created. Aside from the small number of athletes with astronomical salaries, the jobs directly associated with stadiums tend to be part-time, intermittent positions with low wages and few benefits. Hawking hot dogs and beer or cleaning up after the fans go home is not a sure-fire route to prosperity. Stadium construction does generate better-paid work for masons, carpenters, electricians, and the like, but this is of limited duration. The construction jobs evaporate once the stadium is built.

For these reasons, subsidy supporters tend to focus on the *indirect* job-creation impact of stadiums. Team owners pay consulting companies to write reports—or get government agencies to do it for free—estimating how much new economic activity will be generated at bars, restaurants, and other establishments catering to the stadium crowds, as well as estimating the impact of their expanded payroll and purchasing on other businesses.

These reports usually involve some dubious assumptions. For example, in a 1999 report on the expected economic impact of a new stadium in Boston to replace Fenway Park, C. H. Johnson Consulting Inc. assumed that visitors coming to the new facility would spend 20 percent more outside the ballpark than those who visited Fenway.[11] The report's rosy scenario, which included an increase of more than 3,000 jobs, may have had something to do with the fact that the analysis was commissioned by the Greater Boston Convention and Visitors Bureau and the Greater Boston Chamber of Commerce.

Probably the most optimistic estimate of total additional employment was the figure of 10,000 jobs bandied about when the San Francisco 49ers were seeking support for a new taxpayer-financed stadium in 1997. Yet that number consisted almost entirely of temporary construction employment and the thousands of low-wage retail jobs created by the "mega-mall" that 49ers owner Edward DeBartolo wanted to build adjacent to the stadium.[12]

Another common problem with studies justifying stadium subsidies is that they assume all of the dollars spent at the facility are new to the region's economy. In fact, that is only true for those fans who come from far away. Most dollars spent at stadiums are dollars that would have been spent on other leisure activities in the area. You and

I do not have more money and time for fun just because we have another choice in how to spend them.

Economic projections also tend to overlook jobs that might be *eliminated* as the result of a new stadium. For example, construction of the much celebrated Camden Yards baseball stadium in Baltimore required the dislocation of a group of manufacturing businesses that together employed about 1,000 people.[13]

In sum, the projections made by team owners and their paid consultants in support of stadium subsidies are little more than vague or arbitrary promises about job creation and economic stimulus. These cost-benefit analyses rest on faith-based economics: proponents ask the public, in essence, to *believe* that the subsidies will pay off.

This quasi-religious theme was evident in 1997 during a campaign to win public support for a regional sales tax increase in Pittsburgh to finance new stadiums, each costing more than $200 million, for the Pirates and the Steelers. At an event sponsored by the baseball and football teams, U.S. senator Rick Santorum declared: "I know I'm preaching to the choir, but it's time for the choir to start singing." Sounding, according to the account in the *Pittsburgh Post-Gazette*, "more like an old-time evangelist than a politician," Santorum urged the audience to promote the tax at their churches and civic organizations.[14]

It's not often that you hear a right-wing politician urging a mobilization of religious groups in favor of a tax increase, but that's typical of the topsy-turvy politics surrounding the use of public resources to subsidize the business of professional sports. Conservatives embrace tax-and-spend fiscal policies, and liberals endorse giveaways to big business—all in the pursuit of stadium-based economic development.

Not Much Bang for the Bucks

If we go beyond anecdotal information to more formal academic analyses, the results are no different. The overwhelming majority of studies conclude that stadium subsidies do not pay off in terms of economic growth or job creation. The limited number of jobs that might be created exact a high cost from taxpayers—often well above $100,000 each.[15]

This theme of stadium subsidies as a bad investment for cities permeated the most extensive scholarly volume on the subject— *Sports, Jobs, and Taxes,* a 500-plus page anthology published by the Brookings Institution. In their opening chapter, Roger Noll and Andrew Zimbalist conclude that new sports facilities "rarely, if ever, are worthwhile. Sometimes they can be financially catastrophic."[16]

In another chapter of the volume, Robert Baade and Allen Sanderson analyze economic trends in ten metropolitan areas where new stadiums had been built. Overall, they find that professional sports teams tended to "realign economic activity within a city's leisure industry rather than adding to it."[17] In other words, all that public subsidies accomplished was to help shift spending from other forms of entertainment to the stadium, with little in the way of net employment gain. "Professional sports," they write, "are not a major catalyst for economic development."[18]

The Brookings volume also includes case studies of stadium subsidies in several cities, including two of those discussed above— Baltimore and Cleveland, both of which are sometimes claimed to be exceptions to the idea that public investments in stadiums are bad deals for cities. In an analysis of the Camden Yards, Bruce Hamilton and Peter Kahn find that the economic benefits generated by the stadium are far outweighed by the cost to the taxpayers of Maryland.[19] A study by Ziona Austrian and Mark Rosentraub of the early years of Cleveland's Gateway Complex, which encompasses the Jacobs Field baseball stadium and the Gund Arena basketball facility, concludes that there were some economic benefits, but they came at a very high price—more than $200,000 in taxpayer funds for each additional job.[20]

The findings in the Brookings volume are not unique. In a later review of numerous other studies on the subject, John Siegfried and

Andrew Zimbalist write: "Few fields of empirical economic research offer virtual unanimity of findings. Yet, independent work on the economic impact of stadiums and arenas has uniformly found that there is no statistically significant positive correlation between sports facility construction and economic development." The authors note that the results of academic research "stand in distinct contrast to the promotional studies that are typically done by consulting firms under the hire of teams or local chambers of commerce supporting facility development. Typically, such promotional studies project future impact and almost invariably adopt unrealistic assumptions regarding local value added, new spending, and associated multipliers."[21] In other words, the consultants and team owners are peddling snake oil.

Who's Winning?

If taxpayers are footing the bill and the local workforce is not enjoying a boon, then the question is: cui bono? Who is benefiting from stadium subsidies?

The obvious winners are the owners of the teams that inhabit the stadiums erected at public expense. These owners are hardly in need of public assistance. About two dozen of them appear on the *Forbes* list of the 400 wealthiest Americans, with a net worth of more than $750 million each. Paul Allen, owner of the Seattle Seahawks and the Portland Trail Blazers, is said by *Forbes* to be worth $20 billion, making him the third richest person in the country.[22]

Forbes also calculates the current value of franchises in the major sports leagues. The magazine estimates that the most valuable football team, the Washington Redskins, is worth $1.1 billion; the most valuable baseball team, the New York Yankees, is worth $832 million; and the most valuable basketball team, the Los Angeles Lakers, is worth $510 million. For many teams, these amounts have risen smartly in recent years. The value of the Yankees, for instance, has more than doubled since 1998.[23]

New stadiums built at taxpayer expense do a lot to boost franchise values. The Baltimore Orioles, for instance, changed hands for $70 million in 1989, before Camden Yards was completed. In 1993, after the well-received stadium was in operation, the team was resold for $173 million, an increase of 147 percent in only four years.[24] Cases such as these are consistent with a statement made more than a half-century ago by Cleveland Indians owner Bill Veeck: "You don't make money operating a baseball club. You make money selling it."[25] Today, owners may also make money on operations, but selling remains a sure thing.

If you don't believe it, just ask the president of the United States. In 1989 George W. Bush, fresh from an undistinguished stint in the energy business, spent about $600,000 to buy a small stake in the Texas Rangers baseball team while agreeing to serve as a managing general partner. Before long, Bush and his co-investors got voters in the Rangers' home town of Arlington to approve a sales tax increase to pay more than two-thirds of the cost of a lavish new $191 million stadium and a surrounding development that included an amphitheater, shops, and restaurants. The lucrative deal allowed the Rangers to collect rent from all the nearby facilities. Bush and his partners did not even have to provide their share of the construction costs up front. Instead, they borrowed the amount from the public authority in charge of financing the stadium, which was grandly named The Ballpark in Arlington.[26]

Bush dismissed charges that these arrangements were a giveaway to private interests. "Corporate welfare has this sinister tone to it," he said in 1994. "This project has been totally scrutinized, put before the people of Arlington, and voted for overwhelmingly."[27]

Bush stuck to that line during his successful gubernatorial campaign in 1994 and again in 1998, when he and his partners sold the team to leveraged buyout investor Thomas Hicks for $250 million. This was three times its 1989 value, an increase attributable in significant measure to the new taxpayer-subsidized stadium. Bush, still governor, came away from the sale with a profit of $14.9 million (thanks to an enhancement in his share because of his management role). The *New York Times* later wrote that it was due to the whole Arlington stadium experience that Bush "acquired not only wealth but also the resume he would need to triumph in politics."[28]

It is sobering to think that the current political climate of the entire United States—indeed, the current world situation—can be traced back to a single subsidized sports facility. Not all stadium subsidies have quite that global an impact, but it is clear that scores of team owners have exploited America's devotion to professional sports to enrich themselves and contribute very little to the economies of the communities in which they operate.

Too Many Convention Centers

The dubious economics behind stadium subsidies are replicated in cities across the country when it comes to another big-ticket facility—convention centers. Like professional sports, conventions are sold as a way to lure large numbers of free-spending visitors to struggling downtown areas. Consultants—often the same ones who analyze stadium deals—produce reports arguing that this infusion of money into hotels, bars, and other hospitality businesses will greatly boost tax revenues and create substantial numbers of new jobs.

This vision of convention-induced development has prompted city governments to double their capital spending on convention centers over the past decade, reaching an average of more than $2 billion annually. In early 2005, some 40 cities were planning or building at least six million additional square feet of convention space.[29]

It's true that this build-up targets an entirely different market than stadiums serve. Each professional sports franchise is a local monopoly, so stadiums are captive; cities, however, compete for a share of the national convention market. If that market were steadily expanding, then it might make sense for cities to increase their convention center investments.

But the market is *not* growing rapidly. Professor Heywood Sanders of the University of Texas at San Antonio has done a careful study showing that overall national attendance at conventions and trade shows has generally been on the decline since the mid-1990s. He refers to conventions as a "faltering industry."[30] Such weakness means that fewer jobs are created either in the convention centers themselves or in the surrounding hospitality sector.

To bolster his case, Sanders looks at attendance for centers in leading convention cities such as Chicago, New York, Atlanta, and New Orleans. In each case, the numbers are down from the mid-1990s, despite numerous expansions in exhibit space. At the Morial Convention Center in New Orleans, for example, attendance is down more than 40 percent since a peak in 1999.[31]

The bottom line: an increasing number of ever-larger convention centers are chasing fewer events and dollars. Given that convention centers are usually publicly owned, government spending on these facilities does not constitute a direct giveaway to the private sector. Yet, as with stadiums, this use of scarce public dollars to build and operate expensive facilities is creating few good jobs.

Chapter 8

Shifting the Burden

There is a mountain of evidence, from national statistics and from individual states, that over the past 25 years corporations—especially big ones—are getting lower tax rates and paying a smaller share of the cost for public services, shifting the burden onto everyone else. The evidence on income taxes is especially disturbing: data from many states now show that a lot of big companies are paying zero state income taxes, or only tiny minimum taxes.

The evidence comes from government studies of state revenue and corporate expenses, from academics creating financial models of subsidized companies, from taxpayer watchdog groups, from studies of large publicly traded companies—even from a few angry governors and state treasurers. Experts analyzing this data conclude that tax breaks enacted in the name of jobs are a major culprit, along with surging corporate use of loopholes like Delaware Passive Investment Companies.

First, the national evidence. The Congressional Research Service (CRS)—a nonpartisan body that works exclusively for members of Congress—tracks the long-term trend in state and local corporate taxes for all domestic companies except banks and other financial institutions. It reports that the effective corporate rate for all state and local taxes—income, property, sales, excise, and utility taxes, and so on—has declined sharply over the past two decades. Specifically, the CRS found that in the 1980s, companies paid an average of 6.93 percent of their profits in all state and local taxes. In the 1990s, the average rate was 5.12 percent, and by 2002, the last year studied, the rate had declined to just 4.99 percent. That's an overall rate decline of 28 percent.[1]

And why are corporations paying less? "Perhaps the most obvious explanation is the tax competition among states to attract business," the CRS concludes. It specifically cites Single Sales Factor as an example.

More evidence of burden-shifting comes from the Center on Budget and Policy Priorities. It points out that in the second half of the 1990s, when the U.S. economy was sizzling, federal corporate income tax revenues grew an average of 6 percent a year. But *state* corporate income tax collections rose at just half that rate. Same companies, same profits, same years: half the tax.[2] Translation: corporations are gaming the states' tax codes even harder than they're gaming Uncle Sam's.

It's not just the rate of corporate taxes, it is also the share of revenue companies provide. By that measure too, state corporate income taxes are also declining. In 1980, corporate income taxes accounted for 9.7 percent of state tax revenue; by 2000, it was down to 6 percent, and for the next three years, it averaged only 5.2 percent.[3]

Put another way: if corporations contributed the same share to state treasuries in income taxes in 2003 as they did in 1980, the states would have received $27.3 billion more to help pay for smaller class sizes in schools, for public safety, for healthcare and infrastructure. Or they could have avoided raising that much in other taxes, especially the regressive hikes—such as sales taxes—that many states enacted.[4]

Corporate Tax Dodging, State by State

This trend of corporate burden-shifting is not limited to any one region, nor is it unique to manufacturing. Over the past several years, reports from many states have told the same story: companies are paying less—and, in many cases, nothing at all. (To be fair, I must add that not all companies paying zero income taxes do so because they exploit loopholes or get subsidies. Some are unprofitable and therefore have no taxable income.) Here are some stark examples:

- In Arizona, corporations paid 26 percent of all income taxes in 1980–1981, but just 15 percent by 2002–2003. In the same period, the corporate share of property taxes paid declined from 71 percent to 49 percent.[5]
- Arkansas Advocates for Children and Families has revealed that corporations paid about a third of all the state's income taxes in the 1970s, but by 2002, their share had shrunk to just 10 percent. Fully 58 percent of all corporations filing Razorback returns in 2002 paid *zero* income taxes.[6]
- The California Budget Project reported that 73 percent of all companies doing business in the state paid just the $800 minimum franchise tax in 2001. This was true even of the 52 percent of companies that reported making profits—including 46 firms that each had more than $1 billion in receipts.[7]
- In Colorado, companies paid 18 percent of all income taxes in 1980–1981, but just 6 percent by 2002–2003.[8]
- In Florida, *St. Petersburg Times* investigative reporter Sydney Freedberg wrote a major series in late 2003 on corporate tax avoidance. She found that 98 percent of companies in the state paid no income tax in 2002. Among the nonpayers: cruise-ship giant Carnival Corp., with 4,220 employees in the state, more than $1 billion in 2002 profits—and registration in Panama. A Florida Senate report found that the state is losing between one-quarter and one-half billion dollars a year by failing to plug corporate loopholes.[9]
- In Idaho, corporations paid 19 percent of all income taxes in 1980–1981, but only 10 percent by 2002–2003. In the same period, the corporate share of property taxes paid declined from 53 percent to 44 percent.[10]
- Policy Matters Ohio found that corporations paying the state's franchise tax contributed 16 percent of the state's general fund in the mid-1970s; by 2002, their share was only 4.6 percent. All business taxes as a share of state and local revenue also fell in the same period.[11]
- In Oklahoma, the Community Action Project reported that corporate

income tax accounted for more than 6 percent of the state's total tax revenue in 1979, but by 2003, it had declined to just 1.8 percent. In the same period, the share of revenue individuals contributed in personal income taxes rose from 22 percent to 36 percent.[12]

- In Pennsylvania, the Keystone Research Center revealed that 66 percent of all companies subject to the Corporate Net Income tax paid $0 in 1999. The state has a second, lesser tax called Capital Stock and Franchise; 73 percent of companies filing under it paid between $0 and the $200 minimum.[13]

- In Utah, corporations paid 12 percent of all income taxes in 1980–1981; by 2002–2003, their share had declined to 9 percent.[14]

- Washington state does not have an income tax, but between 1980–1981 and 2002–2003, the corporate share of property taxes paid declined from 56 percent to 42 percent.[15]

Professor Richard Pomp, a state tax expert at the University of Connecticut Law School, has a simple analysis of why corporate income tax dodging has become so rampant. "The real explanation is that the corporate tax has become a voluntary tax. The legislature doesn't control it. The tax department doesn't control it. Accountants and lawyers control it."[16]

Artful Dodgers: The Big Companies

Available evidence suggests that big companies have become the most aggressive in dodging state income taxes. Professor Pomp believes that in the wake of the sweeping changes made to the fed eral income tax on corporations during the Reagan administration, multistate companies decided that the greatest tax cuts still to be found were at the state level, so they assigned the job to their accountants and consultants. The results are quite apparent and continue to this day.[17]

Citizens for Tax Justice and the Institute on Taxation and Economic Policy looked at the *Fortune* 500 for the years 2001 through 2003. They found that 264 of the companies both were profitable every year and reported the total dollars they paid in state income taxes (in just one aggregate figure, not state by state). Overall, the 264 companies paid just 2.85 percent of their profits in state income tax in 2001, then 2.61 percent in 2002 and 2.35 percent in 2003. In other words, in just three years, the state income tax rate of these *Fortune* 500 companies dropped by almost a fifth.[18]

The taxes these big companies paid is also a far cry from the statutory rate—that is, for states that have corporate income taxes, if companies had paid the official tax rates, they would have paid not 2.35 overall, but *6.82 percent*.[19] The big reasons for the gap: economic development tax breaks and tax loopholes.

There is also fragmentary data from some states about income taxes paid by large companies (including Alabama, as cited below); in each case, the data indicate that many companies pay none at all, or very little.

Connecticut Voices for Children has found that 38 of the 95 largest corporations in the state paid *zero* income taxes in 1999, and nearly two-thirds of all companies in the state paid only a $250 minimum tax. Net corporate business taxes declined from 9.8 percent of tax revenue in 1992 to just 1.7 percent in 2002, when the Nutmeg State kept only 40 percent of the corporate income tax it was due and *refunded* 60 percent back in credits.[20]

The Maryland Budget and Tax Policy Institute reported that 91 of the largest 131 companies in the state—almost 70 percent—paid zero income taxes in 2002. That includes 29 of the largest 39 manufacturing companies (the year after Maryland adopted Single Sales Factor for manufacturers) plus 11 of the 16 largest retailers and 14 of the 22 biggest banks and financial institutions.[21]

In New Jersey, then-governor James McGreevey revealed in 2002 that of the 50 corporations with the largest payrolls in the state, 30 paid just $200 a year, the state's minimum corporate tax. Corporate tax avoidance is so pervasive, 77 percent of all the state's corporations paid only the $200 minimum. New Jersey Policy Perspective documented the big-picture trend: as recently as 1990, the corporate tax accounted for almost 16 percent of all taxes collected, but by 2002 it was 8.4 percent.[22]

The Oregon Center for Public Policy found that more than half of all corporations with known payrolls of more than $2 million paid just $10 in income tax in 2000. That's the state's corporate minimum tax, set in 1931. Tax credits are so rich there, 26 corporations, each with more than $1 million of taxable Oregon income, paid just the $10 minimum for 2000. Lumber giant Louisiana Pacific and utility Portland General Electric each paid just $10 in 2002.[23] Oregon corporations paid 13 percent of all income and estate taxes in 1980–1981, but their share was down to 5 percent by 2002–2003.[24]

How Subsidies Zero Out Corporate Income Taxes

University of Iowa Professor Peter Fisher, with Hawkeye colleague Alan Peters, has explored the reasons why corporate income taxes have dropped so much. He concludes that job creation tax gimmicks are an important reason. He uses a "representative firm" computer model that enables him to take a hypothetical new factory—with an average-size capital investment and rate of profit for its particular industry—and project what would happen to the company's tax bill if the factory were built in a state's enterprise zone, where tax breaks are the most generous.[25]

Looking at 20 of the most-industrialized states, he finds that "incentive wars have proceeded to the point that state corporate income taxes are on the verge of disappearing in some states, at least with respect to new investment." In other words, new factories in many places get such large tax credits, they pay little or no income tax. In fact, for 12 of those 20 states, his model indicates that typical companies building new factories can actually generate net tax *credits*—that is, the deals create *negative* income taxes. This can happen when a state allows what is called a "refundable credit"; if the credit exceeds the tax, the state refunds the difference to the company.[26]

The other way companies can end up with a negative tax rate is that many states allow them to apply credits against other taxable income they have from other facilities. Here's how it works. Suppose a company already has a facility in the state, and pays $100,000 in state income taxes on it. Then it builds a new plant, which normally would generate another $100,000 in state income taxes. But the credits on the new plant are $150,000. Instead of producing additional tax liability, the new plant pays no taxes at all, and the company also gets to reduce the taxes it was already paying. That's like getting a second job, doubling your income, and paying lower taxes than you did when you had only one job.[27]

Let me repeat it: corporate income tax breaks in some states are now so lavish that when a company builds a new facility, it gets tax credits that mean the company pays zero taxes for at least year one of the new operation. And if the credits are more than the taxes it owes, the company either gets the rest of the credit as an immediate "refund," or it gets to carry the unused credits forward into future years, so that it may not pay taxes for years. Or, if it has profits from other operations in the state, it may apply the credits to cancel out income taxes owed on them.

In fact, economic development tax credits have become so numerous, at least four states—Connecticut, Idaho, Louisiana, and New Jersey—have passed legislation allowing companies to sell their unused credits![28]

Are states mortgaging the candy store because they suffer high unemployment and believe they must "prime the pump"? To the contrary, Fisher finds. "There is no discernable relation between the state's average level of economic distress, as measured by unemployment rates, and that state's adoption of business tax cuts or development incentives between 1990 and 1997," he concludes.[29]

Fisher even broke the story down by 16 industrial sectors (such as food processing, transportation equipment, and so on). For Texas, he found that in 9 out of 16 sectors, companies are getting negative income taxes; in Ohio, it's 13 out of 16; and in Kentucky, 15 out of 16.

In three states—Iowa, Michigan, and South Carolina—he finds that *in all 16 sectors, companies are getting negative tax rates!*[30]

It's not hard to find extreme examples.[31] Alabama offers lavish tax credits, especially since its notorious Mercedes deal in 1993. Through 2002, the Yellowhammer State reported that 462 projects have been approved since 1995 to create 53,581 jobs, with a total of $11,447,358,413 in estimated capital costs. Under this capital credit, a company gets to deduct 5 percent of its capital costs, every year for 20 years, from its state income tax bills. So the companies are entitled to more than $11.4 billion in tax credits—more than $213,000 per job. Actual capital costs for projects placed in service are running higher—almost $275,000 per job.[32]

"The practical effect is they don't pay any income tax for 20 years in Alabama," said George Howell, Jr., director of economic development in the Alabama Department of Revenue. Actually, Howell added, the companies won't claim all of the credits because they will not make enough profits to claim them all. But the state does not know how many billions will be claimed, Howell admitted; it has not estimated the revenue loss. (Of course, this is just one big *income tax* break. Most of those deals undoubtedly received other kinds of subsidies as well.)[33]

Alabama's governor at the time, Don Seigelman, got angry about corporate tax dodging; in the year 2000 alone, there were 619 companies doing business in Alabama with a total of $850 million of profits—and they all paid $0 in state income taxes. He said the companies are "cheating our children out of an education," and "we're not going to let them get away with it." He almost doubled the state's corporate auditing staff and proposed various loophole-closing bills to the legislature.[34]

Kentucky is another big giveaway state, where lumber giant Willamette Industries (later merged into Weyerhaeuser Company) expanded a pulp and paper mill in Hawesville. My analysis of its state financing agreement and county bond deal indicated that the expansion project was entitled to tax credits worth $132.3 million. And how many jobs was the company required to create in return? Fifteen. That's a tax credit entitlement of up to $8.8 million *per job!* Willamette can deduct 100 percent of this capital credit—dollar for dollar—from the project's corporate income tax bill to Kentucky. And if the credits exceed the income tax bill in a given year, it can carry them forward against future tax bills.[35]

The company declined to verify my math, but the Kentucky Cabinet for Economic Development did confirm it. And a Cabinet spokeswoman hastened to add that it's unlikely the project will generate enough profits to use up all the credits. In other words, according to the state agency that did the deal, it's unlikely Willamette Industries will pay any income tax to Kentucky on the Hawesville project for 15 years.[36]

To be fair, a manager at the plant told me that the company had actually hired 105 new full-time employees, with wages averaging $17.50 an hour plus weekend premiums. At 105 jobs, the tax credit entitlement shrinks to a mere $1.26 million per job. Such a deal![37]

The Poor and Middle Class Pay More

When large corporations control the tax system and use that control to pay much less, that means working families and small businesses pay more, because states and cities have to raise taxes to sustain public services. Mainly, they raise sales taxes and property taxes, and those are regressive taxes; that is, they hit low- and middle-income families harder than high-income people.

This combination of corporate tax cuts and personal tax hikes has made the states' tax systems more regressive overall. This happens both because personal taxes have gone up and because corporate tax cuts mostly benefit wealthy people, who own the vast majority of corporate stock. The overall trend toward a more regressive tax system has also been fueled by some states changing their personal income tax schedules. Bowing to corporate lobbies, some states have lowered their top rates for high-income families, making their income tax systems less progressive.

Table 8.1 shows the 50-state trend in taxes becoming more regressive since the late 1980s (with thanks again to the Institute on Taxation and Economic Policy).

Table 8.1. The Share of Income Americans Paid in All State and Local Taxes, 1989 and 2002

Income Group	Income Range	1989	2002
Lowest 20%	Less than $15,000	10.2%	11.4%
Second 20%	$15,000 to $25,000	9.4%	10.3%
Middle 20%	$25,000 to $40,000	8.8%	9.6%
Fourth 20%	$40,000 to $69,000	8.4%	8.8%
Next 15%	$69,000 to $147,000	7.9%	7.7%
Next 4%	$147,000 to $304,000	6.5%	6.5%
Top 1%	$304,000 or more	5.5%	5.2%

Note: Shares of family income, non-elderly taxpayers, after state and local taxes are deducted on federal income tax returns.[38]

Add it up, and we can see that four-fifths of U.S. families—all those with incomes up to $69,000 in 2002—are paying more in state and local taxes and high-income families are paying less. Again, this is chiefly due to increases in sales and property taxes, both of which eat up a much bigger share of low- and middle-income families' paychecks. As well, some states cut personal income taxes.

The trend is much worse in some states, especially in the seven states that lack a personal income tax. That's because most state income taxes are progressive: they have higher rates for high-income folks, so that the income tax helps offset the regressive impact of sales and property taxes. This help is desperately needed; in Florida, for example, the lowest-income families pay 14.4 percent of their income in state and local taxes, while the top 1 percent pay just 2.7

percent. In Texas, the poor pay 11.4 percent vs. 3.2 percent for the ultra-rich.

In Washington state, families making an average of just $9,600 in 2002 paid a whopping 17.6 percent of their income in state and local taxes, while families in the top 1 percent income bracket paid just 3.1 percent. So the world's richest person, Bill Gates (with an estimated net worth of $48 billion), is just like every other Washington state personal resident in paying no state income tax there—while the Evergreen State gives Boeing and the aerospace industry a $3.2 billion subsidy for the 7E7 "Dreamliner" deal. That's some serious redistribution of wealth—upward![39]

If states and cities cannot make up all the revenue lost to corporate tax cuts by raising other taxes and fees, they inevitably have to reduce spending, which means service cuts such as fewer school programs, and deferred infrastructure maintenance of public structures such as schools, roads, and bridges.

Bush's Corporate Tax Cuts Create a "Jobless Recovery"

Corporations have also succeeded in reducing the share of *federal* government revenue they contribute in corporate income taxes. In the 1950s, companies provided almost 28 percent of federal revenues through their income tax payments. By the 1970s, their share was down to 15.5 percent; by the 1990s it was just 10.8 percent. So far this decade, corporate income taxes are averaging just over 9 percent of federal revenue—two-thirds less than they paid in the 1950s.[40]

Another meaningful measure of corporate tax burden is as a percentage of gross domestic product. By that measure, too, the corporate burden is plummeting: from 4.8 percent in the 1950s to 2.7 percent in the 1970s to 1.6 percent so far this decade—also a two-thirds drop.[41]

Finally, there is fresh evidence about the ineffectiveness of creating jobs by giving tax cuts to big corporations. President George W.

Bush's corporate tax cuts were entitled the Job Creation and Worker Assistance Act of 2002 and the Jobs and Growth Tax Relief Reconciliation Act of 2003. Both laws temporarily expanded the amount of "accelerated depreciation" companies were allowed to take on new equipment purchases, so that almost all of the cost could be deducted immediately, rather than spread out over time as the equipment declined in value. That substantially reduced corporations' taxable (as opposed to real) profits. In just three years, the tax cuts were projected to cost the U.S. Treasury $175 billion.[42]

Bush and other backers claimed that this "bonus depreciation" would be a powerful incentive for companies to invest and thereby create new jobs. But instead of creating lots of new jobs, the tax cuts increased corporate profits and made the federal budget deficit bigger, while the nation suffered a "jobless recovery." Between 2001 and 2003, U.S. corporate pretax profits rose 26 percent, yet federal corporate income tax payments *shrank* 21 percent in the same period. Job creation was the worst since the Great Depression. From the start of the recession in March 2001 through November 2004, the U.S. economy had a net loss of 1.2 million private-sector jobs.[43]

Citizens for Tax Justice (CTJ) and the Institute on Taxation and Economic Policy (ITEP) combed through hundreds of corporate reports to investigate why the tax breaks failed so miserably as job creators. They found the same problem we have described in the states: when you hand out huge subsidies with no accountability, no transparency, and no requirements that companies do anything positive in exchange, you often lose twice.

CTJ and ITEP focused on new capital investment made by the nation's largest companies, to see if they were using the "bonus depreciation" tax break to invest more and create jobs. Looking at 275 of the Fortune 500 companies—each of which made a profit every year from 2001 through 2003—CTJ and ITEP found that *the companies actually invested 12 percent less in 2002 than in 2001, and an-*

other 3 percent less in 2003. That was more than twice as bad as the overall national trend. In other words, large corporations were least responsive to the tax break, even though they were getting the biggest subsidies.

The 275 big companies cut their investments, despite the fact that their true federal income tax rate was dropping from 21.4 percent to just 17.2 percent—less than half the official (or statutory) rate of 35 percent. And they invested less despite the fact that 2002 and 2003 were economic recovery years; for example:

- SBC Communications got $5.8 billion in total depreciation tax breaks over the three years and reduced its investment 53 percent
- Verizon paid $4.5 billion less due to the same breaks and cut its investment 35 percent
- Devon Energy's total depreciation tax cut was $4.4 billion and it invested 51 percent less
- General Electric got a $2.6 billion depreciation tax break and reduced its investment 40 percent
- AT&T got $1.5 billion in depreciation "tax relief" and invested 45 percent less[44]

Robert McIntyre, the wry director of Citizens for Tax Justice, emphasized plain old business basics. "[T]he evidence shows, as it has so often in the past, that business investment decisions are primarily driven by supply and demand, not by government attempts to micromanage the economy. The $175 billion in revenue lost to the tax subsidies enacted in 2002 and 2003 appears to have been exceedingly poorly spent."[45]

Indeed, McIntyre reports, with ballooning tax cuts and rampant use of offshore loopholes, the total of all federal, state, and local taxes on corporations in the United States plunged to just 1.6 percent of the Gross Domestic Product in FY2003. That's less than half the average rate in the other 28 industrial democracies of the Organization for Economic Co-operation and Development. It makes the U.S.

the third-lowest corporate-tax nation, cheaper than all but Germany and Iceland.[46]

Working Families' Taxes Up + Wages and Benefits Down

Rising Frustration with Government

As big companies invent more ways to dodge their taxes, public officials still face pressure from taxpayers to maintain public services. That causes state and local governments to do two things: raise taxes on working families and small businesses, and cut corners where public resistance is weakest (such as neglecting schools in poorer areas and deferring infrastructure maintenance).

While big companies have enjoyed lower taxes and working people have suffered higher taxes, most workers' wages and benefits have been stagnant or declining. Between 1979 and 2003, real earnings for workers not in management (that's four out of five wage and salary workers) actually declined by $10 a week. Between 1979 and 2002, the share of workers receiving health insurance coverage from their employers declined from 69 percent to 57.3 percent (not even taking into account more people being pushed into HMOs and bearing higher copays, and other declines in the quality of coverage). And the share of workers receiving any kind of retirement benefits has declined from 50.6 percent to 45.5 percent—plus, more people now have inferior defined contribution plans, such as 401(k) accounts, rather than traditional defined benefit plans. Women, Blacks, Hispanics, and people with only a high-school education have always received fewer benefits, and Hispanics have suffered the greatest losses.[47]

This quadruple squeeze—higher regressive taxes plus poorer public services plus declining wages plus fewer benefits—goes a long way toward explaining why so many working people have grown angry at government. It doesn't help that for 20 years they've read about huge government giveaways that are supposed to create jobs but so often fail. For most families, the economy has already offered a quarter-century of higher taxes, declining wages, and shrinking benefits.

The big picture seems obvious. Big businesses have too much control over economic development and tax policy. They are using that control to dodge their fair share of the burden for public services, sticking everyone else with higher taxes. They are disinvesting the public goods that are key to our economic future, suggesting they don't care about our long-term prosperity.

Is Big Business Pulling Out?

For the last ten years that I lived in Chicago, I consulted for groups in many states trying to prevent factory shutdowns. That's actually how I backed into this issue of job subsidies going awry: some of the plants I investigated had gotten tax breaks, but now they were shutting down.

To help people be proactive and increase the chances of intervening early enough to save jobs, I coauthored an *Early Warning Manual Against Plant Closings* in 1986.[48] I also trained the 50 states' Dislocated Worker Units in the methodology in 1989, as a consultant to the U.S. Department of Labor. The manual and trainings drew upon numerous plant "autopsies," in which I and others interviewed plant-closing victims about events during the last few years of the life of their plants. Over and over, we found that the shutdowns were planned corporate events that involved many kinds of disinvestment, such as letting the equipment run down, moving hot new products to other plants, transferring the most promising managers, and demanding contract concessions if the workers had a union.

We found another kind of disinvestment outside the plant, at the property tax assessor's office. Sometimes companies would appeal their assessments, especially as they let the equipment run down or moved product lines out. Once, I investigated a company that had told the union the plant was "idled" and therefore workers were not eligible for shutdown benefits. But the same company had told the assessor the place was toast.

It makes sense when you think about it: if a company sees no future in the community, if it's not going to be hiring, why would it want to support the schools anymore? So we taught unions, community groups, public officials, and journalists that if they suspected a company was disinvesting they should go look at the property tax records.

Today, as I write about all these tax-dodging scams, my disinvestment antennae are up again. Big Business's behavior on taxes looks like an early warning signal, writ large. Their actions say they don't want to reinvest as much as they used to in our public goods. Instead, they appear to be disinvesting by aggressively cutting the share of the costs they bear for public services that we all rely upon to maintain our standard of living. Their actions suggest that they feel little loyalty, that they see little future here within our borders.

The danger is that, like the disinvestment of an individual plant, the process can become self-fulfilling. That is, once a facility has been bled beyond a certain point, it is so inefficient that the company has little choice but to close it. Likewise, if our nation's public goods continue to be so neglected—if our schools and workforce development systems fail to provide enough skilled labor and our aging infrastructure impedes productivity—the United States will inevitably become a less attractive place to invest and create jobs.

It's a perverse situation. After a quarter-century of slashing corporate taxes in the name of jobs, the two things that are proven job creation winners—our skills and infrastructure—are not in good shape. As I'll argue in the closing chapter, some U.S. industries and regions are already suffering skilled labor shortages, and when the

Baby Boom generation starts retiring en masse around 2008, the problem will become more acute. And our nation's physical infrastructure—which makes all companies more productive—is in poor condition, because states and cities lack the money to maintain and improve it.

★ Chapter Nine ★

Building a New
Consensus for Reform

Given how costly and wasteful this great American jobs scam has become, you'd think that our public officials would be proposing drastic solutions. For the most part, you'd be wrong. Corporate domination of the public dialog on jobs is so complete, the typical debate these days is about cooking up new giveaways—not about fixing the system.

We are, after all, talking about $50 billion a year's worth of entrenched self-interests tied to business as usual: footloose corporations, site location consultants, accounting firms and tax consultants, corporate real estate brokers, mayors and governors.

Given all those self-interests, there is no silver bullet. Only an *organizing approach* to the problem will do. By that I mean reforms that bring lots more people into the process. The real heroes moving this issue are the taxpayers: members of unions and community groups, budget watchdog groups and investigative journalists, environmentalists and land-use activists. We need reforms that make it possible for many more taxpayers to get involved. The politicians will surely follow.

In fairness to those in elected office, as I've recounted here in many ways, this whole job scam system depends upon our government being demeaned and degraded, upon public officials being docile and passive. So at every level the system makes sure it cows and bullies public officials, keeps them in the dark.

Despite all this negativity, some officials have been able to establish a few winning precedents that we can build on. Indeed, there is a rich bipartisan history of elected officials reforming job subsidies. But in almost every case they acted because taxpayers were outraged and demanded action.

I say this having observed public officials on the issue for many years. Because running economic development programs is a function of the executive branch of government, the governors have the first responsibility. Yet the last time the National Governors Association debated the "war among the states" was 1993. The two opposing committees were both led by Republicans: Jim Edgar of Illinois for the pro-accountability caucus; Brereton Jones of Kentucky for the devil-take-the-hindmost caucus. The governors passed a resolution that said a lot of great things, but it was non-binding and expired after two years. There have been other task forces, composed of economic developers and of government finance officers. One could not agree and gave up; the other issued a brief statement that had no binding effect.

In the absence of executive-branch leadership, some terrific reforms have been initiated by legislators. The National Conference of State Legislatures maintains an economic development committee, and it revisits the issue of accountability about every other year in workshops at its annual conference. Attendance at these sessions runs high and participation is spirited. Likewise, the National League of Cities has me teach at its leadership institute about every other year, and the sessions sell out. We do small-group role-plays with characters such as site location consultant, company, mayor, chamber of commerce, city council member, PTA president, and labor council leader. All of the tensions I've described here come to life—in Technicolor. Invariably, the best dramatic performance is given by a city council member playing mayor: you should hear the shameless sales pitches!

Reforms, of course, involve legislation. We need some new laws, but generally I favor fewer subsidies and simpler rules to replace the mess we have today—and then tough, fair enforcement. Don't forget, today's candy-store mess is a dream for lawyers and accountants, since it consists of so many hundreds of convoluted laws and tax gimmicks. We need a smaller, simpler body of laws that are based on common sense. Rules that everyone can understand and work with. Laws with clear intentions that courts cannot pervert.

Here are some common-sense reforms, most of which are already on the books in some states and cities.

Reform #1: Disclosure, Disclosure, Disclosure

History tells us: sunshine is the best antiseptic. When community groups alleged that banks were discriminating against neighborhoods with people of color or older housing stock—that the banks were "red-lining" their communities—they demanded and won the Home Mortgage Disclosure Act. That law requires banks to disclose data about all of their housing loans every year, by census tract. The discriminatory patterns revealed by the data soon led Congress to pass the Community Reinvestment Act, which has enabled hundreds of community groups to win billions of dollars for neighborhood revitalization.

Similarly, when community groups and factory workers alleged that chemical plants and other big polluters were endangering their health with toxic emissions, they demanded and won the "Toxic Right to Know" law,[1] which requires companies to disclose what they emit and how much. Using that data, coalitions across the country have won agreements with companies to reduce emissions and otherwise improve local safety.

Here are a few disclosure requirements that could spread a little sunshine over the murky subsidy landscape.

Annual Deal-Specific Disclosure

Already on the books in some form in 11 states, the idea is simple: annual, company-specific, public reporting of the costs and benefits of every deal. How much did each company get? Which subsidy program did the money come from? What did the company do with the money? How many jobs did it create? How well do the jobs pay? Are they full-time? Do they provide healthcare coverage? Are they accessible by public transportation? The company fills out a simple form with the data; it is certified by the local agency that did the deal and then mailed to the state. The state dumps the data into a spreadsheet, and posts it on the Web, in spreadsheet form. The form also includes the company's street address and, if the deal involved a relocation, the address of the old site and whether that site was accessible by public transit, plus how many jobs were moved.[2]

This rule should apply to every kind of subsidy above, say, $25,000—and not just grants and loans, but also corporate income tax credits and sales tax exemptions that are usually hidden from public view.

Before someone misrepresents what I am saying: I am *not* proposing that corporate income tax returns be disclosed. I am saying that *the amount of money a company gets to deduct from its income tax bill by taking a tax credit in the name of jobs* should be disclosed. From a taxpayer's point of view, there is no difference between the company claiming that credit and the government handing the company a check. It is all government spending. Property tax abatements are visible down at the assessor's office; why aren't income-tax breaks just as open?

Maine enacted disclosure requirements after experiencing a "job blackmail" episode. General Dynamics demanded $60 million in tax cuts from the Pine Tree State in 1997 for its Bath Iron Works—on top of $53 million in state tax credits it qualified for and $80 million in local property tax breaks it had secured.[3] The following year, amid taxpayer furor, Maine enacted an excellent disclosure law that requires annual, company-specific reporting on seven subsidy programs: how much the company got, how many jobs it created, plus wages and benefits.

Hidden Taxpayer Costs Disclosure

Following the legislative lead of Massachusetts and the disclosures by several other states, all states should require that every company with more than 50 enrolled beneficiaries of Medicaid or the State Children's Health Insurance Program be disclosed each year. Taxpayers need to know who they are subsidizing through the back door, whether it is Wal-Mart or any other company.

Big-Company Tax Disclosure to Shareholders

Publicly traded companies (those listed on stock exchanges) already have to disclose how much they pay in federal income tax each year, in their annual reports and Forms 10-K. They also disclose how much they pay in all state income taxes, but only in one aggregate 50-state number. The solution is simple: amend Securities and Exchange Commission rules to require publicly traded companies to include a 50-state matrix in their Form 10-K showing how much tax they paid in each state, grouped in three categories: income tax, property tax, and sales, utility, and excise taxes. This would not be unduly burdensome; these big companies obviously have people who justify their jobs by obsessing about such numbers, and we are only talking about 0.1 percent of all U.S. corporate tax-filers.

Having such data made public would enable taxpayers and elected officials to really see who the tax dodgers are. Given that we already know large numbers of big companies are paying little or no income tax in some states, this would spell out the details. In the early 1980s, there was a Citizens for Tax Justice bumper sticker: "I paid more income tax than General Motors, General Electric, and General Dynamics combined." The ensuing outrage prompted a major progressive reform, closing some corporate loopholes.

Reform #2: Clawbacks, or Money-Back Guarantees

A clawback, or recapture provision in a subsidy contract, simply says that a company must hold up its end of the bargain or else taxpayers have some money-back protection. Nineteen states and dozens of cities already use clawbacks for at least one program.[4] A basic clawback says something like this: starting from when a company receives the subsidy, it has a certain period of time to achieve its goals; that is, to create X number of jobs at X wage and benefit levels, and/or to invest X dollars. If the company does not meet its target(s), the clawback provides a formula for taxpayers getting paid back. It can be prorated so that, for example, if the company falls 10 percent short, it has to pay back 10 percent of the subsidy; a steeper penalty may apply if the company falls far short.

Site location consultants and corporate lobbyists sometimes claim clawbacks are bad for the "business climate." But I think just the opposite is true. When parties on both sides of the table have clear, written expectations, it is much less likely there will be anger or lawsuits down the road. If the rule is simple and fair—and evenly enforced—businesses will accept it.

Reform #3: Job Quality Standards

This is the most widely enacted subsidy reform, thanks in part to the living-wage movement. Increasingly, states and localities are requiring that, as a condition of getting a subsidy, a company must pay a decent wage with full-time hours and health care. The best wage formulas are those that are tied to markets: that is, the average wage for the industry or the labor market, with a poverty-wage floor. Public officials are starting to get it: at least 43 states, 41 cities, and 5 counties now attach such requirements to at least one of their job subsidies (though the vast majority of subsidy programs still lack this safeguard).[5]

The rationale is simple: why give a company the advantage of a subsidy and then allow it to pay less than comparable companies— or even to pay a poverty wage? Lord knows the economy has been producing lots of lousy jobs all by itself. And as we have seen in the case of retail, subsidizing poverty-wage jobs only means taxpayers get stuck with massive hidden costs.

Reform #4: Unified Development Budgets

A Unified Development Budget is an annual document that provides a state's legislators with a comprehensive inventory of all spending line items for economic development—all the tax breaks and all the appropriations. The point here is to make sure that tax breaks get as much scrutiny as appropriations get. It's a big issue because tax breaks for jobs often dwarf appropriations; it's no exaggeration to call appropriations the tip of the iceberg and "tax expenditures" the bulk that lies beneath. But because tax spending is often poorly accounted for, many state legislatures are flying in the dark; they don't see the corporate tax breaks below the radar screen, and that makes the breaks immune from budget cuts, even when states struggle with deficits.[6]

So the idea of a Unified Development Budget is to get the whole iceberg up on the table every year for a checkup. That way, legislators are more likely to treat both kinds of spending fairly and evenly. Today, only about 30 states publish what is called a Tax Expenditure Budget, compiling line items of forgone tax revenues (not just those for economic development), and only about a dozen of those are considered reasonably complete by state tax experts. Watchdog groups have created their own Unified Development Budgets in a few states, and Illinois is slated to start publishing one in mid-2005.[7]

Reform #5:
Give School Boards Full Say on Abatements and TIF

As I explained in chapter 5, very few states effectively protect school funding from revenue losses caused by property tax abatements and TIF. This intergovernmental free lunch is just plain wrong. School boards should control their share of property tax revenue, in the same way they are held accountable for how the money is spent. School boards should have a full voting seat on any board that abates or diverts property tax revenue away from schools. And separately, school boards should have the right to vote up or down on each deal for the school portion that would be abated or diverted.

Protecting education funding matters doubly for job creation. Good schools are a key amenity that helps cities attract and retain good employers, especially those that require highly skilled (read: well-paid) workers. And with the Baby Boom generation approaching retirement, skilled labor matters more than ever.

Reform #6: Close Corporate Loopholes

To reduce corporate tax sheltering, the states where this is out of control should adopt combined reporting and throwback rules. Combined reporting gets at the Delaware Passive Investment Company gimmick, by requiring a company to report its income as if all of its subsidiaries are one entity. And throwback rules reduce "nowhere income" by saying that if a company makes profits in a state but does not get taxed on them there, the income is "thrown back" to its headquarters state.

Reform #7: Repeal Single Sales Factor

To eliminate windfalls for the favored few corporations and restore tax fairness among different kinds of employers, the states with Single Sales Factor should repeal it and restore the three-factor formula.

Reform #8: Register and Regulate Site Location Consultants

Merriam Webster's Collegiate Dictionary defines "lobbying" as "to attempt or influence or sway (as a public official) towards a desired action." That sure sounds like the work of a site location consultant to me—the deals they orchestrate routinely involve the passage of local ordinances for property tax abatements, industrial revenue bonds, or zoning, and bigger deals sometimes involve state legislation as well. Yet somehow site location consultants have created an unusual position of special privilege for themselves, working both sides of the street.

The solution: register and regulate site location consultants as lobbyists. This means they must register with state ethics boards and disclose their clients and fees, they can only take a fee from one party per transaction, and they cannot work for success fees, a.k.a. commissions—removing one of the most outrageous incentives fueling the candy-store arms race. Ideally, with regulation the profession will split into fish and fowl: consultants who work for companies and others who work for cities, counties, and states. There should be a robust, adversarial process with no ambiguity about each party's loyalty and self-interest.

Reform #9: Put Every Deal to an Official Vote

All too often, massive deals are granted by boards made up of people who are appointed. For example, Fantus coached New York City to give more power to appointed boards—the company understood that this would mean less taxpayer accountability and more corporate control. The solution: require that every deal be approved by officials who are elected by taxpayers, so that at election time, people can hold politicians directly accountable. Minnesota has required this since 1995, along with disclosure and other reforms, and this has served the state well.

Reform #10: A Federal "Carrot" Against Job Piracy

The federal government often uses the power of its purse as a "carrot" to encourage state reforms. For example, a small share of federal highway funding was held back from states until they raised their legal drinking age to 21 years.[8] There is no reason the same idea could not apply to job subsidies. Let's withhold, say, 10 percent of a state's appropriation from the U.S. departments of commerce and labor until the state adopts certain reforms. Just a few strategic requirements would suffice: a certification by the governor that the state will not use taxpayer dollars to pirate jobs from another state, and adoption of deal-specific disclosure and a unified development budget.

Reform #11: Smart Growth to End the "Economic War Among the Suburbs"

There are several priorities here, but the big point is efficiency: if we adopt land use policies that bring jobs and tax base back to older areas, there will be less need for subsidies to revitalize them. We need to let the older cities compete fairly in the market instead of exaggerating the advantages newer suburbs already have.

Smart growth means better living *and* good jobs. When we say no to Wal-Mart Supercenters, we protect our Main Street merchants and the community life they foster. We also protect the jobs, wages, and healthcare of grocery store workers. When we say yes to better public transit, we create cleaner air and more economic opportunity for carless workers. We also create family-wage bus and rail jobs. When we preserve the tax base of older areas, we stabilize home equity and create fairer tax systems. We also create better quality of life by keeping public school class sizes reasonable, teachers' wages competitive, and schools well maintained. When we save hospitals and hospital departments in older areas, we save vital services for the neighborhoods and we help our nurses and doctors and aides. Cleaning up brownfields and rehabilitating older buildings helps us make more efficient use of our infrastructure; these projects also create good construction jobs.[9]

Here are some of the specific approaches we can take to achieve smart growth:

Location-Efficient Incentives

These would be state rules stipulating that, for deals occurring in metro areas that have public transit, the company will not qualify for the subsidy unless the work site is transit accessible (within a quarter-mile of a regular stop). These would help ensure that subsidies create new job opportunities for people who cannot afford a car. It would also give more people a choice about how to get to work, improve air quality, and reduce traffic congestion.

Regional Sharing of Local Sales Tax Revenue

This puts an end to point-of-sale revenue going to an individual suburb and thereby creating a perverse incentive to pirate sales and overbuild retail.

Regional Sharing of Some Property Tax Revenue

The Twin Cities region has been sharing 40 percent of the increase in commercial-industrial property taxes since 1971; this has gone a long way toward reducing tax-base disparities, helping older areas remain vital.

No "TIFing" of Sales Tax

TIF is problematic enough as it is with property tax getting diverted; sales tax TIF is just trouble waiting to happen—on steroids.

No Subsidies for Paving Cornfields

Maryland's Smart Growth Act is a model here.[10] It says if you want to build a project in a place that already has infrastructure or is already slated to get it, fine, you are eligible for incentives. If you want to build outside such areas, have a nice day: no job subsidies and you are going to pay for every mile of road and water and sewer and utility hookup; the taxpayers will not subsidize your sprawl. Making developers bear the full infrastructure costs of development on the fringe helps tip the scales in favor of infill construction and urban reinvestment.

No Subsidies to Sprawling Retail

For all the reasons we covered in chapter 6, states should deny subsidies altogether to retail deals, except in truly depressed inner-city markets that are demonstrably underserved for basics such as groceries, prescription drugs and other care needs, and clothing.

Reform #12: Community Benefits Agreements

Pioneered by the Los Angeles Alliance for a New Economy, these are legal contracts negotiated between community coalitions and developers to make sure that city residents benefit from redevelopment of their neighborhoods. Each contract is tailored, but they often include provisions for first-source hiring (to give local workers the first chance to qualify for the jobs), living wage job quality standards, affordable housing assistance, and environmental and/or open space allowances. They may also create space in the development for community priorities such as a child care center or a healthcare clinic. Once the coalition and the developer agree on the Community Benefits Agreement, the coalition supports the developer's application to the city for subsidies and the agreement is attached to the redevelopment agreement between the city and the developer, making it again legally enforceable.

Will Some Subsidies Be Ruled Unconstitutional?

There are legal developments in the "war among the states." Shortly before this book was completed, a potentially significant court decision on subsidies was issued. The U.S. Sixth Circuit of Appeals (which covers Ohio, Michigan, Kentucky, and Tennessee) ruled that a corporate income tax credit Ohio gave DaimlerChrysler for a Jeep plant in Toledo violated the Commerce Clause of the U.S. Constitution. The tax credit was part of a $280 million package used to prevent the plant from locating in Michigan.[11]

The case was conceived by Peter Enrich, professor of law at Northeastern University, who argues that many subsidies are legally vulnerable because they involve one state interfering with another's commerce.[12] In response to the decision, at least two corporate coalitions (one by the Council on State Taxation) have been formed to overturn it; their efforts include proposed federal legislation. Both sides are appealing the decision to the U.S. Supreme Court.

Public Goods: A Positive Alternative for Creating Good Jobs

I conclude with a two-pronged warning about why we can't keep giving money away in wasteful corporate subsidies. We have far more urgent needs to spend our money on to really create good jobs. Instead of steering so much money into private deals that are unaccountable and ineffective, we need to get back to basics and invest in public goods, especially our skilled labor base and our infrastructure. The 12 reforms I just detailed are *how* to do it, and here—in addition to all the jobs scams—are two more big reasons *why* we must do it.

Skills and Infrastructure: Our Neglected Jewels

How'd you like to have surgery in a hospital missing a third of its nurses? Send your child to a school with unqualified teachers? Buy your phone service from a company that lacks enough line installers? Pay your taxes to a government that has trouble remembering how to dismantle a nuclear weapon?

Welcome to America, circa 2020, when most of the Baby Boom generation has retired.

How'd you like to spend more time in traffic jams because roads and bridges are bottlenecked? Send your child to a decrepit school? Pay much higher water and sewer bills because the systems need rebuilding?

Welcome to America, various years and places, thanks to our ballooning infrastructure deficit.

We have two really obvious, predictable train wrecks on the horizon: a skilled-labor shortage that is already evident and will become more acute when Baby Boomers retire en masse, and a crumbling infrastructure system that will harm the private-sector productivity and public services that benefit all employers.

In other words, the two taxpayer investments that are proven winners for creating good jobs—skills and infrastructure—are in deep trouble.

In this era of heightened capital mobility, investments in skills and infrastructure are especially wise because, unlike a call center or a widget plant, they don't up and run away. If a business fails or moves, at least the taxpayers in the area retain the value of their past investments: the dislocated workers will take their skills to new jobs, and the infrastructure will still be there, helping other businesses.

Aging Boomers, Slowing Growth

We who were born between 1946 and 1964 are the 76 million Baby Boomers. By 1980, when we had all come of age, we made up almost half of the U.S. workforce. A few of us have already retired; by 2008, we will be leaving the labor market in droves.[13] You think Florida is crawling with geezers? How about 39 Floridas? By 2025, that's how many states will have as large a share of seniors as Florida has today.[14]

The Baby Boom generation's retirement means we are about to lose an enormous pool of skilled labor. It also means that a dollar spent in the name of jobs that does not produce more skilled labor is a dollar wasted (see chapters 1 through 8).

The combination of Boomers leaving and lower birth rates during the Gen X period (births between 1965 and 1975) and the Echo Boom (1976 to 2001) means the growth rate of the labor force is steadily declining. In the 1970s, the U.S. labor force grew 2.6 percent a year on average. In the 1980s, that rate cooled to 1.6 percent. In the 1990s, it was 1.2 percent. In this decade, the growth rate is projected at only 0.8 to 1.0 percent. In the 2010s, the forecast is only 0.4—and then more declines and a flat line.[15]

Put another way, in the last two decades of the twentieth century, the number of people in their prime-age work years—age 25 to 54—grew by 35 million. In the first two decades of the twenty-first century, the net growth in prime-age workers will be only three million. And the workforce will become far more diverse; only 15 percent of all new workers will be native-born whites.[16]

The Most Vulnerable Industries and Occupations

Government economists, trade associations, and even a couple of book authors have already started sketching this skilled-labor train wreck. We need more skilled workers, but we are about to lose a whole lot of school teachers. Boomers are going to demand much more medical care, but the healthcare professions are already screaming about worker shortages.

Elementary and secondary school teachers will be in short supply because fewer were hired in the 1980s and they tend to retire younger because, like most government workers, about two-thirds are eligible for pensions by age 55 if they have 30 years of service.

Other large occupations that are especially "grey" are farmers, government and school administrators, clergy, librarians, bus drivers, school and vocational counselors, property managers, psychologists, management analysts, phone installers, private household cleaners and servants, tool and die makers, and taxi drivers. Still more occupations that will be significantly affected include airline pilots and navigators, special education teachers and teachers' aides, industrial engineers, postal clerks, plumbers, pipefitters and steamfitters, financial managers, social workers, lawyers, registered nurses, and chemists.

The risk is that we in the United States will have fewer folks who know how to do many complicated things, and we'll be forced to pay those elsewhere to do them for us. That's a surefire recipe for a lower standard of living. We already buy more than half of our manufactured goods from other nations; should it be three-fourths? Pentagon procurement scandals raise the question: do we want even less management expertise watching the store?

Healthcare: Skills Shortages Endanger Patients

Our healthcare system faces a double whammy: rising demand for services (more Baby Boom geezers, living longer) and growing shortages in key skilled positions (not to mention the asthma and the diabetes, heart disease, and other obesity-related problems stemming from car-dependent sprawl). The nursing crisis has received the most attention, but many medical professions—including doctors and numerous technical support occupations—also face shortages.

Health facilities in many places are already struggling with shortages of registered nurses. The U.S. Department of Health and Human Services reports that there was already a shortage of 110,000 registered nurses by 2000, and it projects that the gap between supply and demand will reach 808,000 by 2020—leaving almost a third of nursing positions unfilled. HHS forecasts that the problem will be worst in some rural states, where more than half of all nursing positions will be vacant. The American Health Care Association reports that 15 percent of registered nurse positions at nursing homes were vacant in 2002.[17]

The Joint Commission on Accreditation of Healthcare Organizations (JCAHO) says 90 percent of long-term care organizations already don't have enough nurses to provide just basic care. JCAHO summarizes the issue bluntly: "When there are too few nurses, patient safety is threatened and healthcare quality is diminished."[18]

Corporate Warning Bells

In addition to healthcare associations, other corporate groups have begun to acknowledge this huge issue. The Aspen Institute, a bipartisan think tank, calls for many reforms to improve skills, enhance benefits, and make workplaces more family friendly.[19] Similarly, the

Committee for Economic Development, an elite corporate group, says that slower growth of the labor force means savings and investment will decline, and therefore "growth of productivity and our standard of living will suffer."[20]

The National Association of Manufacturers (NAM) reported in 2003 that, despite millions of factory jobs having recently been lost, 60 percent of its members were experiencing a "moderate shortage" of qualified job applicants and 20 percent were experiencing a "serious shortage." Some companies, especially smaller firms, said they could not accept new orders or add new shifts because they cannot find qualified workers. Engineering and skilled crafts are in especially short supply.[21]

The National Science Foundation forecasts that the growth rate in the number of scientists and engineers will slow and the workforce will grow older. It also estimates that the U.S. growth rate of scientific researchers is already a third less than that of other industrialized nations in the Organization for Economic Co-operation and Development (which does not include China, India, or Russia, each of which has a booming scientist population). The National Aeronautics and Space Administration could lose a fourth of its scientists and engineers to retirement by 2008 and is having trouble finding replacements for them.[22]

The Solution: Put Workforce Development First

The solutions proposed by these trade associations and think tanks are way too tepid. Cajoling some seniors to work longer, making workplaces more family friendly—these are fine, but they miss the big picture. We need much more drastic action to avert our skilled-labor train wreck. At every level of government, we need to put workforce development at the forefront of jobs policy. If we don't make real strides helping workers (and future workers) of all ages gain new skills, then everything else we do in the name of jobs is likely to be wasted.

By workforce development, I mean early childhood and preschool programs; kindergarten through twelfth grade; traditional workforce development programs like vocational education, apprenticeships, and dislocated worker retraining, including those that are jointly managed by labor unions and companies; community colleges and state universities (both institutional budgets and scholarship funds, undergraduate and graduate); every manner of incumbent worker retraining; English as a second language; graduate equivalency degrees; retraining for welfare recipients and people who are chronically unemployed; and training for entrepreneurs and small businesspeople.

We need to take a fine-tooth comb to the $50 billion a year states and cities spend for jobs. Any expenditure that does not create more skilled labor, that undermines funding for skills, or that cannot be retooled to become a strong "carrot" for companies to invest more in skills development, should be seriously considered for elimination.

Despite this urgent need, federal policy has been moving in the other direction: federal support for skills development has been declining. The cuts have been deepest in programs that mostly benefit low-income people, for those workers who might have made real strides in their standards of living. Massive federal budget deficits now threaten to cause additional cuts.

In a comprehensive analysis of four U.S. cabinet agencies between 1985 and 2003, the Workforce Alliance found that federal investment in skills is down substantially. It concluded that we are "skilling" our workforce "on the cheap." The second-biggest federal workforce development program is the Workforce Investment Act. WIA funding is down by a third—with adult and youth services each cut by more than half. Overall, support for workforce development from *all* Department of Labor programs is down by almost a third.[23]

Welfare reform—known as Temporary Assistance for Needy Families (TANF)—pushes many recipients into low-wage jobs under the mantra "work first" instead of helping people gain new skills and better jobs. Spending for education and training of welfare recipients is down by almost half and represents a measly 2 percent of TANF funding.[24]

Pell grants for low-income students to go to college are the biggest federal program for adult education and training. Although spending is up in absolute dollars—by about two-thirds since 1990—it has not kept pace with demand or with the high rate of college tuition inflation. The average Pell grant is now only about one-third of the cost of attending a two-year public institution. The eligibility formula favors students without income, so that working adults often don't qualify. And the rules discourage support for vocational education classes.[25]

America's Crumbling, Disinvested Infrastructure

Good infrastructure is critical to every form of productivity. Children need safe schools with enough rooms to accommodate smaller classes; truck drivers need good roads to deliver their cargo on time; commuters need reliable roads and public transit to get to work; families need safe drinking water free of lead and parasites.

But our nation's physical plant has suffered serious disinvestment and deterioration, especially in the past twenty years, the same period in which states and cities have enacted hundreds of new corporate subsidies in the name of jobs.

The most damning evidence of this problem comes from the American Society of Civil Engineers (ASCE), which issues an infrastructure "report card" grading the key aspects of the nation's physical condition. The ASCE report is highly credible; the grades are issued by prestigious committees composed of civil engineering experts in each respective field. And the results are endorsed by dozens of professional and trade associations whose members build, maintain and use our public systems.[26]

Table 9.1 presents a report card for the past 15 years. Our nation's grades are not pretty.

Table 9.1. American Society of Civil Engineers Infrastructure Report Card

Type of Infrastructure	1988*	1998	2001	2005 Trend
Highways	C+	—	—	—
Roads	—	D–	D+	D
Bridges	—	C–	C	C
Mass Transit	C–	C	C–	D+
Aviation	B–	C–	D	D+
Schools		F	D–	D
Water Supply/ Drinking Water	B–	D	D	D–
Wastewater	C	D+	D	D–
Water Resources	B	—	—	—
Dams	—	D	D	D
Navigable Waterways	—	—	D+	D–
Solid Waste	C–	C–	C+	C+
Hazardous Waste	D	D–	D+	D
Energy	—	—	D+	D
Overall Grade	C	D	D+	D

*The 1988 grades were issued by the National Council of Public Works Improvements, and ASCE added new categories for Energy and Navigable Waterways in later years; hence the category shifts in Highways and Water Resources.

As ASCE summarizes, traffic congestion reduces productivity and wastes fuel—to the tune of $67.5 billion a year. More than a fourth of the nation's bridges are "structurally deficient or functionally obsolete," so they cannot handle all vehicles. Transit spending is half what it needs to be just to maintain the systems. Airport officials are focused more on increasing security than expanding capacity. Three out of four school buildings are inadequate; the cumulative rebuilding deficit is $127 billion. Drinking-water systems are mostly reliable, but aging; they need $11 billion a year more than they are getting to replace or rehabilitate facilities and comply with federal rules. Wastewater systems are in such bad shape that we risk losing all of the gains made in surface water purity since the 1972 Clean Water Act.[27]

Almost 2,600 dams are now deemed unsafe, and more than 10,000 dams are upstream from development, so if they collapsed, people would die (21 dams collapsed in a recent two-year period). Progress remains slow in cleaning up brownfields, or sites contaminated by past industrial activity with hazardous wastes. Half the locks on our inland waterways are older than the 50 years they were designed to last. Investment in power transmission systems has declined since 1975, which contributed to the big power outage in the Northeast in August 2003. The U.S. Department of Energy estimates that the nation's power grid needs $50 billion worth of modernization—a cost consumers will inevitably bear.[28]

Overall, the ASCE estimates that to renew our infrastructure will cost us *$1.6 trillion!* I take the advice of the guys with the pocket protectors very seriously. Having poor infrastructure is a huge disadvantage for job creation.

The Bottom Line: We Need Reinvestment, Not Disinvestment

In addition to the 12 reforms, this is my positive agenda for creating good jobs: reinvestment in skills and infrastructure, not more corporate disinvestment by tax dodging. The "solutions" spawned by narrow corporate interests—like TIF for sprawling big-box retail or Single Sales Factor for manufacturing—were always dumb ideas. Now it is glaringly obvious: they are wasteful handouts we can no longer afford.

Acknowledgments

The staff of Good Jobs First has provided enormous support, enabling me to write this book, and the publisher's contract is with the organization, not myself. Our research director, Philip Mattera, himself the author of four books, provided superb research, sage editing, and fact-checking, and oversaw additional stellar help from research analysts Anna Purinton and Sarah Diehl. Phil also authored the chapter on stadiums. Our Good Jobs New York staffers, project director Bettina Damiani and research analyst Stephanie Greenwood, created the New York City research and also provided editing and feedback. Our Illinois project director Jeff McCourt provided new corporate research and led all of the Illinois work cited in the book. The great work of several former staffers—including Kate Davis, Sara Hinkley, Fiona Hsu, Mafruza Khan, Alice Meaker, Anne Nolan, and Alyssa Talanker—shines through in many of the reports cited here. Finally, our communications/development coordinator Zoë Lane adeptly managed administrative and fundraising affairs for three months while I mostly stayed at home to write, and our administrative assistant Edgar Soto Enciso helped us all with mailings, travel, and training arrangements. Thanks also to Betty Grdina of Heller, Huron, Chertkof, Lerner, Simon & Salzman for her astute legal guidance and clarifications.

The backstage heroine of this book is Johanna Vondeling, editor extraordinaire, who solicited me to conceive it, shepherded the outline, negotiated a contract, and then resigned in protest from her position at another publisher when its corporate executives got cold feet. In a poetic twist, she landed at Berrett-Koehler, where publisher Steve Piersanti had decisively and enthusiastically embraced the project. This book owes its existence to Johanna's savvy insights and Steve's courageous vision. Thanks also to copyeditor Kristi Hein for her sage wordsmithing and spirited content suggestions and to book manager Dave Peattie for his professional handling.

Frank Mauro and James Parrott of the Fiscal Policy Institute are our partners in Good Jobs New York. Frank has been an active colleague since I wrote *No More Candy Store* in 1994, both in our New York work and on the broader issue of the economic war among the states. Ralph Martire and Jennifer Holuj of the Center for Tax and Budget Accountability are our partners in Good Jobs Illinois, where many good things are happening.

Michael Mazerov, former Director of Policy Research of the Multistate Tax Commission and now senior fellow at the Center for Budget and Policy Priorities, has long been an exemplary colleague. He was especially helpful on the chapter on Single Sales Factor, as was Eugene Corrigan, the founding executive director of the Multistate Tax Commission. Jim Peters, retired tax counsel at AT&T and a former chairman of the Council on State Taxation, shared his perspective from the corporate side of those early debates.

Peter Fisher of the Iowa Policy Project and the University of Iowa has done some of the most important work in the field of economic development subsidies and has been unfailingly generous and patient in sharing his work.

The work of Bill Schweke and the Corporation for Enterprise Development has long inspired me and many others seeking to improve economic development policy; he gave helpful comments on several chapters. Thanks also to Massachusetts State Representative

James Marzilli, who shared his insights and files on the Raytheon and Fidelity episodes.

Thanks also to the many people who reviewed passages, have collaborated with us on in-depth projects, or provided materials about their state, city, or other area of expertise: Lenny Goldberg at the California Tax Reform Association; Jean Ross of the California Budget Project; Jessica Goodheart of the Los Angeles Alliance for a New Economy; Howard Greenwich of the East Bay Alliance for a New Economy; Arn Pearson of the Maine Citizen Leadership Fund; Julia Sass Rubin of Rutgers University; Andy Van Kleunen of the Workforce Alliance; Stephen Herzenberg of the Keystone Research Center; Amy Hanauer and Zach Schiller of Policy Matters Ohio; C. Scott Cooper and Beth Fraser of the Minnesota Alliance for Progressive Action; Kimble Forrister of Alabama Arise; Chuck Sheketoff of the Oregon Center for Public Policy; Dick Lavine of the Center for Public Policy Priorities in Texas; Si Kahn of Grassroots Leadership; Kennedy Smith, formerly of the National Trust for Historic Preservation and now of the Community Land Use and Economics Group LLC; Blair Forlaw and Les Sterman of the East-West Gateway Coordinating Council; D. J. Waldie of the City of Lakewood, California; *Field of Schemes* co-author Neil deMause of *HERE* magazine; Doug Hoffer of Vermont; Brett Bursey of the South Carolina Progressive Network; John Ruoff of South Carolina Fair Share; and Mark Vasina of Nebraskans for Peace.

Don Chen at Smart Growth America provided sage feedback on the chapter on sprawl and has been unfailingly helpful to our work on smart growth. Elizabeth Schilling of the Growth Management Leadership Alliance and Anne Canby and her colleagues at the Surface Transportation Policy Project have also opened many doors and advised us on our smart growth work. Thanks also to Ben Starrett of the Funders Network for Smart Growth and Livable Communities and Bruce Katz and Amy Liu of the Brookings Institution for their generous collegiality. Tim Frank and Brett Hulsey of the

Sierra Club's Challenge to Sprawl Committee have actively helped us disseminate our smart growth research, along with other members of the committee and Club staff; thanks especially to Neha Bhatt, Eric Olson, Peter Tyler, and Eric Antebi.

Thanks to Tim also for the supportive role he plays as a member of Good Jobs First's board of directors, and to the other members of the board: Hector Figueroa of Service Employees International Union Local 32B-32J in New York; Mark Harrison of the United Methodist Church; Madeline Janis-Aparicio of the Los Angeles Alliance for a New Economy; Clara Oleson, formerly of the University of Iowa; Cynthia Ward of Northeast Action; and Steve White of the ACT Foundation.

Good Jobs First owes its running start to the collegial hospitality of Robert McIntyre and Michael Ettlinger at the Institute on Taxation and Economic Policy. They sponsored us for our first four years and provided much invaluable assistance, both intellectual and administrative. Mike now directs the Economic Analysis and Research Network at the Economic Policy Institute, where he remains a terrific colleague. Thanks, too, to Ed Meyers, Bonnie Rubenstein, and Matt Gardner of ITEP for their many kindnesses these seven years.

As a measure of the heat that surrounds this issue, several individuals provided invaluable information and assistance but asked to remain anonymous. My gratitude and empathy.

Of course, the opinions expressed and any errors made are my own and not those of my advisers.

The Stern Family Fund made Good Jobs First's birth possible by awarding me its 1998 Public Interest Pioneer Award; my thanks to David Stern, Michael Caudell-Feagan, Elizabeth Collaton, and the other board members for launching direct support and for helping to open so many other doors. Since the Pioneer grant, we have had more than 50 additional major sources of support; thanks especially to other early supporters such as the Alki Fund of the Tides Foundation, the Veatch Unitarian Universalist Program at Shelter Rock, and the Ottinger Foundation. We gratefully acknowledge support for this book project from the Nathan Cummings Foundation and the Arca Foundation.

I dedicated *No More Candy Store* to two dislocated union leaders who went down swinging. Tom Stillman of Duluth, Minnesota, saved his fellow workers' jobs for six years by exposing the abuse of a subsidy, even as he lost his own job. Connie Malloy of Elkhart, Indiana, blew the whistle on a drug company's tax scam and led her fellow union members to a $24 million lawsuit settlement. May we never forget that basic accountability safeguards such as clawbacks were first enacted in this country because people like Tom and Connie, at great personal cost, insisted that taxpayer-subsidized job destruction must end.

Finally, I owe my deepest gratitude to my wife, Shoon Murray. Without her steadfast, insightful, and generous support, this book could never have happened.

Greg LeRoy
January 2005

Notes

Introduction

1. Kenneth Thomas estimated total state and local subsidies at $48.8 billion as of 1996, and many states have enacted new subsidies since then. (*Competing for Capital: Europe and North America in a Global Era* [Georgetown University Press, 2000].) Peter Fisher and Alan Peters conservatively estimated total subsidies at $50 billion. ("The Failures of Economic Development Incentives," *Journal of the American Planning Association*, Vol. 70, No. 1, Winter 2004.)

Chapter One

1. Barbara Carton, "Raytheon Threatens to Relocate Unit Unless Massachusetts Grants Concessions," *Wall Street Journal*, February 15, 1995. Beppi Crosariol, "Tenn. Knockin,'" *Boston Globe*, March 2, 1995; Joan Vennochi, "Raytheon Picks Sasso to be Lobbyist," *Boston Globe*, March 9, 1995.

2. "Raytheon's Proposed Cost Savings Options for Consideration by the Massachusetts Legislature," company presentation March 1995. Raytheon later indicated that because of federal tax law changes and lower earnings, it saved less than $21 million a year.

3. Joan Vennochi, "Poison Pill Strategy," *Boston Globe*, September 6, 1995.

4. David Warsh, "Raytheon Chief: A Football Player Without a Helmet," *Boston Globe*, November 19, 1995.

5. Michael E. Knell and Jeffrey Krasner, "Raytheon Revamps Campaign," *Boston Herald*, March 29, 1995. *Boston Herald* editorial, "A No-Brainer

Way to Tax," May 14, 1995. William H. Swanson, Raytheon senior vice president, "The Fight for Manufacturing Jobs," *Boston Globe* op-ed, February 21, 1995. John Gill, "Tax Shortfall Casts Doubt on Raytheon Aid," *Lawrence Eagle-Tribune*, March 15, 1995.

6. Daniel Golden, "Weld Proposal Expected to Cut Corporate Taxes $160m a Year," *Boston Globe*, September 5, 1995. Phil Primack, "Clearing the Smoke about Tax Breaks," *Boston Globe*, December 15, 1999; Joan Vennochi, "John Sasso for the Defense," *Boston Globe*, November 10, 1995. Summary of Raytheon's jobs rhetoric by the Tax Equity Alliance for Massachusetts, "The Record on 'An Act Relative to Job Retention and Economic Expansion,'" n.d.

7. Testimony of John Gould, president and chief executive officer of Associated Industries of Massachusetts, "Tax Incentives for Jobs in Massachusetts," presented to the Committee on Taxation, March 22, 1995.

8. Separately, the Massachusetts Taxpayers Foundation (which consists of several hundred companies) issued a paper saying the state was high cost. (John J. Gould and John Gill, "Should Raytheon Get Tax Cuts?" *Lawrence Eagle-Tribune*, September 10, 1995.) And the Beacon Hill Institute at Suffolk University, a conservative think tank, issued its own study arguing for applying SSF to all companies, not just manufacturers. (Beacon Hill Institute, "Corporate Tax Proposal Would Mean New Jobs, Higher Wages for Mass. Workers," October 3, 1995.) Phil Primack, "Raytheon Spends $$ to Win Big State Tax Breaks," *Boston Herald*, January 17, 1996.

9. State Representative James Marzilli interview June 18, 2004. DRI/McGraw-Hill, "Commonwealth of Massachusetts Competitive Economic Choices," May 10, 1995. In four different scenarios, the study's job benefits ranged from 63 to 93 percent *retained* jobs, with the remainder being new jobs.

10. The Boston Federal Reserve's senior economist and a widely recognized expert on state corporate taxes, Robert Tannenwald, was reportedly forbidden by his superiors to testify on SSF. (Joan Vennochi, "Muzzled at the Fed," *Boston Globe*, March 8, 1996.)

11. Associated Industries of Massachusetts, "Questions and Answers on Single Sales Factor Apportionment," October 31, 1995.

12. Eric Convey, "Memo: Raytheon Offered Buyouts," *Boston Herald*, May 31, 1996.

13. Raytheon Systems Company, "Raytheon in Massachusetts Overview of Plans," January 23, 1998 report sent to state legislators.

14. Todd Wallack, "Raytheon Job Cuts Criticized," *Boston Herald*, June 15, 1999.

15. Meg Vaillancourt, "Raytheon Defends Itself in Outcry over Tax Breaks," *Boston Globe*, June 17, 1999.

16. Todd Wallack, "Unions: Raytheon Should Lose Tax Breaks Amid Cuts," *Boston Herald*, February 5, 1999. Wallack, "Raytheon Job Cuts Criticized." Marzilli interview.

17. John Gill, "Raytheon Spent $600,000 on Tax Cut," *Lawrence Eagle Tribune*, January 17, 1996.

18. As previously noted, Raytheon later indicated that it received a smaller tax break than it projected. However, the SSF tax cut applied to all defense contractors and all manufacturers.

19. Alton Parker Hatcher, Jr., telephone deposition given March 28, 1995, in *William F. Maready vs. the City of Winston-Salem et al.*, North Carolina Superior Court 95-CVS-623.

20. "Marriott International & Host Marriott Corp. Number of Associates by Income Level and County As of February 1998," spreadsheet dated May 31, 1998, in Virginia Economic Development Partnership project files.

21. Virginia Economic Development Partnership, "The Commonwealth of Virginia Presents Marriott with Incentives to Relocate Their Corporate Headquarters to Northern Virginia," September 1998.

22. Scott Wilson, "Marriott Takes Deal to Stay in Maryland," *Washington Post*, March 12, 1999. Press release, "Marriott Chooses Maryland," State of Maryland, Governor's Press Office, March 11, 1999.

23. Jay Hancock, "Marriott Used Va. as a Ruse to Raise Md. Bid; Public Records Suggest Bethesda Firm's Threat to Leave Was Bluff," *Baltimore Sun*, March 27, 1999.

24. VEDP Opportunity Profile (project log), Bob Gibson (Virginia economic development executive) entry 2/10/99. The Virginia files suggest the company wanted more leverage against Maryland, that Marriott was dissatisfied with Maryland's early bids and by a lack of personal attention to the deal from Maryland governor Glendening. In early December 1998, Marriott told Virginia that it had asked Maryland to resubmit a new subsidy offer. A week later, an unknown source leaked to the *Washington Post* about new developers involved. (VEDP Opportunity Profile, Ann Broadwater, December 10, 1998 entry.)

25. VEDP memo, Ann Broadwater (manager, Global Business Development) to Bob Gibson, November 6, 1998. Other examples of Virginia's skepticism: in late 1997, a Fairfax County official told state officials that it "seemed [Marriott was] 'shopping' but won't leave." (VEDP Opportunity Profile, Ann Broadwater entry, December 5, 1997.) And in a May 1998 meeting with Virginia officials, Marriott "spent a considerable amount of time addressing the rumors regarding whether or not Marriott would seriously consider leaving MD." (VEDP memo.)

26. Timothy B. Wheeler, "Assembly Approves Deal with Marriott; $44 Million Incentives Pass Despite Questions," *Baltimore Sun*, April 8, 1999. Scott Wilson, "Marriott Opts to Renovate Bethesda Site, Rejects Move," *Washington Post*, September 18, 1999.

27. Jonathan Bowles, "Payoffs for Layoffs," Center for an Urban Future, February 10, 2001.

28. Stephanie Greenwood and Bettina Damiani, *Know When to Fold 'Em: Time to Walk Away from New York's Corporate Retention Game*, Good Jobs New York, February 2004.

29. Ibid.

30. Ibid. Tania Padgett, "Staff Cuts at Bank of America," *Newsday*, October 8, 2004.

31. Clint Johnson, "Enterprising Businesses Zone In On Savings," *Plants Sites & Parks*, December 1, 2000 (No. 7, Vol. 27). Kenneth Lovett, "Megadeal: IBM Chips in Billions for N.Y. Plant," *New York Post*, October 11, 2000. Michael Gormley, "IBM to Build Chip-Making Plant, Create 1,000 Jobs," Associated Press, October 10, 2000.

32. "I.B.M. Raises Number of Hudson Valley Cuts," Reuters, February 26, 1993. Mary Voboril, "The Dutchess County Blues: IBM Cutbacks Lay Low a Company Town," *Newsday*, August 29, 1993. Dennis Hevesi, "In I.B.M. Deal, State Offers a Loan to Create 700 Jobs," *New York Times*, January 30, 1994.

33. New York State General Municipal Law, Section 958 (c) as amended in August, 1993. Gov. Cuomo signed the law on August 6, 1993. Under section (C) (iv) an area with "equal to or less than the national average of unemployment" and a labor market that has "experienced or is likely to experience within three years the lesser of a loss of one thousand direct jobs or a dislocation of workers equal to four percent of the employed population of the labor market area" became eligible for zone designation.

34. Barney Beal, "Report: U.S. Call Centers Vanishing," SearchCRM.com, August 27, 2004.

35. Joe Gardaz, "Right on the Money; Sykes Call Centers Command Hefty Price Tags from Cities," *Bismarck Tribune*, July 12, 1998.

36. Jesse Fanciulli, "Incentives for Sykes Totaled $312,000,"*Greeley Tribune*, January 6, 2002. *Regional Economic Review—Northern Region*, October 2002, p. 2. Published by Colorado Legislative Council. The $915,000 figure includes land valued at $203,000, a zero-percent-interest loan of $400,000, and other state, county, and city subsidies totaling $312,000; the company was also due an unknown additional amount of state tax credits for locating in an enterprise zone.

37. "Klamath Falls Call Center to Close," *Portland Business News*, November 20, 2003. Scott Barancik, "Tales of Two Oregon Towns Give Lessons on Lessening Outsourcing's Sting," *St. Petersburg Times*, August 23, 2004. Wendy Culverwell, "High Tech Firm Locating in Klamath," *Klamath Falls Herald & News*, July 20, 1995. Wendy Culverwell, "McMillan County Not to Blame for Sykes Plant Crisis," *Klamath Falls Herald & News*, July 26, 1995.

38. Jeff Olson, "More Jobs Days Away; City OKs $2 Million Incentive Plan for Sykes," *Bismarck Tribune*, September 27, 1995. Joe Gardyasz, "Sykes to Add Building, Jobs," *Bismarck Tribune*, March 21, 1997. "After $3.8 Million, It's Time Sykes Paid Its Own Way," *Bismarck Tribune*, July 17, 1998. "Was Sykes Worth It?" *Bismarck Tribune*, July 12, 2004. Joe Gardyasz, "Incentive Proposed for Sykes; Company Will Build Third Center if Bismarck OKs Funds," *Bismarck Tribune*, July 9, 1998. Associated Press, "Sykes Enterprises Closes Some U.S., European Call Centers," January 2, 2002. Mark Hanson, "Sykes Announces Plans to Lay off Another 71 Employees," *Bismarck Tribune*, August 17, 2003.

39. Melissa O'Neil, "Technical Company to Bring Jobs to Milton-Freewater," *Tri-City Herald*, September 12, 1998. Barancik, "Tales of Two Oregon Towns."

40. Matt Moline, "Manhattan Lures Firm, Gains 432 New Jobs," *Topeka Capital-Journal*, April 24, 1998. Tony Herrman, "Sykes Closes Doors in Manhattan," *Kansas State Collegian*, April 15, 2004 at http://www.kstatecollegian.com/article.php?a=1549. Manhattan Economic Development Opportunity Fund, "Accountability Checklist: Sykes Enterprises, Inc.," July 15, 2003.

41. Helen Huntley, "Hays Weighs Its Investment in Sykes Enterprises," *St. Petersburg Times*, June 23, 1997. "NEW Expands Operations Into Hays, Kansas," N.E.W. Customer Service Companies, Inc., press release, July 14, 2004, http://www.forrelease.com/D20040714/dcw069

.P2.07142004173819.24672.html. Associated Press, "Call Center Having Difficulty Finding Applicants," August 7, 2004. Associated Press, "Sykes Flip-Flops on Closure of Hays Call Center," March 16, 2004.

42. Brenda Tollett, "Sykes Shuts Down Ada OK Location," *Ada Evening News,* January 7, 2004. Associated Press, "Some 440 Layoffs Expected," January 7, 2004. Adam Wilmoth, "Ada Call Center Shutdown to Leave 440 Without Jobs," *The Daily Oklahoman,* January 7, 2004.

43. Virgil Larsen, "Florida Firm to Close Scottsbluff, Neb., Call Center," *Omaha World-Herald,* November 19, 2002. Associated Press, "Scotts-bluff Officials Tout Economic Development Plan," September 12, 1999. John Taylor, "Firm to Hire 150 Workers in Scottsbluff," *Omaha World-Herald,* March 28, 1999.

44. Lee Mueller, "State to Spend $9 Million on Call Centers," *Lexington Herald-Leader,* August 31, 1999. Scott Barancik, "Sykes Says It Will Pull Plug on Ky. Call Center," *St. Petersburg Times* June 26, 2003. Dan Morse, "Jobs Promised to Ky. in Asia, South America: Small Town Blindsided by Company's Move to Offshore Operations, Former Employees Say," *Charleston Gazette,* March 10, 2004.

45. David Streitfeld, "Town's Future Is Leaving the Country," *Los Angeles Times,* March 28, 2004. Lee Mueller, "Pikeville Call Center to Close," *Lexington Herald-Leader,* February 11, 2004. Morse, "Jobs Promised To Ky."

46. Scott Barancik, "Call Center to Close Soon: Nearly 200 Workers at the Sykes Enterprise Facility in Palatka Will Be Laid Off in September and October," *St. Petersburg Times,* July 10, 2004. Associated Press, "Palatka Call Center on Verge of Losing 194 Jobs," July 9, 2004.

47. Marianna Now, "Industry, Sykes Enterprise on the Internet," n.d. Rep. Bev Kilmer, District 7 Fla., "Jackson County to Pick up Over 500 New Jobs," *The Kilmer Konnection,* May 1-5, 2000 (http://www.bevkilmer.com/kc/archives/may1-2000.htm). Scott Barancik, "Sykes to Shut Fla. Call Center: the Marianna Closing is the Ninth Scheduled for 2004, Bringing the Total Layoffs This Year to More Than 2,500," *St. Petersburg Times,* August 5, 2004. Scott Barancik, "Sykes Leaves Marianna a Parting Gift," *St. Petersburg Times,* January 1, 2005.

48. Scott Barancik, "Fortunes Might Be Turning for Sykes: After Moving Most of Its Call Center Jobs Overseas and Downsizing at Home, Sykes Enterprises Had Some Good News," *St. Petersburg Times,* November 3, 2004.

49. Jeff McCourt and Greg LeRoy, *A Better Deal for Illinois: Improving Economic Development Policy*, Good Jobs First, January 2003, p. 28 and pp. 28–35 generally.
50. Although many of the "transplants" were located in heavily unionized states, only those with substantial U.S. ownership became unionized: Mazda in Michigan (because of Ford's large stake in Mazda), Toyota/GM in California (half-owned by General Motors) and Mitsubishi/Chrysler in Illinois (half-owned by Chrysler).
51. Martin and Susan Tolchin, *Buying into America: How Foreign Money Is Changing the Face of Our Nation*. (New York: Berkley Books, 1989), p. 241.
52. Good Jobs First compilation of transplant subsidy reports. The one early transplant that may not have been heavily subsidized was Toyota/GM in Fremont, California.
53. David L. Barkley, Deborah M. Markley, and Julia Sass Rubin, "Certified Capital Companies (CAPCOs): Strengths and Shortcomings of the Latest Wave in State-Assisted Venture Capital Programs," *Economic Development Quarterly*, Vol. 15, No. 4, November 2001, pp. 350–366. Julia Sass Rubin, correspondence, January 6, 2005.
54. Some states' CAPCO rules provide for the state to get a very small cut of profits made on those loans.
55. Barkley, Markley, and Rubin, "Certified Capital Companies (CAPCOs)." David L. Barkley, Deborah M. Markley, and Julia Sass Rubin, "Public Involvement in Venture Capital Funds: Lessons from Three Program Alternatives," Rural Policy Research Institute, PB99-2, November 1999.
56. Christopher Swope, "Economic Development: Risky Ventures," *Governing*, April 2004.
57. Ibid.
58. Bruce Murphy, "Capital Subsidy Bill Raked," *Milwaukee Journal Sentinel*, December 21, 2003.
59. Swope, "Economic Development."
60. Murphy, "Capital Subsidy Bill Raked."
61. Robert Guskind, "The New Civil War," *National Journal*, April 3, 1993.
62. Roy O. Priest (HUD Office of Economic Development), April 12, 1993, letter in response to Gary N. Conley (Los Angeles Economic Development Corporation).

63. Melvin L. Burstein and Arthur J. Rolnick, "Congress Should End the Economic War Among the States," Minneapolis Federal Reserve Bank, 1994 Annual Report Essay, March 1995, at http://minneapolisfed.org/pubs/ar/ar1994.cfm.

64. Paul More et al., *The Other Los Angeles: The Working Poor in the City of the 21st Century*, Los Angeles Alliance for a New Economy, August 2000. Paul Jargowsky, "Stunning Progress, Hidden Problems: The Dramatic Decline of Concentrated Poverty in the 1990s," Brookings Institution, May 2003, p. 9.

65. Paul More et al., "Who Benefits from Redevelopment in Los Angeles? An Evaluation of Commercial Redevelopment Activities in the 1990s," UCLA Center for Labor Research and Education, School of Public Policy and Social Research and Los Angeles Alliance for a New Economy, March 1999.

66. Shea Cunningham et al., "Taking Care of Business? An Evaluation of the Los Angeles Business Team," Los Angeles Alliance for a New Economy and the UCLA Center for Labor Research and Education School of Public Policy and Social Research, October 1999.

67. Greg LeRoy and Tyson Slocum, *Economic Development in Minnesota: High Subsidies, Low Wages, Absent Standards*, Good Jobs First, February 1999, p. 27.

68. Jason Bailey and Liz Natter, "Kentucky's Low Road to Economic Development: What Corporate Subsidies Are Doing to the Commonwealth," Democracy Resource Center, 2000.

69. Bill Bishop, "There's No Such Thing as a 'Free' Factory," *Lexington Herald Leader*, April 4, 1993.

70. Democratic staff of the Committee on Education and the Workforce, U.S. House of Representatives, "Everyday Low Wages: The Hidden Price We All Pay for Wal-Mart," February 16, 2004, at http://edworkforce.house.gov/democrats/WALMARTREPORT.pdf.

71. Kenneth E. Poole et al., *Evaluating Business Development Incentives*, the National Association of State Development Agencies, W. E. Upjohn Institute for Employment Research, and the Urban Center at Cleveland State University for the U.S. Department of Commerce, EDA Project #99-13794, August 1999; see especially chapter 7, pp. 57–94, at http:// www.eda.gov/ImageCache/EDAPublic/documents/pdfdocs/1g3_5febdi_5freport_2epdf/v1/1g3_5febdi_5freport.pdf.

72. Poole et al., *Evaluating Business Development Incentives*.

73. For a full account of the Boeing episode, see Jeff McCourt and Greg LeRoy, *A Better Deal for Illinois: Improving Economic Development Policy*, Good Jobs First, January 2003, chapter 8, pp. 57–65.

74. Ibid.

75. The case was *Bradley Harwood v. Pam McDonough et al.*, Appellate Court of Illinois First District No. 1-02-2714.

76. Philip Mattera and Mafruza Khan, *Jail Breaks: Economic Development Subsidies Given to Private Prisons*, Good Jobs First, October 2001. Philip Mattera, Mafruza Khan, and Stephen Nathan, *Corrections Corporation of America: A Critical Look at Its First Twenty Years*, Grassroots Leadership, December 2003.

77. United Auto Workers interoffice communication, Nat Weinberg to Paul Sifton, September 23, 1953.

78. James C. Cobb, *The Selling of the South* (Chicago: University of Illinois Press, 1993), pp. 8–16.

79. Robert L. Rose, "Job Piracy' Legislation Advances after Company Announces Job Shifts," *Wall Street Journal*, September 20, 1994. Jack Norman, "Ban on Grants to Help Firms Move Gains Support," *Milwaukee Journal*, August 14, 1994. Frank A. Aukofer, "House OKs Bill Against Job 'Piracy,'" *Milwaukee Journal*, July 22, 1994. On the legality of using CDBG money for interstate job transfers, see William J. Gilmartin (Assistant Secretary of HUD) letter to Senator Russ Feingold, August 8, 1994. The anti-piracy language was not attached until HUD's 1998 reauthorization. Then-congressman and now Milwaukee mayor Tom Barrett was most tenacious for the reform. When the HUD money was revealed, Murray, Kentucky, officials withdrew it from their Briggs deal. Officials in Poplar Bluff, Missouri, did not follow suit.

80. Jim DuPlessis, "Bendix Came Here in 1982 to Escape the High Wages . . ." *The State*, March 21, 2004.

81. Zack Nauth, *The Great Louisiana Tax Giveaway*, Louisiana Coalition for Tax Justice, n.d. [1992].

82. Ibid.

83. Marc Breslow, "Connecticut's Development Subsidies: Job Growth Far Short of Projections, High Costs Per Job," *Northeast Action*, February 28, 2002.

84. Jill Barton, "Governor Says Biotech Firm Will Spur Budding Industry in Florida," Associated Press, October 10, 2003. Palm Beach County, "Scripps Florida—Key Messages," at http://www.co.palm-beach.fl.us/

SRI/images/key-messages.pdf, and Scripps Research Institute, "Business Plan for Scripps Florida," December 16, 2003 at http://www.co.palm-beach.fl.us/SRI/BUSINESS_PLAN_010504.pdf.

85. The William S. Lee Act generates tax credits that may be used to offset up to 50 percent of a company's state income and/or franchise tax liability. North Carolina Department of Finance, Commerce Finance Center, http://www.nccommerce.com/finance/incentives/tax/.

86. Terry Hammond, "House OKs Bill to Give Record Tax Breaks to Federal Express Corp. and Nucor Steel," *State Taxes*, July 16, 1998. G. Donald Jud (University of North Carolina at Greensboro, School of Business and Economics), "The Economic Impact of the FedEx Mid-Atlantic Hub on the Piedmont Triad," report for Greensboro Area Chamber of Commerce, April 1998. This report assumed that 1,050 of the 1,500 jobs at FedEx by 2007 would be part-time.

87. Despite the massive subsidy, Dell executives admitted that the real issue was proximity to customers: North Carolina is in the middle of the populous East Coast, and Dell had no production in the region. And the state's Triad area has four interstate highways and Dell moves most of its product by truck. Plus the region has lots of laid-off textile and furniture workers, and a new surge of textile and apparel imports from China starting in 2005 is expected to cause more layoffs in the area. (David Rice, "Dell Picks Triad for New Plant; Company Plans to Hire 700 in First Year," *Winston-Salem Journal*, November 10, 2004.)

88. The Dell deal was rushed through the North Carolina state legislature in a special session that lasted just one day—two days after the November 2004 elections. A Republican state senator proposed a "sunshine" amendment to the deal, a disclosure reform so that taxpayers could see for themselves if Dell is living up to its jobs and production promises. Republicans voted for the sunshine 19 to 1; Democrats voted against 24 to 4. (J. Andrew Curliss, "Dell Takes Offer to Bring Computer Plant, Jobs to Triad; Bill Tried to Open Deal-Makers to Public Accountability," *Raleigh News & Observer*, November 10, 2004.)

89. Press release from North Carolina Governor's Office, "Easley Announces Dell to Locate in Piedmont Triangle," November 9, 2004. "N.C. Should Cheer Dell, But We Must Weigh the Wisdom of Incentive Packages Trend," *Asheville Citizen-Times*, November 10, 2004. Amy Martinez, "Deal Called Unfair Even if Workers Gain," *Raleigh News & Observer*, November 10, 2004. Rice, "Dell Picks Triad for New Plant." Michael Hewlett, "Forsyth, Guilford Get Ready for Dell; City,

County Governments Planning Closed Sessions for Incentives Discussions," *Winston-Salem Journal*, November 11, 2004. "City-county Incentives for Dell Total as Much as $37 Million," Associated Press, December 8, 2004. Jane Seccombe and Victoria Cherrie, "Winston-Salem Wins," *Winston-Salem Journal*, December 23, 2004. The Forsyth County package is especially tragic, since the County's board of commissioners adopted a resolution in 1997 essentially announcing that they wanted to end the use of subsidies by 1999 and would do so if other local governments in the Southeast would do the same. (Gloria Whisenhunt, "Taking a Stand Against the Use of Incentives," *Developments*, September 1, 1998.)

90. Perri Morgan, North Carolina Chapter, National Federation of Independent Business, interview, December 21, 2004. See her analysis of the broader subsidy issue, "The Economic War Between the States: Robbing Families to Enrich Big Business," in *North Carolina Political Review*, February 2004.

91. The quotes in this paragraph were taken from one and usually more of the following news accounts: David Rice, "Dell Pressed to Avoid 20 Years of N.C. Taxes 'Shouldn't You Be Happy with No Revenue?'" *Winston-Salem Journal*, January 19, 2005; Richard M. Barron, "Dell Talks Difficult from Start; The Computer Maker Never Backed Down from Its Initial Demands for Incentives from the State to Locate Here," *Greensboro News & Record*, January 19, 2005; Richard M. Barron and Eric Dyer, "Dell Was Tough from Beginning; Documents Give a Glimpse Inside the Process That Led the Company to the Triad," *Greensboro News & Record*, January 23, 2005. The state records also reportedly revealed that Governor Easley's aides produced widely varied estimates of the deal's effect on state revenues, "from as little as $83 million over 12 years to $886 million over 20 years." The state's final public claim was $743 million. (Associated Press, "Records Show Dell Sought No Taxes for New Plant for 20 Years," January 19, 2005.)

92. Rice, "Dell Pressed to Avoid 20 Years of N.C. Taxes."

93. Richard Locker, "Nashville Wins Dell Computer with Hefty Incentives; Thousands of Jobs Promised," Memphis *Commercial Appeal*, May 7, 1999. West Chester township manager David Gully quoted in Amy Joyner, "Dell Draws Perks from Other Cities: Including North Carolina's Package, Dell Has Landed More Than $429 Million in Incentives Since 1999," *Greensboro News & Record*, November 12, 2004.

94. Richard LeFrak, as quoted in Charles V. Bagli, "Companies Get Second Helping of Tax Breaks," *New York Times*, October 17, 1997.

95. See a database of New York City's retention subsidies at http://www .goodjobsny.org/deals_size.htm.

96. Daniel Gross, "The great state giveaway (Part 1)," *CFO*, January 1996.

97. Release #571-98, "Mayor Giuliani and Governor Pataki Announce Agreement with New York Stock Exchange," December 22, 1998, at http://www.ci.nyc.ny.us/html/om/html/98b/pr571-98.html.

98. Michael Gormley, "Pataki Signs on to Keeping NYSE," Associated Press, December 8, 2000. Charles V. Bagli, "Exchange Considers Move to Trade Center Site," *New York Times*, November 9, 2001.

99. Good Jobs New York research at http://www.goodjobsny.org/nyse _estimates.htm. David Seifman, "$44M Fiasco on Wall St.—City Lost Big on Office Project," *New York Post*, September 19, 2004.

100. Greenwood and Damiani, *Know When to Fold 'Em*.

101. Ibid.

102. Michael Bloomberg, quoted in John Tierney, "The Big City: An Outsider Comes Inside to Run Things," *New York Times*, November 8, 2001.

103. Steve Jordon, "Enron CEO Gave Omaha Black Eye Years Before Firm's Blues: Ken Lay in Omaha," *Omaha World-Herald*, January 22, 2002.

104. Henry J. Cordes, "LB 775: Did It Prime the Pump? Report Questions Economic Incentives," *Omaha World-Herald*, December 28, 1997. ConAgra press release, "ConAgra to solicit location proposals from other states," reproduced in *Omaha World-Herald*, May 15, 1987. Steve Jordon, "Missouri Gets Serious About ConAgra Bid," *Omaha World-Herald*, May 20, 1987. Jordon, "Enron CEO." Dennis Farney, "Nebraska, Hungry for Jobs, Grants Big Business Big Tax Breaks Despite Charges of 'Blackmail,'" *Wall Street Journal*, June 23, 1987.

105. *Lincoln Journal* editorial, "Tax Revolution Completed; Corporate Forces Sweep Field," May 27, 1987.

106. "Major Features of LB 775," *Lincoln Journal*, May 27, 1987. Sen. James D. McFarland, "LB 775 Is Flawed; Revise or Repeal It," *Lincoln Journal*, November 9, 1987. "Firms Not Adding Jobs but Seeking Credits 'Surprises,'" *Omaha World-Herald*, November 2, 1987. "Vard Johnson Supports Incentives for Mutual," *Omaha World-Herald*, October 10, 1987. 2003 Nebraska Department of Revenue Annual Report to the Nebraska Legislature, Summary of LB 775 Benefits Approved Through 12/31/03, Table 2, p. 13.

107. Scott Bauer, "Opponents to LB 775 Say Report Bolsters Their Cause,"

Associated Press, March 17, 2004. $top Big Business $ubsidies: The Committee to Repeal LB 775, "The Case for Repealing LB 775," August 2003.

108. Henry J. Cordes, "LB 775 Report Adds Fuel to Debate; Proponents See the Need for More Incentives; Opponents See Lost Revenue," *Omaha World-Herald*, March 16, 2004.

Chapter Two

1. Hearing Before the Committee on Finance, United States Senate, First Session on the Anticipated Nomination of Paul O'Neill to be Secretary of the Treasury, January 17, 2001, available online at http://www .senate.gov/~finance/SFINANC2.pdf, p. 26.

2. Roger W. Schmenner, "How Corporations Select Communities for New Manufacturing Plants," in "The Economics of Firm Size, Market Structure and Social Performance," Proceedings of a Conference Sponsored by the Bureau of Economics, Federal Trade Commission, July 1980, pp. 185–189.

3. Robert Ady, "Discussion," *New England Economic Review*, March/ April 1997, p. 77.

4. For an overview of alternatives to giveaways, see William Schweke et al., *Improving Your Business Climate: A Guide to Smarter Public Investments in Economic Development*, Corporation for Enterprise Development, 1996.

5. U.S. Department of Labor, "Union Members in 2003," release dated January 21, 2004, at http://www.bls.gov/news.release/union2.nr0.htm.

6. William H. Whyte, cited by Alan Farnham, "The Migratory Habits of the 500," *Fortune*, April 24, 1989.

7. William Fulton, "Growing Pangs," *Governing*, December 2001, p. 62. The company's headquarters remained in Dallas after it was acquired in 2004 by Federal Express.

8. Ady, "Discussion," pp. 78–79.

9. Bruce Maus, Corporate Real Estate, Inc., presentation to "Reining in the Competition for Capital" conference, Humphrey Institute of Public Affairs, University of Minnesota, February 27, 2004.

10. Ady, "Discussion," p. 79.

11. Robert G. Lynch, *Rethinking Growth Strategies: How State and Local Taxes and Services Affect Economic Development*, Economic Policy Institute, 2004. Analysis of the Internal Revenue Service's *Statistics on Income Bulletin*, Spring 2003.

12. Schmenner (p. 200) makes a convincing case for the value of speed over subsidies. For a $10 million plant, he estimates that a six-month delay in the construction of a road or sewer line would cost the company $2.5 million, almost three times the value of a five-year property tax abatement.

13. Dennis J. Donovan, "Trade Secrets Revealed: An Insider's Look at Incentives Negotiations," *Expansion Management* "Incentives 1999" issue, pp. 39–43.

14. According to the *Stanford Encyclopedia of Philosophy,* using the example of a shrewd prosecutor talking to two separated bank robbers: "The 'dilemma' faced by the prisoners here is that, whatever the other does, each is better off confessing than remaining silent. But the outcome obtained when both confess is worse for each than the outcome they would have obtained had both remained silent." ("Prisoners' Dilemma" definition at http://plato.stanford.edu/entries/prisoner-dilemma/.)

15. Stanley Holmes, "Behind Boeing's Sweet 7E7 Deal," *Business Week*, March 18, 2004.

16. Jay Hancock, "Ethics Officials Look at Consultant Fees Tied to Tax Breaks; Pay Linked to Deals As Corporations Move," *Baltimore Sun*, October 29, 1999. Maus, Corporate Real Estate.

17. Bruce Maus, Corporate Real Estate, Inc., January 11, 2004 correspondence.

18. Michael Wasylenko, "Taxation and Economic Development: The State of the Economic Literature," *New England Economic Review* (Federal Reserve Bank of Boston), March/April 1997, available at http://www.bos.frb.org/economic/neer/neer1997/neer297c.pdf.

19. Peter Fisher and Elaine Ditsler, "Taxes and State Economic Growth: The Myths and the Reality," Iowa Policy Project, May 2003.

20. See, for example, Wasylenko, "Taxation and Economic Development."

21. Cecil Andrus, *Politics Western Style* (Seattle: Sasquatch Books, 1998), pp. 22–23.

22. Sara Hinkley and Fiona Hsu, *Minding the Candy Store: State Audits of Economic Development*, Good Jobs First, September 2000, p. 37.

23. Ibid, pp. 43–45. Jeffrey Krasner, "Tax Credits May Violate Vermont Policy," *Wall Street Journal*, September 20, 2000.

24. Elizabeth M. Ready, Vermont State Auditor, "Payoffs and Layoffs: The High Cost of Business Subsidies. A Compliance Audit of the Vermont Economic Advancement Tax Incentives Program, administered by the Vermont Economic Progress Council and the Vermont Tax Department," December 30, 2004.

25. L. A. Lorek, "San Antonio Offered Firm Lowest Incentives," *San Antonio Express News*, February 6, 2003.

26. Toyota executive Dennis Cuneo as quoted in Lorek, "San Antonio Offered Firm Lowest Incentives."

27. Tony Mitchell, spokesman for American Express, as quoted in *Newsday*, June 3, 2002.

28. Clayton Bellamy, "Citgo to Move Headquarters to Houston," Associated Press, April 26, 2004.

29. "Though Incentives Lower, Virginia Lands AOL Facility That Rejected Georgia," *Site Selection Online Insider*, May 1999.

30. Location Management Services, "Location Management Services Announces Web-Based Incentives Management Tool," press release dated January 31, 2003.

31. James Renzas, "Incentives Unrealized: How Companies Are Leaving Millions of Dollars on the Table and What You Can Do," *Corporate Real Estate Leader*, July 2004, pp. 26–28.

32. Local Management Services website at http://www.locationmgmt .com, as accessed September, 2004.

33. Jack Scis, "Consultant Claims Use of Incentives Should Be Stopped," *Greensboro* (North Carolina) *News & Record*, April 24, 1995.

34. Cabela's Initial Public Offering prospectus, Securities and Exchange Commission, Form S-1, 2004, pp. 3, 44.

35. Cabela's quotes and facts from its Initial Public Offering prospectus, Securities and Exchange Commission, Form S-1, 2004, p. 59.

36. Ibid., p. 44, F-10.

37. Ibid., p. 15.

38. Sam Kennedy, "Have Cabela's Tax Breaks Paid Off? No One Can Say Since State Does Not Verify Claims That Any Business Makes About Creating Jobs and Revenue," *Morning Call*, October 17, 2004.

39. Ibid.

40. Ibid.

41. Cabela's IPO prospectus, p. 63.

Chapter Three

1. David Treadwell, Associated Press, February 2, 1977.

2. Jay Hancock, "Ban on Site-Consultant Deals May Return to Haunt State," *Baltimore Sun*, December 19, 2001.

3. Robert E. Bedingfield, "Personality: Sleuth in Search of Plant Sites," *New York Times*, January 24, 1960. Reginald Stuart, "Busy Times for a

Corporate Mover," *New York Times*, June 24, 1977. Associated Press obituary of Leonard Yaseen, "Former Fantus Co. Executive, Realty Consultant to New York," *Chicago Tribune*, October 10, 1989.

4. Fantus Co. press release dated April 17, 1985, announcing the promotion of Norton L. Berman.

5. As detailed in the text that follows, after Fantus performed a "business climate" study in 1975, the accounting firm later known as Grant Thornton issued subsequent studies.

6. This section draws upon Cobb, *The Selling of the South*, chapters 1 and 2.

7. James C. Cobb, *The Selling of the South: The Southern Crusade for Industrial Development, 1936–1960*, pp. 6–9.

8. White proposed the Act after much careful legal work, because the state's constitution, like many others, included prohibitions against public monies aiding private firms or individuals. The state's supreme court had even struck down a local bond deal for a garment plant a few years before. Besides drawing on New Deal rhetoric, White's bill drafters found a U.S. Supreme Court precedent: a decision upholding North Dakota's system of state-sponsored banks, grain elevators, and warehouses. Creating employment was a legitimate way to serve the general welfare, North Dakota had successfully argued. Ibid., pp. 13–14.

9. Ibid., p. 42.

10. Ibid., p. 40.

11. Ibid., p. 63.

12. Ibid., p. 58.

13. Liz Roman Gallese, "Bucking the Trend: A New England Town Stops a Big Employer from Moving South," *Wall Street Journal*, January 9, 1978.

14. Douglas Sease, "Yankee Go Home? Many Northern Firms Seeking Sites in South Get Chilly Reception," *Wall Street Journal*, February 10, 1978, pp. 1, 29.

15. Bedingfield, "Personality," p. F3.

16. John H. Wilford, "One Firm's Dual Aim: Areas for Factories, Factories for Areas," *Wall Street Journal*, December 19, 1956, p. 1.

17. Fantus Company, "Building Illinois: A Five-Year Strategic Plan for the Development of the Illinois Economy," report for the Illinois Department of Commerce and Community Affairs, August 1986, p. 24.

18. Christopher Swope, "Site Seers," *Governing*, November 2001. "After Helping Firms Go, Fantus Lures Them Back," *Wall Street Journal*, October 4, 1977, p. 25. Another concern about such studies is that they

may be "cookie-cutter" products that are recycled by consultants from state to state. The president of the National Association of State Development Agencies spoke in 2004 of an unnamed consultant who delivered a $400,000 study to a state—but forgot to change the name of the client state from a previous job. (Miles Friedman, workshop presentation, National Conference of State Legislatures, July 20, 2004.)

19. Christopher Swope, "Site Seers," *Governing*, November 2001. An angry Philadelphia booster told the *Wall Street Journal* in 1977, "If you don't hire Fantus, you're more likely to get an unfavorable review" in one of its studies. ("After Helping Firms Go, Fantus Lures Them Back," *Wall Street Journal*, October 4, 1977.)

20. "Labor Letter," *Wall Street Journal*, January 30, 1968.

21. Prince M. Carlisle, "Plant Moves Go On Despite Wage Law," *New York Times*, March 26, 1939. Associated Press, "Shift of Vital Defense Plants to Rural Sections Is Noted," *Washington Post*, September 4, 1940. "City Losing Many of Defense Plants," *New York Times*, September 6, 1940. "Lag Seen in Efforts to Disperse Industry," *New York Times*, January 2, 1952. "Policy Is Assailed on Tax Write-Offs," *New York Times*, December 15, 1953, p. 69.

22. Alfred L. Malabre, Jr., "Factories in Flight: More Companies Build Plants in Rural Areas as Cost-Cutting Move," *Wall Street Journal*, September 7, 1962, p. 1.

23. Carlisle, "Plant Moves Go On Despite Wage Law." Reginald Stuart, "Moving-Out Expert Takes City to Task," *New York Times*, August 3, 1974.

24. Vartanig V. Vartan, "Consultant Says He Is Making Studies of Other Areas," *New York Times*, February 17, 1967, p. 37. Alfred L. Malabre, Jr., "New York City: The Crux of the Crisis," *Wall Street Journal*, November 1, 1965. "Labor Letter," *Wall Street Journal*, January 30, 1968.

25. Joseph B. Treaster, "Company That Finds Plant Sites Moving Headquarters from City," *New York Times*, December 16, 1969, p. 51. "Varied Urban Decay Cited by Relocator Who Moved," *Wall Street Journal*, November 10, 1970, p. 8. After leaving New York, the Fantus Company resided in at least three New Jersey jurisdictions: South Orange, Millburn, and Princeton. However, Yaseen apparently maintained his own office in Manhattan until he retired. In 2000, four years after Fantus was acquired by Deloitte & Touche, its New York–area office was relocated back in New York City, where it could be more integral

to the parent company's corporate real estate practice. The Fantus headquarters remained in Chicago. ("Relocation Strategist Comes Full Circle: Fantus Moves Back to New York," *Site Selection*, May 2000, p. 514.)

26. Reginald Stuart, "Moving-Out Expert Takes City to Task," *New York Times*, August 3, 1974, p. 29. See also Yaseen's advocacy of clearing industrial slums in "City Urged to End Industrial Slums," *New York Times*, February 27, 1966.

27. "Former Archenemy of New York City Gets $280,000 Job," *Wall Street Journal*, June 10, 1977, p. 10. A copy of the study could not be obtained, but in his 1979 book *The Last Entrepreneurs* Robert Goodman describes its recommendations. The Fantus study called for a non-profit, quasi-public corporation with the power to research, lobby for, and dispense subsidies, with an appointed board composed of at least two-thirds businesspeople. It would have the "ability to make direct loans to private business, share in ownership and risk, issue bonds, and buy, sell, or lease property without cumbersome public hearings or approvals." Economic development corporations "are insulated more politically than city departments. Elected officials are not as directly responsible for an EDC as they are for a city department." In other words, Fantus's solution was more corporate control and less public accountability. (Robert Goodman, *The Last Entrepreneurs: America's Regional Wars for Jobs and Dollars* [New York: Simon and Schuster, 1979], pp. 19–20.)

28. "After Helping Firms Go, Fantus Lures Them Back," *Wall Street Journal*, October 4, 1977, p. 25. "To Sink Roots or Pull Up Stakes?" *Chemical Week*, August 1, 1979, p. 37. David Treadwell, Associated Press, untitled dispatch, January 26, 1977. "Is the Sunbelt Getting a Little Chilly?" *Industry Week*, September 7, 1981.

29. "The Second War Between the States," *Business Week*, May 17, 1976, p. 92. Gurney Breckenfeld, "Business Loves the Sunbelt (and Vice Versa)," *Fortune*, June 1977. Rochelle L. Stanfield, "Civil War over Cities' Aid— The Battle No One Expected," *National Journal*, August 1977.

30. John M. Winton, "Plant Sites 1977: It's North's Move," *Chemical Week*, November 10, 1976.

31. Ibid. The Fantus/IMA study is also described by Goodman, *Last Entrepreneurs*, pp. 20–21.

32. Jerry Hagstrom and Robert Guskind, "Playing the State Ranking Game—New National Pastime Catches On," *National Journal*, June 30, 1984.

33. See, for example, Alexander Grant & Company, "The Sixth Annual Study of General Manufacturing Climates of the Forty-Eight Contiguous States of America," Chicago, June 1985.

34. Jerry Hagstrom and Robert Guskind, "Playing the State Ranking Game—A New National Pastime Catches On," *National Journal,* June 30, 1984, p. 1268. Fantus Company, "Assessing Illinois' Strengths and Weaknesses in a Changing National Economy," report for the Illinois Department of Commerce and Community Affairs, August 1986. See also Charles F. Harding of Fantus, "Business Climate Studies: How Useful Are They?" *Industrial Development,* January/February 1983.

35. The Corporation for Enterprise Development et al., *Taken for Granted: How Grant Thornton's Business Climate Index Leads States Astray,* November 1986.

36. Corporation for Enterprise Development et al., *Taken for Granted,* p. 87. Today, there are many competing business climate surveys issued annually; for a sample list, go to http://www.dc-intl.com/RCRatingsGame .cfm.

37. Richard Florida, *The Rise of the Creative Class: And How It's Transforming Work, Leisure, Community and Everyday Life* (New York: Basic Books, 2002).

38. Keon Chi, "The States and Business Incentives: An Inventory of Tax and Financial Incentives," Council of State Governments, 1989.

39. Fantus went through four sets of ownership, and along the way, many of its staff left to work for competitors. Yaseen and his fellow partners sold the firm to Dun & Bradstreet in 1967. According to longtime Fantus executive Robert Ady, its next two owners neglected a valuable asset. D&B clumsily tried to merge Fantus with two unrelated firms it had acquired and then took a hands-off approach. PHH Corporation bought Fantus in 1983, hoping to create synergy with its corporate employee relocation business. But PHH did transactions, not consulting, and the benefits did not appear. In the early 1990s, PHH tried to remold Fantus into a general-purpose management consultancy, ignoring its unique value. When that experiment failed, neglect followed, causing many Fantus staffers to leave and strengthening its competitors. PHH auctioned Fantus in 1996, and Deloitte & Touche, which had a modest site selection practice based in Chicago that included some former Fantus staffers, bought it. (Robert Ady, "On Being Acquired," *Journal of Management Consulting,* May 1997, pp. 16–20.)

40. Many sources speak to the industry's fragmentation. See, for example, "Meet the Gurus of Site Selection," *Corporate Location*, March/April 2001.

41. For a website with links to numerous site location consultants, go to http://www.gdi-solutions.com/profsvcs/lists/location_consultants.htm.

42. Ibid. There are also several site location trade magazines; they often blur the lines between infomercials and journalism. *Site Selection* magazine is perhaps the best-known; it issues the annual Governor's Cup Award for the state that announces the most big deals; it also issues an annual business climate ranking based on a blend of data about new facilities and an opinion survey of executives. The magazine also publishes perhaps the most useful publicly available annual listing of state subsidy programs. *Site Selection*'s parent, Conway Data, Inc., has a partnership with the International Economic Development Council, the largest professional association of public and private-sector economic developers (http://www.developmentalliance.com), that exemplifies the explosion of web-based data about locations. *Expansion Management* rates education (2,800 secondary school districts). *Area Development* publishes various surveys, including an annual site selection corporate survey and an annual inventory of incentives. *Plants Sites & Parks* offers fairly substantial journalistic content and also conducts an annual survey, which is a blend of quantitative measures and executives' picks. *Business Facilities* seems to focus more on the nitty-gritty aspects of managing a business when it moves or expands, not just location-choice issues. *Corporate Location* concentrates on European and other international areas.

43. Rhett L. Weiss, "Doing a Deal in the U.S.: Incentives and the Project Negotiation Process," Dealtek website, http://www.dealtek.com/DEALZone/articles/article1.html.

44. "Economic Development Credits and Incentives Bright Idea," Grant Thornton website, http://www.grantthornton.com/content/92346.asp.

45. Tammy Propst, "Are You Missing Out on the Full Benefits of Economic Incentives and Tax Credits?" *Business Facilities*, January 2004.

46. Jay Biggins, "Incentives Owner's Manual," presentation dated June 10, 2003, on Stadtmauer Bailkin Biggins website, http://www.sbb-incentives.com/IncentivesOwnersManual.pps.

47. Christopher Swope, "Site Seers," *Governing*, November 2001.

48. Mintax website, http://www.mintax.com/services/statetax.html and http://www.mintax.com/difference/index.html.

49. Raymond R. Neville, Mintax, Inc., "Retroactive Incentives: It's Christmas All Over Again," *Expansion Management,* January 1999, p. 10.

50. Raymond R. Neville, "Unearthing Secrets from the Incentives Playbook," *Expansion Management,* Ratings 1999, p. 8.

51. Moran, Stahl & Boyer website, http://www.msbconsulting.com/.

52. Stanley Holmes, "Behind Boeing's Sweet 7E7 Deal," *Business Week,* March 18, 2004.

53. David Bowermaster, "State paid $715,000 to Consultants to Aid with 7E7 Bid," *Seattle Times,* January 31, 2004. Holmes, "Behind Boeing's Sweet 7E7 Deal." Rick Anderson, "The State's Two-Timing Consultant," *Seattle Weekly,* March 17, 2004, p. 11. Rick Anderson, "Disinterest in Conflict," *Seattle Weekly,* March 24, 2004.

54. Anderson, "Disinterest in Conflict."

55. "Turning Your State Government Relations Department from a Money Pit into a Cash Cow," PowerPoint presentation delivered to seminar at State Government Affairs Council annual meeting, March 26, 2004, Savannah Georgia. See the PowerPoint itself at http://www .carolinajournal.com/upload/ and choose either "cost_savannah" option. Paul Chesser, "On Milking a State's 'Cash Cow': Ernst & Young Advises Businesses on How to Maximize Subsidies from State Governments," *Carolina Journal,* May 20, 2004 at http://wwwcarolinajournal .com/exclusives/display_exclusive.html?id=1554.

56. "Turning Your State Government Relations Department from a Money Pit into a Cash Cow."

57. Chesser, "On Milking a State's 'Cash Cow.'"

58. International Economic Development Council, 2004 annual meeting, St. Louis, September 22, 2004.

59. Ibid.

Chapter Four

1. About 20 more states have given sales a double weighting, so their formulas are 50 percent based on sales and 25 percent each on property and payroll. A few more states have superweighted sales to as much as 80 percent.

2. Robert Gavin, "As States Cut Corporate Taxes, Incentives Lose Their Advantage," *Wall Street Journal,* February 14, 2001.

3. Michael Mazerov, Center for Budget and Policy Priorities, December 29, 2004 calculation.

4. Dan Rodricks, "A 'Teachable Moment' in Corporate Taxes World," *Baltimore Sun*, February 15, 2002.

5. Michael Mazerov, "The 'Single Sales Factor' Formula for State Corporate Taxes: A Boon to Economic Development or a Costly Giveaway?" Center on Budget and Policy Priorities, September 2001. Daniel Hassell, Pennsylvania Department of Revenue, "The Revenue Effects of a Single Sales Factor Apportionment Formula on the Pennsylvania Corporate Net Income Tax." Paper to the Federation of Tax Administrators Revenue Estimation and Tax Research Conference, September 21, 2004.

6. Hassell, "Revenue Effects."

7. Ibid.

8. Ibid.

9. Mazerov, "The 'Single Sales Factor' Formula."

10. Mary E. Forsberg, "Single Factor: Double Trouble," New Jersey Policy Perspective, 2001.

11. Daniel Gross, "There's No Place Like Home: How Companies Are Cashing In by Staying Put," *CFO*, January 1996, pp. 25–26.

12. William J. Donovan, "Fidelity Reportedly Is Eying Providence," *Providence Journal*, April 15, 1995. "RI Enacts Budget with Cigarette, Bank, and Nursing Home Tax Increases," *State Tax Notes*, August 9, 1995. "Fidelity Looks at RI," *Boston Globe*, August 15, 1995. Jeffrey Krasner, "Fidelity Shifting 2,500 Jobs to R.I.," *Boston Herald*, December 12, 1995.

13. Kimberly Blanton, "Fidelity Considers Expanding in N.H.," *Boston Globe*, October 6, 1995. Richard Kindleberger and Tina Cassidy, "Fidelity Reportedly Expanding; Mutual Fund Giant Eyes N.H., R.I. Sites," *Boston Globe*, December 12, 1995. Jerry Ackerman and Tina Cassidy, "Fidelity Cites Need for State Tax Relief," *Boston Globe*, December 13, 1995. Scott MacKay and Jeffrey Hiday, "Mutual Fund Giant Picks Site in Smithfield," *Providence Journal*, December 13, 1995. Marie Gendron, "Fidelity Move to R.I. Sparks Debate over Bay State's Corporate Tax Policy," *Boston Herald*, December 13, 1995. Jeffrey Hiday, "Mass. Tax Cut Won't Change Fidelity Plan," *Providence Journal*, December 15, 1995. Jordon Rau, "Fidelity Center Could Employ Thousands," *Concord Monitor*, December 13, 1995.

14. Alex Pham, "Fund Firms Push for Tax Cuts; Unveil Study Saying Losses Would Be Offset by Growth," *Boston Globe*, April 26, 1996. Massachusetts Business Roundtable press release, "Study Highlights

Mutual Fund Industry's Pivotal Role in State Economy," April 25, 1996. Jerry Ackerman, "Mutual Funds Take to Beacon Hill in Push for Tax Relief," *Boston Globe*, May 15, 1996.

15. Phil Primack, "Changes Likely for Pending Tax Break Bill," *Boston Herald*, April 26, 1996.

16. Howard Merkowitz, "The Single Sales Factor in Massachusetts," Office of Tax Policy Analysis, Massachusetts Department of Revenue, September 21, 2004 presentation to Federation of Tax Administrators. Beth Healy, "Fidelity Lays Off 760 Workers to Cut Costs," *Boston Globe*, October 31, 2001. Beth Healy, "Fund Giant Fidelity Set to Eliminate 1,695 Jobs," *Boston Globe*, October 1, 2002. "100 Fidelity Jobs Sent to R.I. Raises Questions," *Boston Business Journal*, January 30, 2004. Andrew Caffrey, "Fidelity Transferring Jobs out of Boston," *Boston Globe*, January 22, 2004. Cosmo Macero, Jr., "Fidelity's 'List' Moves Rumor Mill," *Boston Herald*, April 21, 2004.

17. Saritha Rai, "Financial Firms Hasten Their Move to Outsourcing," *New York Times*, August 18, 2004. Carol E. Curtis, "In Offshore Outsourcing, Firms Move Well Beyond Processing: Morgan, Fidelity Leading the Charge in Shifting the Front Office Across Borders," *Securities Industry News*, May 31, 2004.

18. DRI/McGraw-Hill had high credibility with legislators because it had accurately forecast the state's tax revenue in prior years. (State Representative James Marzilli, interview, June 18, 2004.)

19. DRI/McGraw-Hill.

20. Massachusetts Department of Revenue, "Single Sales Factor Tax Cut Summary" (updated June 2003 and subsequently). These figures do not include any spending estimates, which were lumped into the DRI/McGraw Hill numbers. Nor are personal income tax effects estimated. Since the state has lost defense jobs, it has presumably spent additional sums helping the dislocated workers and has lost revenue based on their declining personal incomes. On the other hand, the state has gained mutual fund jobs and revenue from those incomes.

21. Massachusetts Budget and Policy Center, "Tax Expenditures and Economic Development," April 2004 at http://www.massbudget.org/econdev.pdf. This includes both directly enacted state tax credits and the effect of coupling to the federal tax code.

22. Alyssa Na'im and Nancy Wagman, "Real Cuts—Real People—Real Pain: The Effects of the Fiscal Crisis on Women and Girls in Massachusetts," Massachusetts Budget and Policy Center, December 2004,

pp. 35 and 53, at http://www.massbudget.org/article.php?id=266. Andrew Reschovsky, "Mass. Fiscal Crises Hit Education Hard," *Boston Globe* op-ed article, January 31, 2004.

23. This section is based on Jeff McCourt and Greg LeRoy, *A Better Deal for Illinois: Improving Economic Development Policy*, Good Jobs First, January 2003. It also reflects updated data from state revenue and dislocated worker sources.

24. Illinois Department of Revenue, "Senate Bill 1305, Single Sales Factor: Oppose," 1997.

25. McCourt and LeRoy, *A Better Deal for Illinois*. The layoff figure reflects updated data from the Illinois Department of Commerce and Economic Opportunity WARN Act website, http://www.illinoisbiz.biz/wia2/warn/warn.html.

26. Austan Goolsbee and Edward L. Maydew, "The Economic Impact of Single Sales Factor Apportionment in the State of Illinois: Job Creation and Tax Revenue," funded by the Illinois Manufacturers' Association, December 1996.

27. Christi Parsons and Ray Long, "Corporations in Line for Big State Tax Break; Supporters Say Effect Will Trickle Down to All," *Chicago Tribune*, May 25, 1998. McCourt and LeRoy, *A Better Deal for Illinois*, p. 23.

28. U.S. Bureau of Labor Statistics. The two economists have since issued two more papers revising their methodology. Their third stab, if applied to Illinois, would still have predicted job gains—but 78 percent fewer. (Mazerov, "The 'Singles Sales Factor' Formula.")

29. Goolsbee and Maydew, "Economic Impact in the State of Illinois."

30. McCourt and LeRoy, *A Better Deal for Illinois*, p. 24. FY2005 Illinois Budget Book, p. 19, Office of Management and Budget, Illinois Governor's Office.

31. McCourt and LeRoy, *A Better Deal for Illinois*, p. 27.

32. Georgia House Bill 1353, 144th General Assembly, 1997–1998 Regular Session, signed by the governor on February 17, 1998. This section is based upon dozens of articles from 2001–2002, most of them by Karen Setze of *State Tax Notes* and especially Meredith Jordan of the *Atlanta Business Chronicle*. For her terrific work, Jordan was awarded two "Best in Business" awards by the Society of American Business Editors and Writers, Inc.

33. Charles Walston, "Business Tax Plan Goes to Governor; Supporters Say the Bill Could Pave the Way for General Electric to Move Jobs

from New York to Cobb County," *Atlanta Journal and Constitution*, February 17, 1998. Karen Setze, "AG: Special Corporate Tax Breaks Should Stay Secret," *State Tax Notes*, August 13, 2001, p. 466. Meredith Jordan, "Georgia's Corporate Tax Giveaway," *Atlanta Business Chronicle*, September 28, 2001.

34. House Bill 1434, 146th General Assembly, 2001–2002 Regular Session, signed by governor April 11, 2002. Meredith Jordan, "Secret Tax Breaks: Four Officials Decide," *Atlanta Business Chronicle*, October 12, 2001. Meredith Jordan, "State Definds [sic] Secret Tax Breaks," *Atlanta Business Chronicle*, October 26, 2001. "Governor's Chief of Staff Calls Republican Legislators 'Sluts,'" Associated Press, October 30, 2001. Meredith Jordan, "GE Power Confirms It Received Tax Break from State," *Atlanta Business Chronicle*, November 16, 2001. Karen Setze, "Lawmakers Vote to Make Special Tax Deals Public," *State Tax Notes*, April 8, 2002, p. 99. Meredith Jordan, "State Reveals Companies That Got Tax Breaks," *Atlanta Business Chronicle*, May 3, 2002.

35. Meredith Jordan, "Ga. Not Getting Jobs It's Paying For," *Atlanta Business Chronicle*, May 31, 2002. Meredith Jordan and Jim Lovel, "Alltel Will Pay State $11 Million," *Atlanta Business Chronicle*, August 9, 2002.

36. The actual drafting of the model law was performed by University of Michigan Law School Professor William J. Pierce and his students. (Eugene Corrigan, December 9, 2004 correspondence.)

37. UDITPA's three factor formula is, of course, more complicated than as I summarize it here. It exempts banks and utilities, for example. It allows states to directly claim income from in-state rents and capital gains. It even allows companies to appeal their tax bill if the three factors do not fairly reflect their business. And it does not try to tell states how to define their tax base; that is, how to define taxable income, or at what rate to tax it. But for the big issue of how to divvy up, or apportion, all other corporate income for a multistate company, it was a major breakthrough. For the text with accompanying commentary, see "Uniform Division of Income for Tax Purposes Act," drafted by the National Conference of Commissioners on Uniform State Laws and approved at its annual conference, New York, July 8–13, 1957. For additional contemporary interpretation of UDITPA, see also William J. Pierce, "The Uniform Division of Income for State Tax Purposes" in *Taxes*, Vol. 35, No. 10, p. 747 (1957). The MTC's founding executive director, Eugene Corrigan, also points out that adherence to UDITPA's

rules was also critical to making taxation uniform (correspondence, December 9, 2004).

38. Transcript of Proceedings in Committee of the Whole, Uniform Allocation and Apportionment Act, Wednesday, August 22, 1956.

39. *Northwestern States Portland Cement Co. v. Minnesota*, 358 U.S. 450 (U.S., 1959).

40. 15 USCS §§ 381–384.

41. This and other MTC history from Eugene Corrigan, executive director of the Multistate Tax Commission from 1969 to 1987, interview November 4, 2004.

42. Eugene Corrigan, September 9, 2004 correspondence.

43. *U.S. Steel Corp. v. Multistate Tax Commission*, 434 U.S. 452 (1978).

44. Corrigan interview.

45. The *U.S. Steel* case and other attacks on the MTC are recounted by its first executive director, Eugene Corrigan, in the MTC's March 1989 newsletter, *Review*, in a farewell column after his twenty years of work. He concluded: "The increased concern for fairness is a legacy I hope will characterize the MTC and its participating personnel throughout its existence."

46. See COST's account of its history at http://www.statetax.org/template .cfm?Section=About_COST.

47. Corrigan interview.

48. Corrigan interview and correspondence.

49. Corrigan correspondence, December 9, 2004.

50. *Container Corp. v. Franchise Tax Bd.*, 463 U.S. 159 (1983).

51. Corrigan interview. Michael Mazerov interview, November 23, 2004. See also, for example, David Freud and Christian Tyler, "Mr. Reagan's Taxing Problem," *Financial Times*, November 1, 1983, which reported that in Florida "more than 100 businessmen have now written to the governor saying they will drop plans to build plants in the state if the unitary tax system goes ahead." California Business Council, untitled press release of February 26, 1985. Donald H. May, untitled article, United Press International, March 31, 1984. Diane Kiesel, "Tax Wars; Unitary Tax Bite Felt Abroad," *ABA Journal*, June 1984.

52. COST website Meetings and Events page, http://www.statetax.org/ Content/NavigationMenu/Meetings_and_Events/Meetings_and_Events .htm. Joseph R. Crosby, COST Legislative Director, testimony before State of Vermont Ways and Means Committee, March 25, 2004, online

at http://www.statetax.org/Template.cfm?Section=By_State3&template=/ContentManagement/ContentDisplay.cfm&ContentID=5415.

53. Michael Mazerov, "Proposed 'Business Activity Tax Nexus' Legislation Would Seriously Undermine State Taxes on Corporate Profits and Harm the Economy," Center on Budget and Policy Priorities, October 4, 2004, p. 2.

54. MTC Chair Elizabeth Harchenko, as quoted in Mazerov, "Should New Limits on State Corporate Profits Taxes Be a Quid Pro Quo for the States' Ability to Tax Internet Sales? The 'Business Activity Tax Nexus' Issue," Center for Budget and Policy Priorities, September 4, 2001, p. 7.

55. Mazerov, "Proposed 'Business Activity Tax Nexus' Legislation."

56. These discussions derive from Mazerov, "Closing Three Common Corporate Income Tax Loopholes."

57. Technically, Massachusetts has a throwback rule, but it is written in an unusual way that makes it easy for companies to avoid. Mazerov, "Closing Three Common Corporate Income Tax Loopholes."

58. Glenn R. Simpson, "A Tax Maneuver in Delaware Puts Squeeze on Other States," *Wall Street Journal*, August 9, 2002.

59. Maryland and New York have enacted the safeguard since Mazerov's article was published. Five states have no corporate income tax.

60. Multistate Tax Commission, "Corporate Tax Sheltering and the Impact on State Corporate Income Tax Revenue Collections," July 15, 2003.

61. "FTA Roundtable Debates Viability of Corporate Income Tax," *State Tax Notes*, June 10, 2002, p. 1007. "The Swiss Cheese Tax System?" *State Tax Notes*, June 14, 1999, p. 1927.

Chapter Five

1. Robert Ady, "Discussion," *New England Economic Review*, March/April 1997, p. 77.

2. Edward Muir and Krista Schneider, "State Initiatives and Referenda on Bonds: A Comparative Analysis of One Solution for the School Infrastructure Crisis," *Journal of Education Finance*, Vol. 24, No. 4. (1999), pp. 415–433.

3. Andy Gammill, "Tax Abatements Often Fail to Generate Jobs; Allen Governments Have Never Rescinded Breaks," *Fort Wayne Journal Gazette*, July 20, 2003.

4. Sherri Buri McDonald, "Big Property Tax Waivers Yield Patchy Returns in Lane County," *(Eugene) Register Guard*, August 11, 2003.

5. *Houston Business Journal,* "Editorial: Taxpayers Get Break As Abatements Drop," June 1, 2001.

6. Zack Nauth, *The Great Louisiana Tax Giveaway,* Louisiana Coalition for Tax Justice, n.d. [1992]. The OSHA Accident Investigation Summary of the Shell fatalities is at http://www.osha.gov/pls/imis/establishment.inspection_detail?id=100478866.

7. Greg LeRoy, "No More Candy Store: States and Cities Making Job Subsidies Accountable," Federation for Industrial Retention and Renewal, 1994, pp. 99–100.

8. *Protecting Public Education from Tax Giveaways to Corporations,* National Education Association, January 2003, pp. 19–22. Doug Oplinger and Dennis J. Willard, "Business Breaks Costing Schools; Ohio Districts Lose as Much as $115 Million to Tax Abatement Deals," *Akron Beacon Journal,* April 10, 2002.

9. Oplinger and Willard, "Business breaks costing schools."

10. Robert Tomsho, "Heavy Tax Abatements Keep Firms in Toledo but Drain Education Coffers," *Wall Street Journal,* July 18, 2001. Ohio Department of Education statistics for 2002–2003 academic year; Toledo graduated 70.4 percent of its students. Ignazio Messinia, "Ohio's School Report Cards: Toledo Leads Parade of Improving Districts," *Toledo Blade,* August 25, 2004.

11. Dan Monk and Lucy May, "Corporate Tax Breaks Sting City," *Cincinnati Business Courier,* August 17, 2001.

12. *Protecting Public Education,* p. 21.

13. Illinois Tax Increment Association FAQs at http://www.illinois-tif.com/faqs.htm. For analyses of Chicago's TIF districts, see the work of the Neighborhood Capital Budget Group at http://www.ncbg.org, especially "TIF Almanac," "Who Pays for the Only Game in Town?" and "The Chicago TIF Encyclopedia."

14. Trine Tsouderos and Crystal Yednak, "TIF Payoffs Recede for Schools; Towns Seek More Time on Tax Deals," *Chicago Tribune,* May 24, 2004.

15. "Who Pays for the Only Game in Town?" Neighborhood Capital Budget Group, Chicago, 2002.

16. Tsouderos and Yednak, "TIF Payoffs Recede for Schools."

17. Edward D. Murphy, "Group Sees Loophole in Tax Break," *Portland Press Herald,* February 16, 2001. Maine Citizen Leadership Fund, "Making BETR Better," April 3, 2003. "Top Estimated 2001 Double

Dippers," n.d. Press releases on double-dipping, February 15, 2001 and April 3, 2003.

18. Jay Hancock, "S.C. Pays Dearly for Added Jobs," *Baltimore Sun*, October 12, 1999.

19. Douglas P. Woodward et al., "Education and Economic Development in South Carolina," *Business & Economic Review*, Vol. 46, No. 4 (Moore School of Business, University of South Carolina) at http://research .moore.sc.edu/Publications/B&EReview/B&E46/BE46q4/devel.htm.

20. South Carolina Commerce Department website at http://www.teamsc .com/workforce.html. National Highway Traffic Safety Administration, *Traffic Facts 2003 Early Edition*, October 2004; available online at http://www-nrd.nhtsa.dot.gov/pdf/nrd-30/NCSA/TSFAnn/2003/ tbl108.htm. National Vital Statistics Reports, "Infant Mortality Statistics from the 2002 Period," Vol. 53, No. 10, November 24, 2004; available online at http://www.cdc.gov/nchs/data/nvsr/nvsr53/nvsr5_10 .pdf. National Center for Education Statistics, http://www.nces.ed .gov/programs/digest/d02/dt136.asp. Washington, DC ranked lower than South Carolina in both measures.

21. Woodward et al.

22. *Protecting Public Education from Tax Giveaways to Corporations*.

23. Ibid. U.S. Bureau of Labor Statistics, Texas Statewide Total Private Sector.

24. Ady, "Discussion."

25. See *Expansion Management* website, http://www.expansionmanagement .com.

26. U.S. Census Bureau, "The Big Payoff: Educational Attainment and Synthetic Estimates of Work-Life Earnings," Special Study P23-210, July 2002; available online at http://www.census.gov/prod/2002pubs/ p23-210.pdf. For a terrific summary of why education is such a good economic development investment, see William Schweke, *Smart Money: Education and Economic Development* (Economic Policy Institute, 2004).

27. Robert G. Lynch, *Rethinking Growth Strategies: How State and Local Taxes and Services Affect Economic Development* (Economic Policy Institute, 2004).

Chapter Six

1. Eileen Weber, "Corporate Subsidies Often Defeat Own Purposes," *St. Paul Pioneer Press*, February 28, 1999, page 19A.

2. For more indicators, see Dolores Hayden, *A Field Guide to Sprawl* (New York: W.W. Norton and Company, 2004).

3. For basic reading on sprawl, start with *American Metropolitics* by Myron Orfield (Washington, DC: The Brookings Institution, 2002); Hayden, *Field Guide;* and the website of Smart Growth America, http://www.smartgrowthamerica.org.

4. American Farmland Trust Fact Sheet at http://farmland.org/steward/factsheet.htm.

5. See, for example, the Trust for Public Land's 2004 election roundup, which found that 75 percent of open space initiatives passed, at http://www.tpl.org/tier3_cd.cfm?content_item_id=17295&folder_id=186, and the Center for Transportation Excellence's 2004 election summary, which found that 80 percent of transit initiatives succeeded, at http://www.smartgrowthamerica.org/vote04roundup.html.

6. William Fulton et al., "Who Sprawls Most? How Growth Patterns Differ Across the U.S.," Brookings Institution, July 2001, at http://www.brookings.edu/dybdocroot/es/urban/publications/fulton.pdf.

7. See, for example, U.S. Department of Transportation Press Release, "Slater Announces Agreement on Advancing Georgia Transportation Projects and New Environmental Measures," January 16, 1998, at http://www.dot.gov/affairs/1998/fhwa0398.htm.

8. Fulton et al., "Who Sprawls Most?"

9. American Lung Association, *Trends in Asthma Morbidity and Mortality,* April 2004, Table 7, at http://www.lungusa.org/site/apps/s/link.asp?c=dvLUK9O0E&b=44168.

10. Barbara A. McCann and Reid Ewing, "Measuring the Health Effects of Sprawl: A National Analysis of Physical Activity, Obesity and Chronic Disease," September 2003, released jointly by Smart Growth America, Surface Transportation Policy Project, *American Journal of Public Health,* and *American Journal of Health Promotion,* at http://www.smartgrowthamerica.org/report/HealthSprawl8.03.pdf.

11. Don Chen, interview, December 22, 2004.

12. Additional evidence supports this finding. An analysis of factory relocations in the Cincinnati area in the early 1970s found that four-fifths move less than twenty miles. (Roger W. Schmenner, "How Corporations Select Communities for New Manufacturing Plants," in "The Economics of Firm Size, Market Structure and Social Performance," Proceedings of a Conference Sponsored by the Bureau of Economics, Federal Trade Commission, July 1980, p. 197.

13. Mark Cassell, *Zoned Out: Distribution and Benefits in Ohio's Enter-prise Zone Program*, Policy Matters Ohio, 2003, at http://www.policy mattersohio.org/enterprise_zones.htm. "Wealthy Benefit Most from Enterprise Zones," *Cleveland Plain Dealer* op-ed, November 10, 2003.

14. Greg LeRoy and Sara Hinkley, "Another Way Sprawl Happens: Eco-nomic Development Subsidies in a Twin Cities Suburb," Good Jobs First, January 2000.

15. Greg LeRoy, "How Economic Development Programs Are Going Awry," *Multinational Monitor*, October 2003, at http://www .multinationalmonitor.org/mm2003/03october/october03corp1.html.

16. Daniel Immergluck and Erin Mullen, *Economic Development Where It's Needed: Directing SBA 504 Lending to Lower-Income Communities*, Wood-stock Institute, June 1997, at http://woodstockinst.org/document/sba .pdf.

17. Friends of the Earth press release, "SBA to Implement New Environ-mental Policies to Settle Conservationists' Lawsuit," March 27, 2003, at http://www.foe.org/new/releases/0303sba.html.

18. Edgar V. Regan, *Government, Inc.: Creating Accountability for Economic Development Programs*, Government Finance Research Center of the Government Finance Officers Association, 1988, pp. 27–28.

19. Chris Lester and Steve Nicely, "Giveaways Set the Stage for a Loss," *Kansas City Star*, December 20, 1995, p. 1.

20. Jeff McCourt and Greg LeRoy, *A Better Deal for Illinois: Improving Economic Development Policy*, Good Jobs First, January 2003, pp. 38–43.

21. Illinois Tax Increment Association FAQs, at http://www.illinois-tif .com/faqs.htm.

22. U.S. Census Bureau at http://www.factfinder.census.gov. Jeff McCourt and Greg LeRoy, *A Better Deal for Illinois: Improving Economic Develop-ment Policy*, Good Jobs First, January 2003, p. 43.

23. Steve Schultze, "State Pays Out, But Promises of Jobs Don't Always Play Out," *Milwaukee Journal Sentinel*, December 5, 1999, p. 1.

24. Alyssa Talanker and Kate Davis, *Straying from Good Intentions: How States Are Weakening Enterprise Zone and Tax Increment Financing Pro-grams*, Good Jobs First, July 2003, at http://www.goodjobsfirst.org/ pdf/straying.pdf.

25. All of these TIF and EZ examples are from Talanker and Davis, *Stray-ing from Good Intentions*.

26. Talanker and Davis, *Straying from Good Intentions*, pp. 7–23.

27. Talanker and Kate Davis, *Straying from Good Intentions*, pp. 15–17.

28. Barbara McCann, "Driven to Spend," Surface Transportation Policy Project, March 19, 2000, at http://www.transact.org/report.asp?id=36.

29. Thomas W. Sanchez et al., "Moving to Equity: Addressing Inequitable Effects of Transportation Policies on Minorities," Civil Rights Project of Harvard University and Center for Community Change, 2003, at http://www.milwaukeeconnector.com/pdf/MovingtoEquity.pdf.

30. Mafruza Khan and Greg LeRoy, "Missing the Bus: How States Fail to Connect Economic Development with Public Transit," Good Jobs First, September 2003, at http://www.goodjobsfirst.org/pdf/bus.pdf.

31. Khan and LeRoy, "Missing the Bus."

32. Another study, in the Chicago area (of low-interest industrial revenue bonds or IRBs), found an explicitly adverse effect on workers and entrepreneurs of color. The Illinois Advisory Committee to the U.S. Commission on Civil Rights examined 104 deals. The study found that only 3 of the 104 bonds went to African American-owned firms, one to an Asian-owned firm, and none to Hispanic-owned firms. It wasn't just an issue of harm to minority entrepreneurs. One-third of the companies' workforces had a much smaller share of black employees than the region's labor market; two-thirds had disproportionately low Hispanic employment; and about half had disproportionately small numbers of women workers. Incredibly, in fully one-fifth of the deals, either the recipient company or the bank that bought the IRB had recently violated the federal fair employment rules of the Equal Employment Opportunity Commission. (Illinois Advisory Committee to the U.S. Commission on Civil Rights, *Industrial Revenue Bonds: Equal Opportunity in Chicago's IRB Program?* No. 005-907-00183-3, 1986.)

33. Kennedy Lawson Smith, the Main Street program's long-time director, 2001 estimate, relayed in May 21, 2004 correspondence. Retail Forward, Inc., "United States Retail Environment," *Global Economic and Retail Outlook*, May 2003, p. 92.

34. Kennedy Lawson Smith, "Main Street at 15," *Preservation Forum*, 1992.

35. Kennedy Lawson Smith, National Trust for Historic Preservation, "The Impact of Discount Superstores on Traditional Business Districts," testimony before Town of North Elba Planning Board, June 6, 1995.

36. PriceWaterhouseCoopers Global Strategic Real Estate Research Group, "Greyfield Regional Mall Study" for Congress for the New Urbanism, January 2001, at http://www.cnu.org/cnu_reports/Greyfield

_Feb_01.pdf, p. 4. A greyfield or dead mall is one with sales of less than $150 per square foot per year. CNU notes that greyfields tend to be located on suburban arterial streets and are therefore transit-accessible, even transit hubs, whereas thriving malls tend to have "freeway visibility and direct ramp access." "Greyfields into Goldfields," CNU and PWC, February 2001, at http://www.cnu.org/cnu_reports/Executive _summary.pdf, p. 3.

37. Matt Kures, "Greyfields and Ghostboxes: Evolving Real Estate Challenges," *Let's Talk Business*, May 2003, Publication of the University of Wisconsin-Extension, Center for Community Economic Development.

38. "Everyday Low Wages: The Hidden Price We All Pay for Wal-Mart," a report by the Democratic staff of the Committee on Education and the Workforce, U.S. House of Representatives, Representative George Miller (D-CA), senior Democrat. February 16, 2004, at http://edworkforce .house.gov/democrats/WALMARTREPORT.pdf.

39. The Massachusetts disclosure legislation can be found in Section 304 of Chapter 149 of the Acts of 2004; available online at http://www .mass.gov/legis/05budget/outside_sections.htm. The Massachusetts report is online at http://www.mass.gov/Eeohhs2/docs/dhcfp/pdf/50+ _ees_ph_assist.pdf and the accompanying spreadsheet at http://www .mass.gov/Eeohhs2/docs/dhcfp/pdf/50+_ees_ph_assist_ss.pdf. Robin K. Cohen, HUSKY A and B—Enrollment and Employer Data, Connecticut Office of Legislative Research Report 2005-R-0017, January 10, 2005; available online at http://www.cga.ct.gov/2005/rpt/2005-R -0017.htm. On Florida: Rocky Scott, "50,000 Workers Qualify for Medicaid: Some Say Companies Taking Advantage," Tallahassee Democrat, December 19, 2004, p. 1. According to a private communication with the author, the headline was incorrect and should have referred to 50,000 employers. Andy Miller, "Wal-Mart Stands Out on Rolls of PeachCare," Atlanta Journal-Constitution, February 27, 2004, p. 1B. John Commins, Dave Flessner, and Ashley M. Heher, "On the Job and on TennCare," *Chattanooga Times Free Press*, January 20, 2005, p. A1. Rebecca Ferrar, "Big Companies Have a Large Number of Workers in Program," *Knoxville News-Sentinel*, January 30, 2005, p. C1. On Washington state: Rebecca Cook (Associated Press writer), "Legislature: Bill Has Employers Pay Share of Health Care," *Vancouver Columbian* (Vancouver, WA), February 28, 2003, p. C2; and Andrew Garber, "Enrollments in State's Health Plan Questioned," *Seattle Times*, February 3, 2004. John Heys and Paul Wilson, "Wal-Mart

Culture: Wal-Mart Tops State CHIP List," *Charleston Sunday Gazette-Mail,* December 26, 2004, p. 1A. Anita Weier, "Wal-Mart Workers Need State Health Aid," *The Capital Times* (Madison, WI), November 4, 2004, p. 1A.

40. David Schrank and Tim Lomax, *The 2004 Urban Mobility Report,* Texas Transportation Institute, September 2004, table 4, p. 18, at http://tti.tamu.edu/documents/mobility_report_2004.pdf.

41. The Missouri narrative draws from Greg LeRoy, "Subsidizing Sprawl: How Economic Development Programs Are Going Awry," *Multinational Monitor,* October 2003.

42. LeRoy, "Subsidizing Sprawl." East-West Gateway Council of Governments school revenue computation for 2001–2002.

43. Ibid.

44. Joe Ortwerth, April 1, 2005 interview.

45. Ibid.

46. *St. Louis Post-Dispatch* editorial, "A Tale of Two TIFs," February 20, 2003, p. B6.

47. Josh Reinert, "Comment: Tax Increment Financing in Missouri: Is It Time for Blight and But-For to Go?" 45 *St. Louis U. L.J.,* Summer 2001, pp. 1019–1053.

48. This section is informed by the work of Lenny Goldberg, whose arguments are summarized in: "The Empire Has No Clothes: Infrastructure, Sprawl, Local Government Finance, and the Property Tax," *State Tax Notes,* October 2, 2000, pp. 899–905.

49. See, for example, Paul G. Lewis and Eliza Barbour, *California Cities and the Local Sales Tax,* Public Policy Institute of California, 1999. Their survey of all 471 California cities in existence in 1998 found that retail was the most desirable land use for both new development and redevelopment. Despite heavy subsidization of retail, they find that California cities' total revenue from the sales tax is stagnant, given that retail spending per capita grows very slowly, while growing shares of consumer spending—such as services and catalog sales—are not taxed. See also Michael Coleman, "City Budget Impacts of Land Development: The Roots of Fiscalization," League of California Cities, December 2002.

50. Greg LeRoy testimony (for Lakewood) before U.S. Navy hearing, March 2, 1995.

51. D. J. Waldie, *Holy Land: A Suburban Memoir,* Norton, 1996.

52. Donald J. Waldie, interview, October 28, 2004.

53. Goldberg, "The Empire Has No Clothes."

54. California Tax Reform Association, "California Commercial Tax Study: Statewide Study Finds Huge Disparities in Property Taxes Paid for Similar Properties; Highlights Need to Reform System," April 2004 at http://www.caltaxreform.org/cpts.pdf.

55. Goldberg, "The Empire Has No Clothes," p. 3.

56. It may also explain why Wal-Mart has rolled out new marketing and philanthropic efforts targeting people of color.

57. National Trust for Historic Preservation, "America's 11 Most Endangered Historic Places 2004," at http://www.nationaltrust.org/11most/2004/vermont.html.

58. Wal-Mart Realty available buildings list as of January 2005, at http://www.wal-martrealty.com/Buildings/PrintableBuilding/BasicBldgListOnly.html.

59. Al Norman, "The Case Against Sprawl," from the book *Slam-Dunking Wal-Mart* (Raphel Marketing, 1999); excerpt at http://www.sprawl-busters.com/caseagainstsprawl.html.

60. Philip Mattera and Anna Purinton, *Shopping for Subsidies: How Wal-Mart Uses Taxpayer Money to Finance Its Never-Ending Growth*, Good Jobs First, May 2004, p. 14.

61. Mattera and Purinton, *Shopping for Subsidies*, p. 7.

62. Mattera and Purinton, *Shopping for Subsidies*, p. 6.

63. See the following two articles by Becky Sisco in the *Telegraph Herald*: "Wal-Mart Takes Galena Off the Shelf" (April 6, 2001, p. A1) and "Lawsuit Will Not Slow Wal-Mart's Galena Plans" (July 3, 2002, p. A3). The project later ran into other legal difficulties.

64. Mattera and Purinton, *Shopping for Subsidies*, pp. 22–23. "Land Buy OK'd for Wal-Mart," *Rockford Register Star*, August 5, 2003, p. 7A.

65. 1000 Friends of Wisconsin, *Wisconsin's Tax Incremental Finance Law: Lending a Hand to Blighted Areas or Turning Cornfields into Parking Lots?* October 1999, online at http://www.1kfriends.org/Publications/Online_Documents/TIF.htm. An addendum to the original posting of the full report included a July 28, 1999 letter sent by Wal-Mart corporate real estate manager Randy Crossno to Sauk County Supervisor Bart Olson, saying: "In response to your question, the answer is simply, yes. We would relocate our existing store to this location regardless of the city's execution of the TIF request." (Mattera and Purinton, *Shopping for Subsidies*, footnote 20, p. 63.)

66. Linda Billingsly, "Olivette Voters Reject Shopping Center," *St. Louis Post-Dispatch*, February 9, 2000, p. B1.

67. Fran Spielman and David Roeder, "City Scoffs at Wal-Mart Subsidy Request," *Chicago Sun-Times*, February 27, 2002, p. 57.

68. See April M. Washington, "City Calls Off Threat to Condemn Parcel," *Rocky Mountain News*, January 16, 2004, p. 20A. For several publications analyzing the proposed deal, see the website of the Front Range Economic Strategy Center, www.fresc.org.

69. See, for example, Jim Tankersley, "A Placid Pond, A Pound of Woe," *Rocky Mountain News*, November 21, 2003.

70. See Al Lewis, "Wal-Mart Lake Grab Sleeps with the Fishes," *Denver Post*, March 2, 2004, p. C1. The citation for the court ruling is: *Arvada Urban Renewal Authority v. Columbine Professional Plaza Association*, 2004 Colo. LEXIS 113 (Colo., 2004).

71. Kristen Go, "Voters Reject Districts and Los Arcos Subsidy," *Arizona Republic*, March 10, 2004.

72. Mattera and Purinton, *Shopping for Subsidies*, p. 21.

73. Forbes.com, "400 Richest Americans" at http://www.forbes.com/lists/forbes400/2003/09/17/rich400land.html.

74. Anita French, "Report Critical of Wal-Mart Incentives," *Northwest Arkansas Morning News*, May 25, 2004. E-mail correspondence from August Whitcomb, Director of Corporate Communications, Wal-Mart Stores, Inc., June 7, 2004.

Chapter Seven

1. Quote from an interview in the September 1996 issue of *Cleveland* magazine, reproduced in Leonard Pitts Jr., "A Man Who Could Use a Library," *Miami Herald*, August 29, 1996, p. 1F.

2. See estimates for the various categories on the website of the *Sports Business Journal*, at http://www.sportsbusinessjournal.com/index.cfm?fuseaction=page.feature&featureId=43.

3. Links to the compilations can be found at http://law.marquette.edu/cgi-bin/site.pl?2130&pageID=1680#sfr.

4. Calculated from the stadium profiles cited in the previous note. The amounts were not adjusted for inflation.

5. John Siegfried and Andrew Zimbalist, "The Economics of Sports Facilities and Their Communities," *Journal of Economic Perspectives*, Vol. 14, No. 3, Summer 2000, p. 96.

6. David Davis, "Calling for Forgiveness from Brooklyn Dodgers Fans," *Forward*, April 18, 2003.

7. Joanna Cagan and Neil deMause, *Field of Schemes: How the Great Stadium Swindle Turns Public Money Into Private Profit* (Monroe, Maine: Common Courage Press, rev. ed. 1998), p. vii.

8. This section is based heavily on chapter 1 of *Field of Schemes*.

9. "Book Says Deal to Move Twins to North Carolina Was Phony from the Start," Associated Press, March 29, 2000.

10. See, for example, David Nakamura and Thomas Heath, "Amended Deal on Stadium Approved," *Washington Post*, December 22, 2004, p. A1.

11. *Economic Impact Analysis of the Proposed Ballpark for the Boston Red Sox*, prepared by C. H. Johnson Consulting Inc. for the Greater Boston Convention and Visitors Bureau and the Greater Boston Chamber of Commerce, June 30, 1999, p. 13; available online at http://www .fenwayaction.org/darchive/CHJohnsonReport.pdf.

12. See, for example, Ilana DeBare, "Stadium Jobs—A Boon or an Illusion?" *San Francisco Chronicle*, May 16, 1997, p. A1.

13. *Field of Schemes*, p. 24. It is not clear how many of the jobs survived the move.

14. Tom Barnes, "Santorum Tells Backers of Tax Plan to Speak Out," *Pittsburgh Post-Gazette*, September 6, 1997, p. A-9.

15. See, for example, Virginia Rybin, "Ballpark Boon?" *St. Paul Pioneer Press*, October 10, 1999, p. 1A.

16. Roger G. Noll and Andrew Zimbalist, "'Build the Stadium—Create the Jobs!'" in Roger G. Noll and Andrew Zimbalist, editors, *Sports, Jobs, and Taxes: The Economic Impact of Sports Teams and Stadiums* (Washington, DC: Brookings Institution Press, 1997), p. 30.

17. Robert A. Baade and Allen R. Sanderson, "Employment Effect of Teams and Sports Facilities," in *Sports, Jobs, and Taxes*, p. 112.

18. Ibid., p. 114.

19. Bruce W. Hamilton and Peter Kahn, "Baltimore's Camden Yards Ballparks," in *Sports, Jobs, and Taxes*, pp. 246 and 274. The authors note that a complete cost-benefit analysis would also factor in "public consumption benefits" relating to the presence of the stadiums, but they admit that there is no way of measuring those benefits.

20. Ziona Austrian and Mark S. Rosentraub, "Cleveland's Gateway to the Future," in *Sports, Jobs, and Taxes*, p. 382.

21. Siegfried and Zimbalist, "Economics of Sports Facilities," p. 103.

22. The *Forbes* 400 list is published each October in *Forbes* (at this writing, the most recent such issue is October 11, 2004).

23. Links to the various *Forbes* lists can be found at http://www.forbes.com/lists/.

24. *Field of Schemes*, p. 26.

25. Quoted in *Field of Schemes*, p. 45.

26. This section is based on information from a variety of sources, including the following: Wayne Slater and David Jackson, "Ballpark Deals Draws Criticism," *Dallas Morning News*, April 16, 1994, p. 1A; Wayne Slater and Richard A. Oppel Jr., "Rangers Sold," *Dallas Morning News*, January 8, 1998, p. 1A; Wayne Slater and Richard Oppel Jr., "Bush Nets Millions from Sale," *Arlington Morning News*, June 18, 1998, p. 1C; Byron York, "George's Road to Riches," *The American Spectator*, June 1999; Joe Conason, "Notes on a Native Son," *Harper's*, February 2000; and Nicholas Kristof, "Breaking Into Baseball: Road to Politics Ran Through a Texas Ballpark," *New York Times*, September 24, 2000, p. 1.

27. Quoted in Slater and Jackson, "Ballpark Deal Draws Criticism."

28. Kristof, "Breaking Into Baseball."

29. All the information in the paragraph is taken from Heywood Sanders, *Space Available: The Realities of Convention Centers as Economic Development Strategy*, Brookings Institution Metropolitan Policy Program Research Brief, January 2005, p. 2.

30. Ibid., pp. 4–5.

31. Ibid., pp. 6–9.

Chapter Eight

1. Steven Maguire, "Average Effective Corporate Tax Rates: 1959 to 2002," Congressional Research Service, Government and Finance Division, September 5, 2003.

2. Michael Mazerov, "Closing Three Common Corporate Income Tax Loopholes Could Raise Additional Revenue for Many States," Center on Budget and Policy Priorities, May 23, 2003, p. 3.

3. U.S. Census Bureau, State Government Tax Collections series.

4. Revenue calculation by Michael Mazerov, Center for Budget and Policy Priorities.

5. Utah State Tax Commission, "Western States' Tax Burdens," annual surveys for Fiscal Years 1980–1981 and 2002–2003. The 2002–2003 data refer to a combination of income and estate taxes.

6. Arkansas Advocates for Children and Families, "The Vanishing Arkansas Corporate Income Tax: Should We Close the Loopholes?" *Paychecks and Politics*, April 2004, issue 24.

7. Jean Ross, "All Gain, No Pain: California's 'No Tax' Corporations," California Budget Project, September 23, 2004.

8. Utah State Tax Commission, "Western States' Tax Burdens."

9. A Carnival spokesman told the *St. Petersburg Times* that two of its subsidiaries pay Florida income tax. Sydney Freedberg, "Loophole, Inc.: A Special Report on Florida's Corporate Income Tax," *St. Petersburg Times*, October 26, 2003. The Florida Senate, Committee on Finance and Taxation, Interim Project Summary 2004-137, "Why Did Florida's Corporate Income Tax Revenue Fall While Corporate Profits Rose?" November 2003. *St. Petersburg Times* Editorial, "Corporations' Free Ride," November 19, 2003.

10. Utah State Tax Commission, "Western States' Tax Burdens."

11. Zach Schiller, *Ohio's Vanishing Corporate Franchise Tax*, Policy Matters Ohio, October 2002.

12. David Blatt, Community Action Project (Tulsa), September 30, 2004 communication.

13. David H. Bradley, "The Truth about Business Taxes in Pennsylvania, Part Two—The Uneven Distribution of the Business Tax Burden," Keystone Research Center, February 2003.

14. Utah State Tax Commission, "Western States' Tax Burdens."

15. Ibid.

16. Prof. Richard Pomp as quoted in a *St. Petersburg Times* editorial, "Unfair share," October 30, 2003.

17. Richard D. Pomp, "The Future of the State Corporate Income Tax: Reflections (and Confessions) of a Tax Lawyer," *State Tax Notes*, March 22, 1999. With the top federal corporate income tax rate lowered in 1986, state and local taxes were worth less as deductible business expenses: another reason for companies to target them.

18. Robert McIntyre et al., "State Corporate Income Taxes, 2001–2003," Citizens for Tax Justice and Institute on Taxation and Economic Policy, January 2005.

19. McIntyre et al., "State Corporate Income Taxes." The average corporate income tax rate is computed on a weighted basis.

20. Shelley Geballe and Douglas Hall, "Connecticut's Corporation Business Tax: It's Time for Repair," Connecticut Voices for Children, July 2003, at http://www.ctkidslink.org/pub_detail_61.html.

21. Maryland Budget and Tax Policy Institute, "Two-Thirds of Maryland's Largest Corporations Pay NO Corporate Income Tax," Maryland Policy Reports, Vol. 4, No. 8, March 2004.

22. Mary E. Forsberg, "A Question of Balance: Taxing Business in the 21st Century," New Jersey Policy Perspective, January 2003, at http://www.njpp.org/rpt_cbt-report.html.

23. Michael Leachman, "Time to Raise the Corporate Minimum Tax: Top Execs Get Pay Raises While Oregon Gets Just $10," Oregon Center for Public Policy, February 23, 2004 statement. Chuck Sheketoff, Oregon Center for Public Policy, correspondence December 21, 2004.

24. Utah State Tax Commission, "Western States' Tax Burdens."

25. Peter Fisher, "Tax Incentives and the Disappearing State Corporate Income Tax," State Tax Notes, March 4, 2002.

26. Ibid.

27. Peter Fisher, correspondence, December 20, 2004.

28. Alyssa Talanker, unpublished legislative memo, Good Jobs First, March 3, 2004. See also Mintax's National Tax Benefit Exchange, which offers to "facilitate the acquisition of benefits," at http:www.mintax.com/services/printfriendly/ntbe_buy.html.

29. Peter S. Fisher and Alan H. Peters, "Tax Incentives, Enterprise Zones and Job Redistribution, 1990–1997," paper presented to the Association of Collegiate Schools of Planning annual conference, November, 1998, p. 8.

30. Fisher, "Tax Incentives and the Disappearing State Corporate Income Tax."

31. Greg LeRoy, "The Terrible Ten Corporate Candy Store Deals of 1998," The Progressive, May 1999.

32. Alabama Department of Revenue, 2002 Annual Report, p. 24.

33. LeRoy, "The Terrible Ten."

34. Shailagh Murray, "Business-Friendly Alabama Puts Brakes on Tax Breaks," Wall Street Journal, September 30, 2002.

35. LeRoy, "The Terrible Ten."

36. Ibid.

37. Ibid.

38. Robert S. McIntyre et al., "Who Pays? A Distributional Analysis of the Tax Systems in All 50 States," pp. 12, 118. Institute on Taxation and Economic Policy, January 2003.

39. Interestingly, Bill Gates, Sr., father of the Microsoft cofounder, is an

active crusader for preserving the federal estate tax; he even coauthored a book on the issue, *Wealth and Our Commonwealth*.

40. Robert McIntyre computations from the U.S. Census.

41. Ibid.

42. Robert McIntyre and T. D. Coo Nguyen, "Corporate Income Taxes in the Bush Years," September 2004, Citizens for Tax Justice and the Institute on Taxation and Economic Policy.

43. McIntyre and Nguyen, "Corporate Income Taxes in the Bush Years." Employment statistics from U.S. Bureau of Labor Statistics.

44. McIntyre and Nguyen, "Corporate Income Taxes in the Bush Years."

45. Ibid.

46. Robert S. McIntyre, correspondence, January 4, 2005.

47. Lawrence Mishel et al., *The State of Working America 2004–2005* (Ithaca, NY: ILR Press, 2005), pp. 119, 138, 139, and 141.

48. Greg LeRoy, Dan Swinney, and Elaine Charpentier, *Early Warning Manual Against Plant Closings*, Midwest Center for Labor Research, 1986 and 1988.

Chapter Nine

1. The law's formal name is the Emergency Planning and Community Right-to-Know Act of 1986.

2. The eleven states are Connecticut, Illinois, Louisiana, Maine, Minnesota, Nebraska, North Carolina, Ohio, Texas, Washington, and West Virginia. They vary widely in the quality and completeness of their disclosure. You can see details about each state's disclosure law in chapter 3 of *No More Secret Candy Store: A Grassroots Guide to Investigating Job Subsidies*, at www.goodjobsfirst.org/research/ch3.pdf. At least four states—Minnesota, Texas, Ohio, and North Carolina—put some of their disclosure data on the Web, and Illinois is slated to start in mid-2005.

3. Francis X. Quinn, "Gov. King Quietly Signs BIW Tax Bill," Associated Press, June 12, 1997.

4. Good Jobs First lists the 18 states using clawbacks, at http://www.goodjobsfirst.org/pdf/clawbacks.pdf.

5. Anna Purinton et al., *The Policy Shift to Good Jobs: States, Cities and Counties Attaching Job Quality Standards to Economic Development Subsidies*, Good Jobs First, 2003.

6. Though we have educated estimates about the total fifty-state cost of

subsidies, many states still have poor accounting—or no accounting—of their subsidies. That's because the Government Accounting Standards Board (GASB), the official body that lays out uniform accounting formats that public agencies have to use to satisfy bond investors and the credit ratings agencies, has never mandated a full accounting of tax spending for economic development. The National Association of State Budget Officers has not engaged on the overall issue of tax spending for two decades; see "Tax Expenditure Reporting: Closing the Loophole in State Budget Oversight," National Association of State Budget Officers, December 1985.

7. Matt Hull et al., "Budgeting and Economic Development Performance: A Guide to Unified Development Budgets," Corporation for Enterprise Development, November 2000.

8. The law is Title 23 U.S.C. 158, and the Supreme Court decision upholding it was *South Dakota v. Dole*, 483 U.S. 203 (1987).

9. For more on smart growth and good jobs, see Greg LeRoy and Sara Hinkley, *Smart Growth and Workforce Development*, Good Jobs First, 2000, at http://www.goodjobsfirst.org/pdf/workforce.pdf; Greg LeRoy, *Talking to Union Leaders About Smart Growth*, Good Jobs First, 2001, at http://www.goodjobsfirst.org/pdf/talking.pdf; and Philip Mattera and Greg LeRoy, *The Jobs Are Back in Town: Urban Smart Growth and Construction Employment*, Good Jobs First, 2003.

10. Maryland Economic Growth, Resource Protection, and Planning Act of 1992.

11. *Cuno v. DaimlerChrysler*, U.S. Court of Appeals for the Sixth District, Case No. 01-3960, ruling filed September 2, 2004.

12. Peter Enrich, "Saving the States from Themselves: Commerce Clause Constraints on State Tax Incentives for Business," *Harvard Law Review*, December 1996.

13. Sources for this chapter include Arlene Dohm, "Gauging the Labor Force Effects of Retiring Baby-Boomers," *Monthly Labor Review*, U.S. Department of Labor, July 2000; David Ellwood, "The Sputtering Labor Force of the 21st Century: Can Social Policy Help?" National Bureau of Economic Research Working Paper 8321, June 2001 at www.nber.org/papers/w8321; Lynn A. Karoly and Constantijn W.A. Panis, "The 21st Century at Work," RAND Corporation MG-164-DOL, 2004 for the U.S. Department of Labor at www.rand.org/pubs/monographs/2004/RAND_MG164.pdf; and Jessica R. Sincavage,

"The Labor Force and Unemployment: Three Generations of Change," *Monthly Labor Review*, U.S. Department of Labor, June 2004.

14. Committee for Economic Development, *New Opportunities for Older Workers*, 1999, p. 7.
15. "Too Many Workers? Not For Long," *Business Week*, May 20, 2002.
16. Ellwood, "Sputtering Labor Force," p. 16. Some people may work a little longer. The age at which you get a full Social Security benefit is getting phased back; by 2022, it will be age 67. People with inferior defined contribution pensions may need to supplement their income. And Social Security recipients can now earn all they want before age 69 without losing benefits (after reaching "full retirement age"). However, the average retirement age of 62 to 63 has remained quite steady; more than two thirds of all workers—and more than three fourths of women—have left their jobs by age 65. Even if a few percent more boomers work past age 62, as is projected, there will still be a huge exodus. (Howard N. Fullerton, Jr. and Mitra Toossi, "Labor Force Projections to 2010: Steady Growth and Changing Composition," *Monthly Labor Review*, U.S. Department of Labor, November 2001. Murray Gendell, "Retirement Age Declines Again in 1990s," *Monthly Labor Review*, October 2001.)

It's not just a matter of the quantity of workers who will be available; of equal concern is the quality of their skills and whether those skills match what the economy needs. Even if the total-worker squeeze turns out to be less severe than some people predict, many observers—from differing political perspectives—argue that the skills needed in our economy are changing faster than our ability to supply them. They advocate big increases in education and workforce development efforts. (See, for example, *America's Choice: High Skills or Low Wages*, report of the Commission on the Skills of the American Workforce, National Center on Education and the Economy, 1990, and writings and statements of people as different as Alan Greenspan and Richard Florida.)

Finally, some observers predict that an increase in immigration will cushion the impact of the boomers' departures. The rate of immigration into the United States has increased greatly in the last two decades, and traditionally we have attracted many highly skilled immigrants. However, many other countries are lowering their entry barriers to attract high-skill immigrants, whereas the Department of Homeland Security is making entry to the U.S. more difficult in the post–September 11 era. And broad public disapproval of U.S. foreign policy in many nations is causing some immigrants, including promising entrepreneurs and graduate students, to avoid this country. If that trend holds, it would be a real blow: more than half of foreign-born scientists and engineers who receive their doctorates in the United States stay here, and Chinese and Indian immigrants founded almost a third of the new Silicon Valley businesses in the 1990s. (Electronics Industries Alliance, "The Technology Industry at an Innovation Crossroads," March 2004. Thomas L. Friedman, "Losing Our Edge," *New York Times,* April 22, 2004. Richard Florida, "Creative Class War: How the GOP's Anti-Elitism Could Ruin America's Economy," *Washington Monthly*, January 2004. National Science Foundation, "Science and Engineering Indicators 2004," Vol. 1, pp. 3-37, 3-38.)

17. U.S. Department of Health and Human Services, Health Resources and Services Administration, "Projected Supply, Demand and Shortages of Registered Nurses: 2000–2020," July 2002. American Health Care Association, "Results of the 2002 AHCA Survey of Nursing Staff Vacancy and Turnover in Nursing Homes," February 12, 2003.

18. Joint Commission on Accreditation of Healthcare Organizations, "Health Care at the Crossroads: Strategies for Addressing the Evolving Nursing Crisis," August 2002. Other observers blame managed care for causing many nurses to quit, making the shortage worse. Labor unions and public officials have responded by advocating for legislation to require nurse staffing plans or mandatory nurse-to-patient ratios. (Linda H. Aiken et al., "Hospital Nurse Staffing and Patient Mortality, Nurse Burnout, and Job Dissatisfaction," *Journal of the American Medical Association*, October 23/30, 2002.)

19. Aspen Institute, Domestic Strategy Group, "Grow Faster Together. Or Grow Slowly Apart. How Will America Work in the 21st Century?" 2003.

20. Committee for Economic Development, *New Opportunities for Older Workers*, 1999, p. 1.

21. The National Association of Manufacturers, the Manufacturing Institute, and Deloitte & Touche, "Keeping America Competitive: How a Talent Shortage Threatens U.S. Manufacturing," white paper, April 2003.

22. National Science Foundation, "Science and Engineering Indicators 2004," Vol. 1, p. 3-32. U.S. General Accounting Office, "Major Management Challenges and Program Risks: National Aeronautics and Space Administration," January 2003, GAO-03-114.

23. Robin Spence and Brendan Kiel, "Skilling the American Workforce 'On the Cheap,'" The Workforce Alliance, September 2003, at http://www.workforcealliance.org/twa-funding-analysis-09.pdf.

24. Ibid.

25. Ibid.

26. American Society of Civil Engineers, "2005 Report Card for America's Infrastructure," at http://www.asce.org/reportcard/2005/page.cfm?id=103. 2001 grades at http://www.asce.org/reportcard/index.cfm?reaction=full&page=2. 1988 data provided by ASCE staff.

27. Ibid.

28. Ibid.

Index

Bed Bath & Beyond, 149
  sales tax, 145
bedroom suburbs, 130
Belvidere, Illinois, Wal-Mart site location, 153
Bendix, 34
benefits, 3, 9
  few associated with stadium jobs, 160–161
  fewer, 181
Bertelsmann AG, 40
Bethlehem Steel Corp., 107–108
big-box power center, 149
big-box retailers, 129
  tax increment financing, 135
big business, disinvesting, 182–184
big companies. *See also* corporations
  economic development control, 182
  lower taxes for, 181
  tax dodging, 181
  tax policy control, 182
birth rates, effect on labor force, 198–199
Bishop, Bill, 28–29
Bismarck, North Dakota, Sykes Enterprises, 19
Black & Decker, layoffs, 96
"blighted" areas
  enterprise zone programs, 137
  new TIF rules and, 138
  tax increment financing, 117, 122, 147–148
  Wal-Mart, 153
"blighted" malls, 130
Bloomberg, 40
Bloomberg LP, 43
Bloomberg, Michael, 42, 43
Board of Commerce and Industry (Louisiana), 119
Boeing Corp., 88. *See also* 7E7 "Dreamliner" project (Boeing)
  conflict of interest, 87–88
  ripple effect claim of, 30–31
  in Seattle, 48
  site location of, 56–57
  subsidy for, 178
Boise, Idaho, Hewlett-Packard, 59
bond issues, 115
Bonneville Power Administration, 48

bonus depreciation, claims of, 179
Borders, sales tax, 145
Boston Braves, 158
Boston, Massachusetts, hospitality jobs, 161
BP/Amoco, 102
branch plants, site location and, 49
bridges, state of nation's, 204
Briggs & Stratton, 33
Bristol Myers Co., 107–108
Brockway Glass Company, relocation blocked, 74
Brookings Institution, 163
Brooklyn Dodgers, move to Los Angeles, 158–159
brownfields, 205
  smart growth and, 194
Bucks, Dan, 114
budget deficits, structural, 3
Budget Rent-A-Car Corp., 113
budgets, state, corrosion of, 5
Buffalo County, 136
Buffalo, New York, GEICO outside, 136
Buffett, Warren, 136
Burger King, 113
Bush, George W., 165–166
  corporate tax cuts of, 178–179
  profit from Texas Rangers and Arlington stadium, 165–166
Bush, Jeb, job subsidies in Florida, 34–35
Business Activity Tax Simplification Act of 2003, 111
business climate, 28
  clawbacks and, 190
  definition vague, 80
  experts, 2
  ideology, 5
  ranking, 81
  rating, 81
  relationship to education, 127
  school boards and, 126
  what constitutes a good, 69–70
business climatologists, 84
"business climatology," 79–84
business-friendly signals, site location and, 53–54, 54
Business Week, 80
"but for" deals, claims of, 60

cities
  Leonard Yaseen's dislike of, 77
  revenue sharing, 145
Citizens for Tax Justice (CTJ), 171–
    172, 179–180, 180–181, 189
clawbacks, 98
  use of, 189–190
Clean Water Act, 205
Cleveland Browns, 159
Cleveland Indians, 165
Cleveland, Ohio, 79
  Gateway Complex, 163
  revenue losses in, 121
  stadium subsidies, 163
Clift Hotel, 150
Clinton, Bill, 23
Coalition for Rational and Fair Taxation
    (CRAFT), 111
Cobb County, Georgia, America On-
    line, 62
Cobb, James C., 73
Coffman, Mike, 26
cold war, Leonard Yaseen on, 77
Colorado
  CAPCOs and, 26
  corporate tax dodging, 170
  Denver, Boeing, 30, 56
  Greeley, Sykes Enterprises, 18
  opposition to Wal-Mart subsidies,
    153–154
  school boards in, 125
  Sykes Enterprises, 18
Colorado Supreme Court, 154
combined reporting, 192
  for audits, 109–110
  tax return requirement, 114
Commerce Clause of the U.S. Constitu-
    tion, subsidies and, 196
commissions, site location consultants
    and, 57, 70. *See also* site location
    consultants
Committee for Economic Development,
    200–201
Community Action Project (Oklahoma),
    170–171
Community Development Block Grant,
    funding, 33–34
Community Redevelopment Agency, 27
Community Reinvestment Act, 187

commuting times, increase as sprawl
    result, 130
competition, 143
  among governments, 3–4
  corrupted definitions of, 3
  role in scams, 9
  need for healthy, 6
  worship of, 137–139
competitor, bogus, 14–16
CompUSA, 113
ConAgra, 44, 113
Conde Nast, 39
Conference of State Manufacturers'
    Associations (COSMA), 81
conflict of interest
  Boeing, 87–88
  Fantus Area Research, 75
  site location consultants, 69, 74–75
Congress for the New Urbanism, 141–
    142
Congressional Research Service (CRS),
    168–169
Connecticut
  economic development tax credits, 174
  EZ tax breaks outside zones, 138
  hidden taxpayer costs in, 143
  job blackmail, 38
  "job creation," 34
  job piracy, 26–27
  Single Sales Factor and, 93
  state income taxes paid by corpora-
    tions, 172
  "throwback rule" in, 112
  Wal-Mart, 143
Connecticut Development Agency, 34
Connecticut Voices for Children, 172
conservatives, professional sports stadi-
    ums, 162
consultants, reports on hospitality busi-
    nesses, 166
consulting companies
  estimating impact of stadiums, 161
  impact of stadiums, 164
  rosy scenarios of, 161
Container Corp. vs. California Tax Board,
    110
contracts
  job "retention" and, 42
  New York, 42

education system. *See* public education

Edwards, Edwin (Louisiana governor), 120

elasticity, taxes and growth, 57–58

Eltra Corp., 107–108

emerging companies, site location and, 49

Empire Insurance Group, 39

Empire Zone program, New York State, 17, 136

Empire Zones, 90

Employment and Investment Growth Act. *See* LB 775

Enrich, Peter, 196

Enron, 43–44, 45. *See also* InterNorth, Inc.

enterprise zone program, typical, 17

enterprise zone rebates, Louisiana, 119

enterprise zone tax breaks, Wal-Mart, 152

enterprise zones (EZs)
  competition and, 137
  Ohio, 120, 134, 135
  property tax abatement restricted to in some states, 117
  sprawl and, 129
  subsidies, 133

entertainment "destinations," Cabela's, 64–66

Equitable Companies/Equitable Life Assurance Society, 39

Erie County, 136

Ernst & Young, corporate income tax study, 110

Ernst & Young International Location Advisory Services, 85

Ernst & Young's Business Incentives Practice, 88–89

escapees, from private prisons, 32

Eugene Register-Guard, 118

Eveleth, Minnesota, Sykes Enterprises, 20–21

Evergreen Freedome Foundation, 87

excise tax, publicly traded companies disclosure needed, 189

exclusionary zoning ordinances, racial inequality, 144

Expansion Management, 54–55, 127

Exxon, 119
  in Louisiana, 34

factory jobs, loss of in New York City, 77–78

factory relocation, 77–78. *See also* corporate relocations; site location
  American Federation of Labor, 72

factory shutdowns, 182

Fain, Commerce Secretary Jim, 37

Fall Audit Session, 110

Fantus, 79, 91
  New York City and, 193
  site location consulting industry, 84

Fantus Area Research, 75–76
  clients, 76

Fantus Company, 50, 68
  TIF rules, 136

Fantus Corporate Real Estate Solutions, 84

Fantus Factory Locating Service, site location, 69

Fantus, Felix, 33, 68–71, 74, 81
  "business climate" study, 80–81
  business relocation and, 70
  clients, 78

Fantus process, 69–70

farmland
  sprawl and, 130
  tax increment financing and, 135

Federal Reserve Bank of Boston, Massachusetts business tax burden study, 12

Federated Department Stores Inc., 40

FedEx hub, jop subsidies, 35

Fenway Park, 161

Fidelity Investments, 39, 99–100
  corporate income tax, 105
  layoffs, 100
  outsourcing, 100
  relocation, 99
  Single Sales Factor, 99
  tax exemptions, 100

Field of Schemes, 159

"fiscalization of land use," 143–144
  zoning ordinances and, 144

Fisher, Peter (professor), 58, 173–176

Flaherty, Charles, and Raytheon, 11

Flat Rock, Michigan, Mazda in, 22

Great American Jobs Scam, 2, 7
  damage done by, 5
  disinvestment and, 6
Greater Boston Chamber of Commerce, 161
Greater Boston Convention and Visitors Bureau, 161
Greeley, Colorado, Sykes Enterprises, 18
Green Giant Co., 107–108
greenfield locations, Wal-Mart siting, 151
greyfields (dead malls), 141–142
gross domestic product, corporate tax burden as percentage of, 178, 180
Guardian Life Insurance, 40
Guiliani, Rudolph (New York City Mayor), 38–43
Gulf States Utilities, 119
Gund Arena, 163

Hallidie Building, 150
Hamburg, Pennsylvania
  Cabela's, 66, 67
  tourism strategy, 67
Hamilton, Bruce, 163
Hamilton County, Ohio, revenue losses in, 121
Hancock, Jay, 68, 124
Harding, Charles, 81
Harris County, Texas, property tax abatement, 118
Hawesville, Kentucky, 175–176
Hays, Kansas, Sykes Enterprises, 19–20
Hazard, Kentucky
  Cintas, 28
  Sykes Enterprises, 20
headquarters
  relocation, 78
  site location and, 49
health insurance coverage, 181
health, sprawl's effects on, 129, 131
healthcare, 3
  condition of getting subsidy, 190
  disclosure needed, 187–188
  skills shortage, 200
Hewlett-Packard, site location and, 59
Hicks, Thomas, 165
hidden taxpayer costs, 27–29
  Cintas, 28–29
  poverty-wage jobs, 190

public assistance to low-wage workers, 142
Wal-Mart, 29
Hilton Tower Hotel, 150
hired economists. *See also* rented economists
  rosy forecasts of, 102
Hoffman Estates, TIF program, 136
Holy Land: A Suburban Memoir, 149
Home Depot USA, 113, 140, 147
  sales tax, 145
Home Mortgage Disclosure Act, 187
Honda
  Lincoln, Alabama, 23
  Marysville, Ohio, 22
  "transplant" siting, 22
hospitality jobs, 161, 167
  convention centers and, 166
hospitals, smart growth and, 194
housing
  affordable, 130, 144
  racial discrimination and, 140
Housing and Urban Development (HUD)
  Community Development Block Grant funds, 33–34
  job piracy, 26
Houston Business Journal, 118
Houston Natural Gas, 43
Houston, Texas
  Enron in, 43–44
  site location and, 61–62
Howell, George, Jr., 175
HUD. *See* Housing and Urban Development (HUD)
human capital, 83
Hynix, 118
hypertension, sprawl and, 132
Hyundai, Montgomery, Alabama, 23

IBEW. *See* International Brotherhood of Electrical Workers (IBEW)
IBM. *See* International Business Machines Corp. (IBM)
IBM Business Consulting Services-Plant Location International, 85
Idaho
  Boise, Hewlett-Packard, 59
  corporate tax dodging, 170

revenue losses *(continued)*
  due to subsidies, 100–101, 103
  due to tax shelters, 114
  Ohio, 120–121
Rhode Island
  Fidelity, 99
  passive investment companies allowed
    in, 114
  Single Sales Factor, 99
  "throwback rule" in, 112
"right to work" states, 23
  "business climate" and, 81
  site location and, 50–51
  union busting, 33
Rinne, Tim, 45
ripple effects, 29–31
  measuring, 140–141
  terrible in retail, 140–141
Rosentraub, Mark, 163
Roxboro, North Carolina, union unwel-
  come, 74
RR Donnelley, 102
Rubin, Julia Sass, 26
rural areas, Leonard Yaseen's preferance
  for, 77
Rust Belt, 79–80

sales tax breaks, 135
  enterprise zones, 133
  tax increment financing and, 135
sales tax increment, TIFed, 146
sales tax rebates, Wal-Mart, 152
sales tax revenue, 148–149
  sharing local, smart growth and, 195
sales taxes
  exemptions, deal-specific disclosure
    needed for, 188
  perverse incentive to subsidize retail,
    148
  publicly traded companies disclosure
    needed, 189
  regional perspective, 145
  regressive, 176, 177
  retailing and, 145
  tax increment financing of, 146–148
  Wal-Mart, 154–155
Sam's Club, opposition to, 154
San Antonio, Texas, Toyota in, 23, 61
San Diego, California, 150

San Francisco, California, property
  assessment inequities in, 150
San Francisco 49ers, 161
Sanders, Heywood, 166–167
Sanderson, Allen, 163
Santa Clara County, California, 150
Santorum, Rick, 162
Sasso, John, 11
  lobbying records and, 14
Saturn, Spring Hill, Tennessee, 23
SBC Ameritech, 102
SBC Communications, 180
Schenectady, New York, General Electric, 105
SCHIP, hidden taxpayer costs, 143
Schnuck's, 147
school-age children, 144
school board associations, 126
school boards
  control over property tax revenue
    needed, 191–192
  lack of power of, 124–126
  Missouri, 146
  tax abatement approval and, 125
school districts, enterprise zones and, 134
school finance, 116
  Illinois, 121–122
  Ohio, 120–121
  property tax revenue, 124
school-funding formulas, 116
school lunches
  hidden taxpayer costs, 142
  Wal-Mart, 154–155
schools
  disinvestment in, 183
  infrastructure of, 181
  neglect of, 183
Scottsbluff, Nebraska, Sykes Enterprises,
  20
Scottsdale, Arizona, opposition to Supercenter and Sam's Club subsidies,
  154
Scripps Research Institute, job subsidies,
  34–35
Scudder (fund), 100
Sears
  ripple effect claims and, 30–31
  TIF program, 136
Seattle Seahawks, 164

Seattle, Washington, Boeing in, 48, 56
Section 8 housing assistance, hidden
    taxpayer costs, 29, 142
Securities and Exchange Commission,
    64, 189
Security Pacific National Bank, layoffs
    from merge with Bank of America,
    16
Seigleman, Don, 175
Selling of the South, The, 73
service sector, Grant Thornton index, 83
7E7 "Dreamliner" project (Boeing), 56–
    57, 87–88, 88
Shareholders, tax disclosure to, 189
Shell Oil, 119
Sherwin Williams, 113
Siegfried, John, 163–164
Silicon Valley, site location and, 48
Single Sales Factor (SSF), 44, 92–114
    AIM and, 12
    corporate income tax, 104–105
    demand for in Massachusetts, 11
    how it works, 93–94
    Illinois, 103
    lack of accountability, 98
    Massachusetts, 12, 13
    provision intended to prevent, 13
    repeal, 192
    states that have enacted, 93
    tax break law, 10
    tax competition among states, 169
    theory versus reality, 94–96
    we can no longer afford, 205
site location
    cost factors, 52
    factors that drive, 48–54
    manufacturing, 5
    subsidies don't determine, 59–64
    Wal-Mart, 152–153
site location consultants, 2, 23, 47–48,
    84, 89–90, 186
    Bruce Maus, 51–52, 57
    on clawbacks, 190
    commissions, 57, 70
    commissions should not be allowed,
        193
    conflict of interest, 70, 74–75
    Dennis Donovan, 54–55, 69
    entrenched power of, 89–90, 185

fees for, 55–56
Gene DePrez, 69
James Renzas, 62–64
junkets for, 76
power of, 90
"prisoners' dilemma" and, 55
registration and regulation needed,
    192–193
Robert Ady, 50–51, 69
on subsidies, 62–64
subsidy demands and, 54
site location consulting
    Fantus Factory Locating Service, 69
    industry today, 84–87
site location firms, 85. *See also* site loca-
    tion consultants
Site Selection magazine, 62
skilled labor
    corporate acknowledgment of short-
        age, 200–201
    eliminate expenditure that does not
        create more, 202
    federal policy regarding, 202
    growth rate declining, 198
    need for investment in, 197–199, 199–
        200
    need urgent, 192
    neglect of, 183–184, 197–199
    public education and, 126
    reinvestment needed, 205
    shortages, 183–184, 200–201
    site location and, 49–50
"slippery slope," Single Sales Factor, 94,
    98
Small Business Administration (SBA)
    504 loan guarantee program, 135
smart growth
    ballot measures approved for, 131
    ending the "economic war among the
        suburbs," 194–196
Smart Growth America, 133
"smokestack-chasing," 146
Smyrna, Tennessee, Nissan in, 22
Snap-on, Inc., 113
Sonangol, 118
Sony, Springfield, Oregon, 118
South
    cheap labor, 91
    factory relocation, 69

About the Author

Greg LeRoy has been dubbed "the leading national watchdog of state and local economic development subsidies" and "God's witness to corporate welfare." For more than 20 years, mostly from Chicago, he has been writing, consulting, and training for unions, community groups, environmental and smart growth advocates, labor-management committees, professional associations of development officials, elected officials, journalists, and state and local government agencies. His 1994 book, *No More Candy Store: States and Cities Making Job Subsidies Accountable,* was the first compilation of economic development safeguards such as clawbacks and job quality standards. Upon winning the Stern Family Fund's 1998 Public Interest Pioneer Award, he founded Good Jobs First (http://www.goodjobsfirst.org). Based in Washington, DC, Good Jobs First promotes corporate and government accountability in economic development and smart growth for working families. It also includes Good Jobs New York, the Corporate Research Project, and Good Jobs Illinois. Greg holds degrees in journalism and U.S. history.

Good Jobs First
A Resource Center for Winning Accountability

Good Jobs First (www.goodjobsfirst.org) is a user-friendly resource center for grassroots groups and public officials who want to end the Great American Jobs Scam. We provide training, consulting, research, and technical assistance, and our website is full of practical toolkit materials on issues such as: Job Quality Standards, Researching Subsidies, Smart Growth for Working Familics, and Clawbacks. You can also sign up for our Activist E-mail List, or click to our Good Jobs New York project for research on Job Blackmail in New York City and Post-9/11 Scams. Our Corporate Research Project provides strategic research assistance.

About Berrett-Koehler Publishers

Berrett-Koehler is an independent publisher dedicated to an ambitious mission: Creating a World That Works for All.

We believe that to truly create a better world, action is needed at all levels—individual, organizational, and societal. At the individual level, our publications help people align their lives and work with their deepest values. At the organizational level, our publications promote progressive leadership and management practices, socially responsible approaches to business, and humane and effective organizations. At the societal level, our publications advance social and economic justice, shared prosperity, sustainable development, and new solutions to national and global issues.

A major theme of our publications is "Opening Up New Space." They challenge conventional thinking, introduce new points of view, and offer new alternatives for change. Their common quest is changing the underlying beliefs, mindsets, institutions, and structures that keep generating the same cycles of problems, no matter who our leaders are or what improvement programs we adopt.

We strive to practice what we preach—to operate our publishing company in line with the ideas in our books. At the core of our approach is *stewardship*, which we define as a deep sense of responsibility to administer the company for the benefit of all of our "stakeholder" groups: authors, customers, employees, investors, service providers, and the communities and environment around us. We seek to establish a partnering relationship with each stakeholder that is open, equitable, and collaborative.

We are gratified that thousands of readers, authors, and other friends of the company consider themselves to be part of the "BK Community." We hope that you, too, will join our community and connect with us through the ways described on our website at www.bkconnection.com.

A BK Currents Title

This book is part of our BK Currents series. BK Currents titles advance social and economic justice by exploring the critical intersections between business and society. Offering a unique combination of thoughtful analysis and progressive alternatives, BK Currents titles promote positive change at the national and global levels. To find out more, visit www.bkcurrents.com.

Be Connected

Visit Our Website

Go to www.bkconnection.com to read exclusive previews and excerpts of new books, find detailed information on all Berrett-Koehler titles and authors, browse subject-area libraries of books, and get special discounts.

Subscribe to Our Free E-Newsletter

Be the first to hear about new publications, special discount offers, exclusive articles, news about bestsellers, and more! Get on the list for our free e-newsletter by going to www.bkconnection.com.

Participate in the Discussion

To see what others are saying about our books and post your own thoughts, check out our blogs at www.bkblogs.com.

Get Quantity Discounts

Berrett-Koehler books are available at quantity discounts for orders of ten or more copies. Please call us toll-free at (800) 929-2929 or e-mail us at bkp.orders@aidcvt.com.

Host a Reading Group

For tips on how to form and carry on a book reading group in your workplace or community, see our website at www.bkconnection.com.

Join the BK Community

Thousands of readers of our books have become part of the "BK Community" by participating in events featuring our authors, reviewing draft manuscripts of forthcoming books, spreading the word about their favorite books, and supporting our publishing program in other ways. If you would like to join the BK Community, please contact us at bkcommunity@bkpub.com.